GORDON PAPE'S
INVESTING
STRATEGIES 2000
MUTUAL FUNDS AND BEYOND

GORDON PAPE   RICHARD CROFT   ERIC KIRZNER

PRENTICE HALL CANADA

Canadian Cataloguing in Publication Data

Pape, Gordon, 1936–
    Gordon Pape's investing strategies 2000

Annual.
2000–
"Mutual funds and beyond".
ISSN 1490-6740
ISBN 0-13-015294-3 (2000 edition)

1. Finance, Personal – Canada. 2. Investments – Canada. I. Title. II. Title:
Investing Strategies.

HG4530.P365   332.024'00971   C99-900985-0

Prentice-Hall Canada Inc.
Scarborough, Ontario

Prentice-Hall, Inc., Upper Saddle River, New Jersey
Prentice-Hall International (UK) Limited, London
Prentice-Hall of Australia, Pty. Limited, Sydney
Prentice-Hall Hispanoamericana, S.A., Mexico City
Prentice-Hall of India Private Limited, New Delhi
Prentice-Hall of Japan, Inc., Tokyo
Simon & Schuster Southeast Asia Private Limited, Singapore
Editora Prentice-Hall do Brasil, Ltda., Rio de Janeiro

ISBN 0-13-015294-3 (2000 edition)

Editorial Director, Trade Group: Andrea Crozier
Copy Editor: Martha Wilson
Production Editor: Jodi Lewchuk
Art Direction and Cover Design: Mary Opper
Cover Illustration: Sandra Dionisi
Production Coordinator: Kathrine Pummell
Page Layout: Dave McKay

1 2 3 4 5 W 03 02 01 00 99

Printed and bound in Canada.

Every reasonable effort has been made to obtain permission for all articles
and data used in this edition. If errors or omissions have occurred, they will
be corrected in future editions provided written notification has been
received by the publisher. In this publication the author and publisher are
not engaged in rendering any professional services. Readers should consult
a professional for advice applying to their particular circumstances.

Visit the Prentice Hall Canada Web site! Send us your comments, browse
our catalogues, and more. www.phcanada.com.

Also by Gordon Pape

INVESTMENT ADVICE

Retiring Wealthy in the 21st Century

Gordon Pape's 2000 Buyer's Guide to Mutual Funds
(with Richard Croft and Eric Kirzner)

Gordon Pape's 2000 Buyer's Guide to RRSPs
(with David Tafler)

Gordon Pape's 2000 Buyer's Guide to RRIFs
(with David Tafler)

Making Money in Mutual Funds

The Canadian Mortgage Book
(with Bruce MacDougall)

The Best of Pape's Notes

Head Start
(with Frank Jones)

Building Wealth in the '90s

Low-Risk Investing in the '90s

CONSUMER ADVICE

Gordon Pape's International Shopping Guide
(with Deborah Pape)

HUMOUR

The $50,000 Stove Handle

FICTION
(With Tony Aspler)

Chain Reaction

The Scorpion Sanction

The Music Wars

NON-FICTION
(With Donna Gabeline and Dane Lanken)

Montreal at the Crossroads

Also by Richard Croft and Eric Kirzner

The Beginner's Guide to Investing

Also by Richard Croft

Aggressive Investing

Also by Eric Kirzner

Global Investing the Templeton Way

VISIT THE GORDON PAPE WEB SITE
(www.gordonpape.com)
for
CBC radio transcripts
Gordon Pape's e-mail newsletter
Weekly Mutual Fund Minute commentary
Answers to your financial questions
Links to all mutual fund sites
Comprehensive Fund Directory
New fund ratings
Book excerpts
Seminar dates and locations
And much more

CONTENTS

A PERSONAL CANCER-FIGHTING APPEAL FROM GORDON PAPE

As I write these words, I'm about to depart for the funeral of my very dear friend, Bruce Smith. Bruce was one of the finest people I have ever known, a man of absolute integrity who loved life and who deeply understood the fundamental importance of family and friendships in the human experience.

Bruce died on August 17, 1999 of cancer. He was the third close friend we lost to this disease within a year. That was three too many.

Cancer has become a modern-day scourge, the plague of our times. There is probably not a family in Canada that hasn't been touched by it, or will be at some point.

We need to do something about it, now. That's why I am launching this personal appeal for your support, asking you to contribute generously to a new program that will save many Canadians and significantly improve the quality of their lives after treatment. You'll find an address where you can send your donations at the end of this message.

I only came to fully appreciate the pervasiveness and personal devastation of cancer two years ago, when I had my own personal encounter with it. I can still remember how appalled I was at the standing-room-only situation I encountered at my first visit to a clinic at Toronto's Princess Margaret Hospital, the nation's largest cancer facility. An entire floor of the massive building was filled with people waiting for assessment and treatment. A few were quite old. Most were disconcertingly young.

As I went through the lengthy and unpleasant process of treatment, I vowed that if I could do anything, however small, to speed up the process of conquering cancer and to improve the lives of those who were successful in their fight against it, I would do so. The deaths of Bruce and my other friends, Stu Strebel and Shirley Winterton, only served to reinforce that personal pledge.

However, being a practical person, I wanted whatever I did to have a tangible result — something that demonstrably helped in the fight. We all know general cancer research is essential. But I wanted to be associated with something more specifically targeted.

I have now found that program. This message is to ask for your help in making it a reality.

I'm sure you have seen the disquieting news reports. Canadians being sent to U.S. hospitals for cancer procedures because waiting lists here are too long. Studies that conclude we are lagging well behind most of the developed world in terms of the availability of state-of-the-art equipment. That we should find ourselves in such a condition, in a wealthy nation such as ours, is shocking.

This is not the time to be pointing fingers of blame for this sorry state. It is the time to start fixing it!

Most people know that radiation, or radiotherapy as it is technically known, is one of the most effective curative cancer treatments available in the health care system today. Unfortunately, it is also one of the most dangerous because it causes irreversible changes to normal tissues which may result in severe complications later. Radiotherapy can have adverse consequences for the patient if the tumour is not completely treated or if excessive normal tissue is irradiated.

Think about it in terms of the role of air traffic control in aviation. Few of us would fly if we lacked confidence in the safety of our air travel industry. Like air traffic control, radiotherapy requires intense attention to detail, alertness, precision and adequate human and material resources to minimize the risk of irreversible consequences.

Conventional radiotherapy techniques have been limited for decades by an inability to directly and adequately target cancerous tissues while minimizing the impact on the surrounding normal tissue. The result is often undesirable collateral damage. For example, I lost a perfectly good salivary gland during my own neck radiation procedure, with the result that I now experience chronic dryness of the mouth. Radiotherapy treatments in other areas of the body can produce much worse after-effects than that, including damage to the lungs, heart, kidneys, etc. The patient may be cured, but the quality of life thereafter is severely impaired. In addition, in some instances it may be impossible to use radiotherapy effectively for fear of major complications. The radiation dose chosen or the volume irradiated may be insufficient, leading to loss of opportunity for cure.

We need to improve our radiation treatment delivery program in Canada in two critical ways:

1) We must be able to better target the cancerous tumours to maximize the likelihood of destroying them.

2) We must protect normal tissue from the damaging sideeffects of radiation to ensure that recovered patients can return to a full and rewarding lifestyle.

Currently, techniques are being developed to deliver radiation therapy in a manner that allows the dose to conform to the precise three-dimensional (3-D) configuration of the tumour. At the same time, these techniques should permit the damage to surrounding issues to be minimized. The technical term for the process is "Three-dimensional conformal radiation therapy" (3D-CRT). Development has been made possible through recent advances in computer technology. This is leading-edge, twenty-first century medical magic which could have a tremendous impact in saving people and greatly improving their ongoing lives in the years to come.

If you're interested in the technical details, this "magic" will be achieved through high-speed automated workstations, computer-controlled radiation machines, automated multileaf collimators (which shape the edges of a radiation beam) and on-line portal imaging, all of which represent some of the recent technological advances that enable implementation of 3D-CRT.

An even more precise method is Intensity Modulated Radiation Therapy (IMRT), in which the radiation treatment is crafted in such a way as to focus tightly on the tumour while protecting normal tissues.

These approaches can be applied to many cancers, but at present can be expected to have maximum impact on tumours located in critical and highly vulnerable parts of the body. These include the head and neck, where the proximity of eyes, spinal cord and brain to the tumour present a major obstacle to precise high-dose radiotherapy delivery.

These types of high precision radiotherapy comprise the next generation of radiation treatment. They have been pioneered in Europe and the United States over the past decade, but regrettably have not been developed or implemented in Canada to date. This is, to me, shocking. Canadian institutions and professionals have the skill and tradition of developing innovative radiotherapy approaches in cancer management. But it isn't happening. Why? Because we aren't providing the financial resources to make it happen!

At the Princess Margaret Hospital, there is great interest in developing these approaches and making them available to Canadians as quickly as possible. But it can't happen without our help. As a result, I have agreed to lend my name to fundraising efforts on behalf of this program, as have my co-authors, Richard Croft and Eric Kirzner.

We ask that you join with us in generously supporting this program. We believe that its implementation will save thousands of lives, perhaps the life of someone dear to you. And we also believe that many of those people who are cured, will, as a result, enjoy much happier, more satisfying lives for the rest of their days.

If you would like to participate, please send a donation to the High Precision Radiation Therapy Research Fund at the Princess Margaret Hospital Foundation. You may address it to:

High Precision Radiation Therapy Research Fund
c/o The Princess Margaret Hospital Foundation
610 University Avenue
Toronto, Ontario M5G 2M9

Of course, all donations are tax-deductible. So please give generously. Thousands of future cancer patients will be forever thankful to you.

Gordon Pape
Richard Croft
Eric Kirzner
Toronto, 1999

INTRODUCTION

During the early years of its publication, *Gordon Pape's Buyer's Guide to Mutual Funds* was divided into two main sections. The front of the book contained basic information about mutual funds plus a range of investing strategies that explained how to profit from funds. The back of the book was devoted to reviews and ratings of all the funds in Canada with at least a three-year track record.

As the mutual fund universe expanded, the ratings section did too. For a time, it was still possible to accommodate both aspects of the book in a single volume. But as the number of mutual funds grew to 500, then 700, and now 1,000+, more of the portfolio-building and investment advice had to be dropped to keep the book size within manageable levels. This year, the front-of-the-book material disappeared altogether.

Many readers bemoaned the loss of this information and guidance. Now *Investing Strategies 2000* restores it all, plus a great deal more.

When Gordon Pape, Richard Croft and Eric Kirzner agreed to collaborate on the 2000 edition of the *Buyer's Guide to Mutual Funds*, Croft and Kirzner decided to suspend publication of their own annual mutual fund guide *The FundLine Advisor*. However, none of the authors wanted to lose the valuable portfolio advice that it contained.

As a result, the concept of this book was born. *Investing Strategies 2000* draws on the basic portfolio concepts advanced in *The FundLine Advisor*, but goes much farther. A wide range of new material has been added, including information on closed-end funds, the new RRSP-eligible clone funds, guidelines for buying segregated funds, royalty trusts, index participation units, tax-advantaged fund investing and much more.

This book is intended to function as a companion to the *Buyer's Guide to Mutual Funds*. The latter helps you to zero in on the best funds in each category. *Investing Strategies 2000* is designed to show you how to use those funds to maximum advantage for your specific needs.

We hope you'll find it a valuable addition to your investment bookshelf.

Gordon Pape	Richard Croft	Eric Kirzner
Toronto, Ontario	*Toronto, Ontario*	*Toronto, Ontario*

PICKING GOOD FUNDS ISN'T ENOUGH

In the 1970s there were fewer than 100 mutual funds in Canada. Ten years ago, there were fewer than 600. Today, there are more than 2,000 such products available to the Canadian investor. With so many options out there, it's no longer just about good mutual funds. It's about good portfolios.

Our goal is to build a portfolio within your comfort zone. Understanding the building process will reassure you that the end results will get you where you want to go, helping you meet your long-term financial objectives.

When we talk about portfolios, we are really talking about an investment process. In this book, the process begins with a get-to-know-yourself exercise. That's followed by an asset mix decision, with a strategy that brings geographic diversification into the equation. The final step is selecting funds with different objectives and management styles.

There's been a major change in mindset from ten years ago. Remember when the purchase of a mutual fund was, in itself, enough to provide diversification? One Canadian equity fund could replace a portfolio of ten or twenty well-thought-out Canadian stocks. And, for added comfort, you could rely on a professional port-folio manager.

Same with a bond portfolio. One Canadian bond fund provided instant diversification within that market. It was more convenient, and more cost-effective, than trying to buy a laddered bond portfolio.

Today that's all changed — perhaps for the better. We still see diversification as a tool to help smooth out the fluctuations in your investment portfolio. And until the latter part of the 1980s we thought that individual mutual funds could do that.

October 1987 was a watershed. Before that, few investors believed market risk would ever have much of an impact on their pocketbooks. But when the Canadian stock market fell more than 20 percent in one day, so did most Canadian equity mutual funds.

While it took some time to lick the wounds, investors eventually adapted. A little further along the evolutionary track came the idea of building portfolios of mutual funds. Each fund eliminated company-specific risk; the portfolio as a whole reduced market risk. (It couldn't eliminate risk itself, mind you. But a portfolio of funds representing different asset classes and geographic boundaries does reduce some of the volatility attached to market risk.)

A portfolio of six to ten mutual funds lets you sleep at night. The problem, of course, is making sure that each fund you choose is actually bringing something special. It doesn't help much to have three funds doing exactly the same thing.

It also doesn't help much if your advisor recommends a portfolio of funds, but you really don't know what each fund has to offer. They may be the right choices, but without a frame of reference, you don't know. This uncertainty can make you question your advisor's motives. Was this or that fund recommended because your advisor earns a higher commission on it? (We don't believe that many advisors really recommend funds on the basis of commission. The industry has taken a number of steps to prevent such practices.) Unfortunately, a lot of financial advisors aren't that adept at building portfolios, and the investor suffers as a result.

THE BETTER WAY

There is a better way to build portfolios: Buy the best funds in each category, without regard to specific fund families. Build a portfolio from the bottom up, using a clear, straightforward process. Add the four levels of diversification we mentioned earlier: asset mix, geographic region, fund objectives, and management style.

Will your portfolio be immune to the ebbs and flows of the business cycle? Not by a long shot. However, it will be as insulated as possible from the economic shocks. You can rest assured that you did all you could do to smooth out the fluctuations. But most important, you will have a framework for examining your advisor's recommendations. If both you and your advisor come to similar conclusions, that helps build mutual respect. Mutual respect brings with it confidence, the cornerstone of a long-term relationship.

So what's new? The realization that selecting the right portfolio involves a bit of science and a lot of art. The science lays the foundation for making decisions; the art is mixing and matching within a portfolio to provide above-average risk-adjusted performance.

BEYOND MUTUAL FUNDS

As baby boomers age, and take a greater interest in their financial affairs, they have sought opportunities beyond traditional mutual funds. The costs associated with traditional mutual funds have become an issue. When investors are paying average management expense ratios (MERs) of 2.5 percent a year, they have a right to ask, "Where's the value added?"

And when investors talk about value added, they aren't just talking about raw performance numbers. Back in the early days of double-digit returns, people didn't question MERs — but today, they are asking the questions despite double-digit returns. Why? Because there are alternatives to traditional mutual funds.

Over the last five years, the average U.S. equity fund returned 19.6 percent a year — impressive numbers by any count. And five years ago, if anyone had told you that you would earn that much, you would have questioned their sanity.

But today that's not the case. Individuals know more about investing, and they know it's not enough to accept the actual performance number; it's important to question the quality of that performance. Think about that!

It's one thing to look at the performance of the average U.S. equity fund. But how did that performance compare to a passive low-cost alternative, like the Dow Jones Industrial Average?

The DJIA is the granddaddy of all stock market indexes. In fact, it isn't even an index, but rather an average designed to track the average performance of the 30 biggest, bluest-chip U.S. stocks, representing a cross-section of sectors within the U.S. economy. In 1998, the DJIA returned 25.3 percent without accounting for reinvested dividends. That's what we mean by quality of earnings.

Of course, it's one thing to look enviously at the performance of some well-known benchmark over the last five years. The fact is, you couldn't buy the DJIA. So the comparison was moot.

Today, however, you can go online through a discount broker, or you can even call your full service broker, and actually buy the DJIA. The security known as DIAMONDS (symbol DIA) trades on the American Stock Exchange and represents a passive investment in the DJIA. And if that weren't enough, DIAMONDS pay a quarterly dividend equal to the dividend paid by the stocks in the DJIA.

There's a cost, of course. The commission to buy DIAMONDS can be as little as a tenth of a percent of the total value, or as high as one percent — it depends on your broker's commission schedule. There is also an ongoing MER. But that's only 18 basis points (0.18 percent) per annum. That's a far cry from the 2.14 percent average MER for U.S. equity funds. So if you are being asked to pay the higher MERs, then you have a right to expect the fund's performance to beat a passive, and now investable, low-cost alternative.

That's what we mean when we talk about investments that go beyond traditional mutual funds. We'll show you a whole range of passive index-based securities that provide alternatives to almost any fund group.

We're not suggesting you opt for the low-cost alternatives. Traditional mutual funds may be the right choice for you. But knowing that you have alternatives helps you assess a fund's quality and performance.

WE'RE HERE TO HELP

These are the questions we are seeing among investors. They want to know about mutual funds, about the managers of those funds, and how we rate them for year-ahead performance. *Gordon Pape's Buyer's Guide to Mutual Funds*, the encyclopedia for mutual fund investors, addresses all those questions. It provides the raw performance data, the fund manager's profile, our own $$$$ rating system, and now the MVA (Manager Value Added index).

This book is designed to work side by side with the *Buyer's Guide to Mutual Funds*, which arms you with information about each individual fund. *Investment Strategies* tells you how to build a long-term portfolio using actively managed mutual funds, passive alternatives, and various types of mutual fund "cousins," such as royalty income trusts and unit trusts.

In the process, we'll introduce you to a number of tools to help you build the right portfolio, beginning in the chapter titled "Your Investment Persona" with the questionnaire. This is a personality profile that asks a series of questions to help establish the best asset mix for you. Whether you're a very conservative investor or a super-aggressive investor, you will find yourself in one of our investor profiles.

This profile will guide you to your asset mix decision, and that's the foundation of any long-term investment plan. Defining your investment personality without defining an asset mix defeats the purpose of the exercise. So we'll accept that there may be more detailed questionnaires, perhaps more complete psychological profiles. Perhaps more questions on your risk profile might give us a better idea of how you can tolerate the roller coaster ride along the business cycle. Perhaps, but we prefer to keep things simple. And we're proud that the Toronto Stock Exchange features our investor questionnaire in their Investor Centre. Maybe it's not the best, but it serves a clear purpose: to get you to an asset mix decision.

THE SIMPLE CASE FOR ASSET ALLOCATION

Imagine a pie baked with four cups of flour and ten pounds of sugar. Even those with a sweet tooth — something we have often been accused of — would find that a little rich! Unfortunately, we often find investors willing to mix their assets with the same regard as our imaginary baker.

While there are four basic asset classes, we tend to think only in terms of the three major financial assets: equities, fixed income, and cash. (We assume that most Canadians own a home, or intend to buy one someday; and we believe that represents sufficient exposure to another asset class, real estate.)

If you own shares of an equity mutual fund, you own an equity asset. It's the same if you own shares of Nortel Networks, General Motors, or IBM. In short, then, equity assets are long on growth, tend to be more volatile, usually lead the performance parade, and, generally speaking, do not provide much in the way of income.

On the other hand, let's say you own shares of a Canadian bond fund. Bonds are considered fixed-income assets. We think of this asset class as income-producing, generally less volatile than equity assets, and, at times, capable of producing better-than-average capital gains.

Those capital gains are produced by changes in the level of interest rates. When rates are falling, as they were for much of the 1990s, bond prices — and the value of bond funds — rise, producing capital gains. On the other hand, when interest rates are rising, bond prices fall, along with the value of your bond fund. Think of this as the bond price/interest rate teeter-totter.

Interest rates are an important consideration when building a portfolio. Rising interest rates not only have a negative impact on bond prices, they can also push down the value of equities (and, of course, equity mutual funds). Interest rates also play an important role in how we tilt the asset mixes based on our long- and short-term economic forecasts, which we discuss in the sections "How to Prosper in the Twenty-First Century" and "The Outlook for the Year 2000."

Finally, cash is the lowest-risk asset in our portfolio models. In fact, cash investments are risk-free, and are normally represented by money market funds. These funds simply invest in short-term government Treasury bills or corporate notes. The yield on such funds is equivalent to the yield on the short-term cash investments they make, except for the management expense ratio — normally 50 basis points (0.50 percent) annually. Money market funds usually have a fixed net asset value per share, and the price is usually set at $10 per unit.

Think of these three asset classes as the "ingredients" of your portfolio. Just as with our imaginary pie, choosing the right recipe, or asset mix, is the most important decision you and your financial advisor will make.

The asset mix is the percentage of a portfolio represented by each class of investment. For example, a portfolio mix might look something like "40 percent equities, 50 percent fixed income, and 10 percent cash."

There is a reason for choosing that kind of description — and it's not because it's easier to say than "I'm holding $40,000 of the Altamira Equity Fund, 500 shares of General Motors, $50,000 in Government bonds, and $50,000 in GICs. ..." Portfolio managers talk in terms of asset mix because they understand the importance that asset mix decisions play on the portfolio's overall return.

Just how important? Studies have shown that 85 to 90 percent of your overall return can be pegged to the asset mix decision. Another five to 10 percent comes from market timing (shifting in and out of investments in response to economic changes). The remainder of your success depends on selecting one specific security over another (for example, buying IBM rather than General Motors, or Microsoft rather than Nortel).

In other words, by determining which percentage of your portfolio is committed to fixed income assets, which percentage to equity assets, and which percentage to any other asset class, you have laid the basis for at least 85 percent of your total return.

Consider a hypothetical portfolio that has only two funds: the Bissett Canadian Equity Fund and the AGF Canadian Bond Fund. The first represents your equity assets, the second your fixed-income assets.

For the ten year period ending June 30, 1999, the Bissett Canadian Equity Fund averaged 12.9 percent a year. A $10,000 investment made in July, 1989 would have been worth $33,646.46 a decade later.

The AGF Canadian Bond fund also has a decent ten year track record, returning 9.3 percent, compounded annually. A $10,000 investment in the AGF Canadian Bond Fund would have grown to $24,333.34 at the end of June, 1999.

Now we are going to mix and match these two assets in a home-grown portfolio. Think of it as our version of investment taste-testing. We'll use the following table (1.1) to examine a number of variations on this theme, giving you a closer look at the importance of asset mix decisions.

TABLE 1.1 - THE IMPORTANCE OF ASSET MIX

	EQUITIES	BONDS	AVERAGE ANNUAL RETURN	END VALUE
Portfolio A	100%	0.0%	12.90%	$33,646.46
Portfolio B	80%	20%	12.18 %	$ 31,783.84
Portfolio C	60%	40%	11.46%	$ 29,921.21
Portfolio D	50%	50%	11.10 %	$28,989.90
Portfolio E	40%	60%	11.74 %	$28,058.59
Portfolio F	20%	80%	10.02%	$ 26,195.96
Portfolio G	0%	100%	9.30%	$24,333.33

Forget for the moment that either fund would have produced decent risk-adjusted returns over the last ten years. In this taste test we are simply looking at what happens when different weights are applied to each asset within the portfolio.

If, for example, you used Portfolio D — 50 percent Bissett and 50 percent AGF — you would have locked in a base return of 11.1 percent without ever having selected a single security. Your $10,000 investment in July, 1989 would have almost tripled, to $28,989.90, by the end of June, 1999.

Perhaps, rather than holding a 50/50 split between these two funds, you decided to practice some nimble trading — say, buying and selling the funds at different points of the business cycle. Assuming that your timing was right on, and that your pocketbook can withstand the tax implications of switching in and out of funds, how much do you think it enhanced your bottom line?

Well, if you shifted your asset mix up a couple of notches, from Portfolio D to Portfolio B, you add 108 basis points (1.08 percent) in compounded annual return. One decision made ten years ago would have had as much impact as shifting in and out of the funds along the way.

And there's more. The incremental return that comes from the right asset mix decision goes beyond year-over-year excess returns. That's because returns compound over time. The value of the $10,000 invested in portfolio B is worth 9.6 percent more than portfolio D at the end of the ten year period.

If those returns remained consistent over the next ten years, portfolio B would be worth $102,408.98, compared with $86,209.78 for portfolio D. That's a difference of $16,199.20, which means that portfolio B would then be worth 18.7 percent more than portfolio D after twenty years.

The difference in performance is the direct result of one asset mix decision made at some point in the distant past. So even modest changes in your asset mix can lead to significant changes over the life of your portfolio.

Why mix and match at all?

One other question about asset mix needs to be addressed. From Table 1.1, we see that the best of our hypothetical portfolios was one in which 100 percent of the assets were invested in the Bissett Canadian Equity Fund.

Not surprising, really. Over the long term, higher-risk equity assets tend to outperform fixed-income assets, which tend to outperform risk-free cash assets. If that's the case, and you are really a long-term investor, why not simply put all your money in equity funds, and take the profits to the bank?

The problem is, investors don't work that way. Remember that risk profile we talked about earlier? There's a reason for trying to ascertain how much volatility you can withstand in your portfolio. If a portfolio is too volatile, investors tend to sell too soon, usually at the bottom of a cycle. If you leave the party too early, it doesn't help you to know that equity assets tend to outperform over the long haul. You won't be there to reap the rewards.

We mix and match portfolios to help smooth out the volatility. Our considerable history in this business tells us that investors only stay for the long term when they are comfortable with the ride. So think of the questionnaire and the asset mix decision that flows from it as your opportunity to test drive a portfolio at speeds that will help you sleep at night.

And don't forget, Canadian equity and Canadian bonds are only two potential classes of assets. Your selection of portfolio ingredients will likely also include cash, some U.S. and international equity funds, and perhaps even a global bond fund. One low-risk asset mix might include 20 percent equities, 50 percent bonds, and 30 percent cash. More speculative investors might choose a spicier mix — say, five percent cash, 25 percent bonds, 70 percent equities.

Once you've determined your asset mix, look at particular securities, or, better yet, specific funds, to represent each asset class. Unfortunately, most investors reverse the process, focusing on security and/or fund selection to the exclusion of all other considerations. The result: when you add up the numbers, you find that your asset mix has been determined by default — not by design. And that means that more than 85 percent of your return has been determined without your conscious control, which is probably a recipe for disappointment.

HOMEMADE VERSUS STORE-BOUGHT DIVERSIFICATION

Should you mix and match funds to build your own portfolio based on the asset mix decision that's right for you? Or can you skip right through the process and just buy a balanced fund?

With the knowledge this book provides, you have all the tools to build your own personalized portfolio. The next question: Do you have the time? And is it worth the effort?

Let's accept for the moment that there is nothing wrong with good balanced funds. And for beginning investors — with less than $25,000 to invest — a balanced fund is probably the best place to start. Balanced funds provide a built-in asset mix based on the fund manager's view of the world.

Well, maybe the asset mix doesn't completely fit the manager's view of the world. The fact is that balanced fund managers are given specific mandates for structuring and changing asset mixes. For example, the Sceptre Balanced Growth Fund, according to Pal Trak, strives "to earn the highest possible return that is consistent with a conservative fundamental investment philosophy." Read: a balanced asset mix, somewhere around 50 percent stocks and 50 percent bonds.

That's all right, if you're looking for that type of asset mix. But if you're a growth investor, a 50/50 split isn't likely to meet your long-term needs. Your homemade asset mix can deal with that. Put that decision into the hands of a fund manager, and you eliminate any possibility of making adjustments that suit your circumstances.

There are also some issues on the performance side. Look at Table 1.2, which shows the median compounded return over the last ten years for Canadian balanced funds, Canadian equity funds, Canadian bond funds, and Canadian money market funds and U.S. large cap funds.

TABLE 1.2 - TEN YEAR RETURNS

CDN BALANCED	CDN EQUITY	U.S. LARGE CAP	CDN BOND	CDN MONEY MKT
8.90%	9.80%	16.50%	8.90%	6.10%

We know that the average Canadian balanced fund returned 8.9 percent, compounded annually, over the past ten years (to June 30th, 1999). So a $10,000 investment in the average Canadian balanced fund ten years ago would have grown to $23,457.34. That's what we call store-bought diversification.

Homemade diversification is when you decide on the asset mix that's right for you, and then find the best people to manage the assets you choose. In Table 1.3, we have structured a simple balanced portfolio using Canadian investments plus 20 percent foreign content, as represented by the median large cap U.S. equity fund.

Remember, we're trying to compare homemade Canadian diversification with a Canadian balanced fund.

So let's assume you put 30 percent of your capital into the median Canadian equity fund, 20 percent into the median large cap U.S. equity fund, 40 percent into the median Canadian bond fund, and 10 percent in the median Canadian money market fund. Those percentages, by the way, are a typical asset mix for a balanced investor.

Did the homemade portfolio do better than an off-the-shelf portfolio? That's important, because if it doesn't beat the off-the-shelf model, why spend the time and effort to build a portfolio from scratch?

TABLE 1.3 - HOMEMADE PORTFOLIO

	PORTFOLIO PERCENTAGES	TEN YEAR COMPOUNDED	VALUE OF COMPONENTS
Cdn Equity Funds	30.00%	9.90%	$7,640.90
U S Equity	20.00%	15.00%	$9,210.63
Cdn Bond Funds	40.00%	9.50%	$9,382.94
Cdn Money Mkt	10.00%	6.10%	$1,807.81
Totals	100.00%	9.87%	$28,042.28

Our homemade balanced portfolio produced a compound annual return of 9.87 percent and is worth $28,042.28. That's $4,584.94 more in your pocket, and a 19.5 percent improvement over the store-bought model. And remember, returns compound over time. Plus, our hypothetical homemade balanced portfolio assumes we can only find the median performing funds in each category. We think we can show you how to do even better.

Why did our homemade model do better? We think it has to do with the 10 to 15 percent of the returns that are attributable to security selection. By finding managers who specialize in specific markets, you define the asset mix decision and let the portfolio managers do what they do best.

By determining your personal asset mix, you tailor your investments to your personal policy statement. And, coincidentally, the numbers tell us that by selecting funds to represent your own personal asset mix, you enhance your overall return. And that assumes you purchase only the median funds in each class, and make no changes to the asset mix for the five year holding period.

We also think that mutual fund managers add more value by bringing their stock-picking or bond-selection ability to the table than they do by arbitrarily deciding which asset mix makes the most sense at a certain point in the business cycle. With the homemade portfolio you decide the asset mix and let the fund managers decide on security selection.

WRAPPING UP

If we accept the proposition that "it's not just about funds anymore; it's about portfolios," then we should also take the position that it's important to learn about portfolio construction. Even if you choose to work with a financial advisor — something we encourage — you ought to have some understanding of the process. (If only to check on the professionalism of the advisor! It doesn't make much sense to pay someone if you can do better yourself.)

So think of this book as your blueprint towards building better mutual fund portfolios. Not just for now, but for the next century.

YOUR INVESTMENT PERSONA

The first step in any sensible investment program is to understand your investment personality. It's also one of the more difficult areas. Personality traits dictate how much risk you can tolerate and help you quantify the trade-off between risk and return.

Conservative investors, for example, are more interested in the safety of their principal than in earning big returns. And in many cases, conservative investors require an income from their portfolios. Aggressive investors are more concerned about their rate of return than the safety of their principal. Income is not usually a priority.

It seems simple enough when we're looking at extremes. Of course, in reality, most people fall somewhere between these two positions. Even conservative investors sometimes have to take on risk in order to meet their financial objectives. GICs may not offer enough return to provide the income or growth necessary for the lifestyle they want. Similarly, some aggressive investors don't have the cash flow or net worth to handle the roller coaster action of the stock market. Psychologically they can do it; financially they can't! So they compromise by investing in less risky alternatives.

Generally, there are probably as many categories of individual investors as there are individual personalities. Unfortunately, if we tried to fine-tune the asset mix to suit all of the possibilities, we would be micromanaging to the extreme. A better approach is an investment personality assessment that attempts to be, as author George Hartman puts it in *Risk Is a Four-Letter Word*, "approximately right rather than precisely wrong." The questionnaire in this chapter attempts to provide this kind of assessment.

This Investor Assessment questionnaire has four basic cornerstones: net worth, financial goals, risk tolerance, and time horizon (see Figure 2.1). All four pieces of this puzzle are interrelated.

FIGURE 2.1

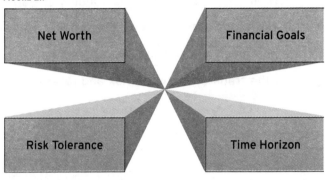

Your net worth (your total assets minus your total liabilities) can influence your risk tolerance. For example, individuals with a higher net worth can be more aggressive, or more tolerant of risk. (They aren't necessarily more aggressive, but they can be.) That's because, with a larger asset base, they can bring more elements of diversification into the portfolio. The greater the level of diversification, the less volatile their portfolio is likely to be, and the more risk can be absorbed. So larger portfolios get higher scores on risk tolerance.

Similarly, your financial objectives go hand in hand with net worth. You might have heard the story of the billionaire who had all his money invested in low-risk, low-return U.S. Treasury bills. When asked why, he answered, "Because I feel I can live comfortably on $45 million a year." The billionaire would have the highest possible score on the net worth section of the questionnaire, but would have the lowest possible score on financial objectives.

Financial goals are also linked to time horizons; that is, whether your objectives are short-term or long-term. And in turn, your time horizon can influence your tolerance for risk, since risk diminishes over the long term.

With these issues in mind, we have categorized investors into six personalities. Later in the chapter, after we've helped you identify which type of investor you are, you'll find an investment policy statement for each personality, along with a minimum and maximum weighting of investments in each asset class.

Safety investors are uncomfortable with risk. They lean toward investments that provide regular returns, even if these returns are low. Their attitude toward financial planning is apprehensive and, at times, pessimistic. Whereas others dream of wealth when they invest, safety investors are motivated by the dread of poverty.

Safety/Income investors are concerned about safety, but often require a specific income stream to meet their financial obligations. They recognize the need for a trade-off. Safety/Income investors want to make certain their principal investment is secure, but they have a keen interest in earning income on that principal. We find many retirees who may be living off a fixed income, and require the receipts from their portfolio to supplement their living standards, in this investment category.

Income/Growth investors focus their attention primarily on the income side of the investment equation. However, unlike safety/income investors, these people don't consider their portfolio's income stream a critical supplement to their standard of living — at least not yet. Often we find that income/growth investors will reinvest the income stream into more securities within the portfolio, effectively dollar-cost-averaging their investment program. Income/Growth investors understand that financial security depends on achieving some growth within the portfolio. They will spend a lot of time understanding the return required to meet their long-range financial objectives. These investors often set reasonable goals that, for the most part, can be attained with their investment style.

Growth/Income investors understand that risk is a natural part of investing. With this in mind, they set out to structure the perfect portfolio, usually a balanced investment scheme. The assets are chosen for their ability to survive the ups and downs of the business cycle. There is one drawback, however: The portfolio is designed to be left alone. Balanced investors are often so absorbed with day-to-day survival that they neglect tomorrow's opportunities.

Growth investors are not at all concerned about income. Usually, this group of investors has a long time horizon and often a sizeable net worth. The objective here is to maximize the potential growth within the portfolio, with reasonable risks. Growth investors have an appreciation of the trade-off between risk and return, and are willing to assume higher levels of risk for greater returns.

Aggressive Growth investors are the quick-draw artists of the investment world, fingers often poised to move from one opportunity to another. They switch from asset to asset, thriving on risk, seeking the thrills that accompany a profitable trade, and are willing to accept (or, some would say, to ignore) the risks associated with their investment philosophy. Aggressive growth investors are often young, have a reasonable income base, and, although they tend to look for results over the short term, are seeking some long-term guidance.

Setting Your Financial Objectives

Where do you see yourself in ten years? Retired and enjoying the finer things in life, nestled in the home of your dreams? Content and pleased with the accomplishments of the past and your aspirations for the future? Or maybe you'll be climbing the career ladder, developing a successful foundation in the career of your choice.

Many of us are unclear about our financial goals, because most of us have never been taught just how important goals are in the context of investment management. In fact, goals are critical. They will define your performance objectives.

It's also important to establish financial goals that are reasonable. You can't simply say, for example, that you want to be a millionaire some day. It may be possible to reach that goal, but how much do you need to set aside, over what period of time, and at what rate of return? And having figured that out, is it realistic?

Having realistic expectations is important, because you need to establish some successes in order to maintain a solid footing on your way to financial independence. Failing to meet unrealistic expectations can be discouraging, and that can have a negative impact on your long-range plans.

Take a few minutes with your family and think about some of the financial objectives you want to meet. Everything is on the table at this point, from an island vacation or a new car to a new cabin cruiser. Name your own dream!

Investment objectives can include such things as growth of capital, protection of principal, and income and tax considerations. There are also short-term and long-term goals, including things like the future education needs of your children, retirement planning, saving for a house, or simply improving your lifestyle. So write down your goals in order of importance, and in terms of timing.

For example, a trip to Hawaii may be a short-term goal, especially if you hope to take the trip within, say, the next five years. In fact, any goal that comes within the next five years should be included on your list of short-term goals. Anything with a time horizon beyond five years probably should go on your list of long-term goals. Your children's education is a longer-term goal. And, obviously, retirement planning deserves some special attention.

We often hear questions about registered retirement income funds. What happens when you are drawing money from your portfolio? Should the design of that portfolio fit within the context of a short-term or long-term goal?

Retired individuals have very long-term goals. When you retire, the real risk is that you will outlive your assets. If you die immediately after you set up your RRIF, there is no financial impact on you. Perhaps on your estate, but not on you personally. So the real risk is of outliving your assets. And since an RRIF begins to pay out at age 70, and life expectancy for men is 76 and for women 82, there is a very long time horizon for your investments to meet your goals.

Some studies conducted at York University attempted to address this issue. What are the odds that you will run out of money before you reach life expectancy? What the studies discovered is that although investors may be drawing an income, they still need some assets in their portfolio to provide growth. Without the growth element, there is a real chance that an individual might outlive his or her assets.

On the other hand, you need to draw income from your RRIF immediately. That affects your time horizon, which raises a very basic question: How long before you need this money? The answer, if you are in an RRIF, is "in less than two years," which would give you a score of 0 in our Investor Assessment questionnaire. We think that's the right answer to the question, and we suspect that RRIF investors will generally fall within the three most conservative of our investment portfolios. But in each of those portfolios, we still leave some room for growth. All six investor personalities need some equity in their final asset mix.

Once you have put together a list of potential goals, try to rank them in terms of importance and then put some realistic prices on them. For example, your retirement income should be at least 70 percent of your current income and, to be safe, you should adjust that number to reflect some inflation expectations.

The Retirement Planner below will help you calculate on paper what rate of return you'll need to meet your goals. However, we recognize that this is bit more cumbersome than you might like. With that in mind, and if you have access to the World Wide Web, we have an alternative to paper-based calculations.

Go to www.quicken.ca web site. From there, click on the RRSP Planner, and then click on the question "How Much Should I Invest?" That will take you to a calculator which will help you decide how much you need in order to retire. You can also use that calculator to help you with Question 2 of our questionnaire ("What is your required rate of return?"). Just plug in your numbers and ask the calculator to give you a rate of return.

RETIREMENT PLANNER

Years to retirement?
Annual household income?
Estimated annual retirement expenses in today's dollars? [1]
Total amount required to provide for retirement expenses?
Annual contribution to retirement goal?
Required compound annual return to meet retirement goal? [2]

[1] Assume 70% of current income

[2] What rate of return do you require in order to meet your retirement goal assuming regular annual contributions

As for the cost of a college education, a number of financial advisors and planners attach an assumed rate of inflation to the current tuition level. With cutbacks from all levels of government, particularly in the area of college and university tuitions, it's important to attach reasonable inflation assumptions to future education costs.

With that in mind, many advisors and planners inflate current education costs by some fixed rate — say, seven percent per year, a figure that is reasonably close to the cost increases experienced over the last ten years. At that rate, a university education that costs $10,000 today will cost about $20,000 ten years from now, or $40,000 by the year 2015.

However, adjusting costs by any fixed rate can be dangerous. If your child is two feet tall at one year old, and four feet tall at age six, that equals a 14 percent annual growth rate. If we maintained that assumption for the next five years, your child would be over eight feet tall at age eleven, and should be receiving scholarship offers to play collegiate basketball.

Past trends, then, are not necessarily indicative of the future. For example, if government cutbacks mean fewer students can afford to attend college or university, that will eventually create cash-flow problems at these institutions. This in turn may bring back some good old-fashioned cost-cutting measures — and by extension, some competitive tuition fees.

EDUCATION PLANNER

Annual cost of the college of your choice?	
How many years before your child enters college?	
How many years attending college?	
Amount needed to meet goal?	

Fixing the rate of return on your investments assumes that you never need to review your investment objectives and goals. And the fact is, over time, they change. A regular annual review is in order and, of course, when personal circumstances change — when there is a death in the family, a marriage, a divorce, the birth of a child — you will need to take a few moments to rethink your priorities.

Finally, it is always important to keep some funds set aside for emergencies. A good rule of thumb is to have enough savings to cover three to six months' worth of expenses.

Time Horizons

For most of us, the longest-term financial goal is our retirement. In all likelihood, we will be drawing on our retirement income long after having met our shorter-term goals. In other words, our retirement goals will be financed with income left over after meeting our shorter-term goals.

The following investment portfolio worksheets will help you to clarify some of your ideas about the future in terms of three time horizons: short, medium, and long term.

SHORT-TERM PORTFOLIO (UP TO THREE YEARS)

1	What are your short-term goals, in today's dollars?	$
2	What percentage of your yearly gross income is that?	%
3	What existing savings can you put toward this goal?	$
4	What are your savings as a percentage of your income?	%
5	Subtract your savings (4) from your goal (2) to get the percentage of your income you need to invest:	%
6	How many years can you wait to reach this goal?	years
7	Divide the amount you need to invest (5) by the years (6) to get the portion of monthly gross income you'll have to set aside:	%

MID-TERM PORTFOLIO (FOUR TO TEN YEARS)

1	What are your mid-term goals, in today's dollars?	$
2	What percentage or multiple of your yearly gross income is that?	%
3	What existing savings can you put toward this goal?	$
4	What are your savings as a percentage of your income?	%
5	If the time you have to reach your goal is more than $\times$ ___ seven years, multiply savings (4) by 2:	%
6	Subtract savings (4 or 5) from goal (2) for required investment:	%
7	How many years can you wait to reach your goal?	years
8	Divide the required investment (6) by the years (7) to get the percentage of your monthly gross income you'll have to invest:	%
9	Add two percentage points if you're saving for college	%
10	Mid-term investment required: (8 + 9)	

LONG-TERM (RETIREMENT) PORTFOLIO (MORE THAN TEN YEARS)

1	Retirement goal as a multiple of annual gross income:	
2	What existing savings can you put toward this goal?	$
3	What are your savings as a multiple of your income?	
4	Savings multiple from Table 1	$\times$
5	Multiply savings (3) by multiple (4) for adjusted savings:	%
6	Subtract adjusted savings (5) from goal (1) for required investment:	%
7	How many years until you plan to retire?	years
8	Find appropriate investment rate on Table 2	$\times$
9	Multiply investment rate (8) by investment goal (6) to get the percentage of gross income you need to set aside each month:	%
10	Total Investment Required (all goals)	%

TABLE 1

YOUR CURRENT SAVINGS WILL GROW BY THIS FACTOR OVER TIME:

Years until retirement																			
11	12	13	14	15	16	17	18	19	20	21	22	23	24	25	26	27	28	29	30
Taxable Account																			
2	2	2	2	3	3	3	3	3	4	4	4	4	5	5	5	6	6	7	7
Tax-Advantaged Acct.																			
3	3	3	3	4	4	5	5	6	6	7	7	8	9	10	11	12	13	14	16

TABLE 2

HERE'S THE RATE YOU NEED TO INVEST FOR EVERY 1 X OF THE INCOME YOU NEED

Years to retirement	10	15	20	25	30
Savings Rate	8.20%	5.10%	3.60%	2.60%	2.00%

Risk as a Function of Time

Now that you've established your financial goals, and the rates of return required to achieve them, how can you invest your money to realize these rates of return? The investment choices you make are inextricably linked to your level of risk tolerance. That's why our Personal Investment Profile looks at risk and return as two sides of the same coin.

Let's say you were considering investing in mutual funds. If performance were the only criterion for screening potential funds, then it would simply be a case of matching your required rate of return to a fund that has generated that rate compounded over, say, the last five or ten years. Mission accomplished!

Of course, as you might imagine, things are never really that simple. The problem is that our tolerance for risk defines for each of us how well we can adapt to the ebbs and flows of our investment returns. The impact of those changes defines for us our ability to remain invested for long periods.

Stocks are one of the few investment assets that can deliver growth over the long term. But too many individual investors looking for growth are preoccupied with safety of principal, and so are unwilling to assume the risk that accompanies an investment in equities. (On the other hand, veteran money managers will tell you that many investors are reluctant to sell when faced with a loss. Many investors find it difficult to admit to a mistake, or believe (falsely) that they do not incur a true loss until a security is sold.)

On the other side of the risk/return coin, you have to be able to maintain your positions for the long term, being careful not to take profits quickly. Many of the same investors who will let their losses run will just as quickly take a profit. There is, of course, some psychological satisfaction in making money. But over the long term this reduces your chances for gains. All too often it takes you out of a market that is performing well. In this case, a little patience is its own reward.

Discussing risk is really talking about the potential for loss. And within that context, equity investments are risky because over short periods there is a reasonable chance that you could lose money. However, if you are willing to take a longer-term view, the risk of loss diminishes dramatically. Knowing your time horizon is important, since it will determine the amount of equity in your investment program.

The Investor Assessment questionnaire below begins with your current financial condition (your net worth), and goes on to address the issues we've covered in this chapter: your financial goals, your tolerance for risk, and the time horizon you envision for achieving these goals. Once you've tallied your scores you will arrive at your Personal Investment Profile, which will give you a foundation for making investment decisions that are right for you.

Try to answer each of the following questions as honestly as you can. Where it's necessary, work with your spouse or partner — investment planning should be a family affair.

INVESTOR ASSESSMENT QUESTIONNAIRE

Question 1

Net Worth

We'll begin at the beginning — with your current net worth. But before firing up the calculator, you should decide whether or not to include your principal residence.

The bottom line: You will always need a place to live. Of course, you may decide to rent at some point in the future. In that case, you may want to sell your principal residence and invest the tax-free profits into upgrading your lifestyle. Or you may prefer to retain your residence and use other forms of disposable income to meet your financial needs.

If you fall into the former camp, and are clear about your long-term plans, then by all means, include the principal residence as part of your net worth. For those of you who fall into the latter camp, or have no plans to sell the family homestead, we suggest you not include your home as part of your net worth.

Is your approximate net worth:

Less than $25,000?	1
Between $25,000 and $50,000?	3
Between $50,001 and $100,000?	5
Between $100,001 and $250,000?	7
Greater than $250,000?	10
NET WORTH SCORE:	

Question 2

Financial Goals

Having determined your financial goals (i.e., retirement, saving for a home, children's education), you must assess the rate of return required to attain these goals. Is your required rate of return:

Less than 6%?	1
Between 6% and 9%?	5
Greater than 9% but no more than 12%?	10
Greater than 12%	15
FINANCIAL GOALS SCORE:	

Questions 3 to 9 will help you determine your ability to deal with risk, or the ebb and flow of the business cycle.

Question 3
Liquidity
How important is it that you have access to your investment capital in case of emergencies or other investment opportunities?

It is extremely important.	1
It is important.	2
It is slightly important.	4
It isn't important at all.	5
LIQUIDITY SCORE:	

Question 4
Safety
After one year of investing, how much would the value of your long-term investment capital have to decline before you would sell it and take a loss?

I would sell if my investment declined by 5%.	1
I would sell if my investment declined by 15%.	2
I would sell if my investment declined by 25%.	3
I would sell if my investment declined by 50%.	4
I would not sell my investment.	5
SAFETY SCORE:	

Question 5
Current Income
How important is it that you receive an income stream from your investments over the period of your investment horizon?

It is extremely important.	1
It is important.	2
It is slightly important.	3
It isn't important at all.	4
CURRENT INCOME SCORE:	

Question 6

Reaction to Events

How would you describe your reaction to financial news that could have a detrimental effect on your investments?

I would be very anxious and likely sell my investments.	1
I would be fearful and consider selling my investments.	2
I would be uncomfortable but would hold my investments.	3
I would remain calm and definitely hold my investments.	4
FUTURE GAINS SCORE:	

Question 7

Portfolio Variability

How important is it that you never experience a loss in your portfolio during a given time period?

It is extremely important.	1
It is important.	2
It is only slightly important.	3
It isn't important at all.	4
PORTFOLIO VARIABILITY SCORE:	

Question 8

Performance Review

Which performance numbers most concern you?

Monthly performance numbers	1
Quarterly performance numbers	3
Annual performance numbers	5
PERFORMANCE REVIEW SCORE:	

Question 9

Speculation

Within the past five years, how often have you invested money into speculative investments?

I have never invested speculatively.	1
I have invested speculatively once.	2

...

I have invested speculatively twice.	3
I have invested speculatively three or more times.	4
SPECULATION SCORE:	

Your time horizon has a great deal to do with risk and with how much equity you can tolerate in your investment program. This last question will help you pinpoint just what your time horizon is.

Question 10

Investment Time Horizon
How long do you plan to hold your investments?

Less than two years?	0
Between two and five years?	3
More than five and less than ten years?	6
Ten to twenty years?	10
More than twenty years?	15
INVESTMENT TIME HORIZON SCORE:	

Your Personal Investor Score

CATEGORY	INFORMATION FOUND WHERE?	TOTAL SCORE
A NET WORTH	Question 1	—
B Financial Objectives	Question 2	—
C Risk Assessment Profile	Questions 3 – 9	—
D Time Horizon	Question 10	—
Total Score (A + B + C + D)		—

WHAT DOES IT ALL MEAN?

The final tally tells you your Personal Investment Profile. But remember, financial circumstances and goals change, so take the time to re-evaluate your situation at periodic intervals.

Your Personal Investment Profile is structured as an aggressiveness index and provides the foundation on which to establish your personal asset mix. The higher the score, the more aggressive the asset mix. The investor categories that follow are distinguished according the six personality types that we listed at the beginning of this chapter.

INVESTOR CATEGORIES

SCORE	INVESTOR CATEGORY
< 15	Safety
15-25	Safety / Income
25-35	Income
35-45	Income / Growth
45-55	Growth
> 55	Aggressive Growth

The first step when constructing a long-term portfolio is deciding how much emphasis should be given to each asset class. With that in mind, we start the process by defining your "policy statement," as shown in the following asset mix chart. That is the average weighting we would expect you to hold in each asset class. Your policy statement is defined as the midpoint for each asset class.

You will also note two other percentages, a maximum and a minimum, wrapped around the policy statement. These are the maximum and minimum commitments you should make to each asset class at any point in time. Each year this book will be updated, and each year we may suggest you overweight, underweight, or maintain your policy statement for the year ahead.

By doing this, we hope to enhance your returns when the economy is strengthening and reduce your risk when the economy is slowing down. In other words, it's another way of trying to smooth your ride through the ups and downs of the business cycle.

PERSONAL POLICY STATEMENTS

SAFETY PORTFOLIO								SCORE: UNDER 15
Equities			Fixed Income			Cash		
Min	Policy	Max	Min	Policy	Max	Min	Policy	Max
0%	10%	20%	60%	75%	90%	10%	15%	30%

SAFETY INCOME PORTFOLIO   SCORE: 15 - 24

Equities			Fixed Income			Cash		
Min	Policy	Max	Min	Policy	Max	Min	Policy	Max
10%	20%	30%	50%	65%	80%	10%	15%	25%

INCOME GROWTH PORTFOLIO   SCORE: 25 - 34

Equities			Fixed Income			Cash		
Min	Policy	Max	Min	Policy	Max	Min	Policy	Max
20%	35%	50%	30%	50%	70%	10%	15%	25%

GROWTH INCOME PORTFOLIO   SCORE: 35 - 44

Equities			Fixed Income			Cash		
Min	Policy	Max	Min	Policy	Max	Min	Policy	Max
30%	50%	70%	25%	40%	55%	5%	10%	15%

GROWTH PORTFOLIO   SCORE: 45 - 54

Equities			Fixed Income			Cash		
Min	Policy	Max	Min	Policy	Max	Min	Policy	Max
40%	60%	80%	20%	30%	40%	5%	10%	15%

AGGRESSIVE GROWTH PORTFOLIO   SCORE: OVER 55

Equities			Fixed Income			Cash		
Min	Policy	Max	Min	Policy	Max	Min	Policy	Max
50%	75%	100%	0%	20%	30%	0%	5%	10%

Remember, your personal policy statement is just the first step in the selection of an ideal portfolio. Later we will add other dimensions of diversification to your portfolio and help you find the right funds or products beyond funds to fill in your portfolio.

A CLOSER LOOK AT RATES OF RETURN

Understanding how rates of return work can give you a better grasp of how your investments can grow — and how much you need to earn on your investments, and over what period of time, dictates how far up the performance ladder you need to go. What follows is mostly the mathematics of the matter, and that's why we've put it at the end of the chapter.

The Magic of Compounding

One of the world's wealthiest bankers, Baron Rothschild, was once asked if he could name the seven wonders of the world. "I cannot recall all the world's seven wonders, but let me suggest to you the eighth wonder of the world. It can be utilized by each and every one of us to get what we want," he replied. "It is compound interest."

The concept of compound interest is not difficult. Suppose you place money in an investment that pays interest compounded annually. During the first year you would earn interest on the principal. However, in subsequent years, you would not only earn interest on the original principal, but also on the interest earned in the first year.

Let's say you were committed to saving $100 a month earning eight percent interest. In five years that $100 per month will be worth $7,347.68. Shop at a few more financial institutions and you might get 10 percent interest on the $100 per month. At that rate, your savings program would net you $7,743.71 after five years.

The longer money is left to compound, the more dramatic the effect on the value of your portfolio. Setting aside $100 per month for ten years at eight percent leaves you with a nest egg of $18,294.60. At 10 percent, you would have $20,484.50.

Once you start saving, the feeling becomes contagious, which is why we suggest you set up a regular savings plan and stick to it. But it's important that your saving not force you to change your lifestyle. Save an amount that you can live with, and over time it will become second nature.

Now let's see what is required to reach millionaire status. Let's begin with a saving program of $200 per month, and an interest rate of 10 percent per year. At that rate, it will take you 37.75 years to reach your million-dollar goal. Earn 12 percent on your $200 per month, and it takes just under 33 years to reach the goal.

If you can save $400 per month and earn 12 percent per year, it will take you just over 27 years to reach $1 million; at 10 percent, it will take just under 31 years.

Here's another example. Assume that $1,000 was invested today, earning 10 percent interest, compounded annually. At the end of the first year your investment would have grown to $1,100. This represents the original investment ($1,000) plus $100 ($1000 x 1.10) interest earned on the principal. Assuming you reinvested the entire amount for another year; the investment would appreciate to $1210 ($1,100 x 1.10). During the second year, you would make $100 interest on the original investment, plus $10 interest on the interest earned in the first year. The amount at the end of two years can be broken down as follows:

Original investment	$1,000.00
First years interest	100.00
Second years interest on original investment	100.00
Second years interest on interest	10.00
TOTAL RETURN	$1,210.00

Reinvestment for the third year would produce $1,331.00 ($1,210 x 1.10). The third year's interest of $121 accounts for $100 on the original principal, plus $21 on the interest earned during the first two years. The interest-on-interest component of the investment is what causes the snowballing effect on the growth of money.

To underline the importance of this, assume the original $1,000 investment was left to compound for 50 years. The investment would have grown to $117,390.85. The interest payable the fiftieth year would be made up of $100 on the original principal, plus $10,671.89 on the $105,781.96 interest earned during the first 49 years.

Had the interest on the original $1,000 principal been calculated using simple interest, the investment would not have grown nearly as much. When earning simple interest, the investment only earns interest on the original investment. Interest is not earned on interest earned in the previous years. To put this into perspective, our original $1,000 investment would be worth $6,000 at the end of the 50-year period ($100 interest x 50 years, plus $1,000 original principal).

The Rule of 72

We trust you get the picture. It is one thing to plan for the future; it is quite another to understand what it will take to meet those goals. Needless to say, there are a number of tables that can be used to calculate the future value of a lump sum of money put aside today.

But while tables can be useful in determining the value of an investment at some point in the future, they are not a tool that you carry with you to the local bank or trust company. Fortunately, there is an easier way to calculate the future value of a fixed investment today. It is known as the "rule of 72." If you divide 72 by the return on a particular investment, it will tell you how many years it will take for your money to double.

For example, if the current rate of return were nine percent, your funds would double in eight years (72 divided by 9 = 8). If the interest rate were 12 percent, your original investment would double every six years (72 divided by 12 = 6).

Now, assuming you invested $10,000 in a bond fund that, historically, has been compounding at 10 percent a year. How soon will your money double? The answer is 7.2 years (72 divided by 10).

How about this: Suppose you have $10,000 you want to double in 10 years to fund your retirement nest egg. What compound rate of return must you earn? Divide 72 by the number of years, and you get 7.2 percent. To double it in five years, you'll have to earn an annual return of 14.4 percent on your investment — 72 divided by five.

Simplicity at work, yet the rule of 72 illustrates some powerful investment principles — most notably the magic of compounding. It also drives home the advantages of mutual funds, where dividends and interest can be automatically reinvested into additional shares. Interest makes your investments grow; compound interest makes them grow faster.

And how about the role 72 plays in assessing the impact of changes in the level of your potential return? Money compounding at six percent annually will take 12 years to double. Compounding at 12 percent, it will double in half the time.

The flip side of this compounding debate is the impact inflation can have on your investments. And there, too, the rule of 72 plays a role. An inflation rate of three percent means that a dollar today will be worth roughly 50 cents in 24 years. A five percent inflation rate means that your cost of living will double every 14.4 years. Tell that to a 40-year-old just beginning to establish a retirement fund.

HOW TO PROSPER IN THE TWENTY-FIRST CENTURY

In the recorded history of mankind, few people have stood where we are standing — not just on the brink of a new century, but a new millennium. The last time it happened was in 999-1000 and not many people in those Dark Ages were very concerned with economic trends and investing decisions. Staying alive was the main preoccupation.

So let's flash forward nine hundred years, to 1899-1900. Imagine we were living then, with the twentieth century about to unfold before us. What wonders would it bring, and how could we profit from them?

The real visionaries of the day might have been able to predict that fortunes would be made from motor cars, from moving pictures, from telephones, from electric lights. All these had been invented before the birth of the new century, but all were still in their infancy. A seer might even have forecast the astounding growth of air travel. (Although the airplane itself was yet to be born, lighter-than-air flight was already a reality.) But radio? Television? Computers? Even kitchen appliances that we take for granted, like dishwashers and microwaves? Who could have foreseen them back in 1900, much less developed a plan to profit from them?

The dawn of the twenty-first century is no different. From this point in time we can see with near certainty that some technologies already in place offer great potential for investors going forward. Just think about the growth prospects for wireless voice and data transmission, the Internet, virtual reality, satellite TV. We're only at the beginning in these areas, about where the automobile and motion picture industries were in 1900.

But what incredible things lie beyond them? What remarkable inventions of the future will have become as mundane as the VCR by the turn of the next century? Let your imagination soar, think about the most improbable creations, and you probably still won't come close.

Robots to wait on us hand and foot in our homes — our own R2D2s? Why not? Just watch the share price soar of the company that figures out how to make them affordable and market them effectively.

Adventure tourism to the moon and Mars? The technology will certainly be in place.

Home entertainment systems in which you become an active participant, not a passive observer? Almost certain to happen.

Personal travel vehicles that ride on cushions of air and follow pre-programmed routes without driver intervention? Urban congestion dictates it must occur, and the companies that perfect these successors to the automobile will be the Fords and GMs of the future — or, perhaps, it will be Ford and GM themselves.

Life without end for those who can afford it, through gene manipulation? Think of the ethical debate that will produce and the profits it will reap for whomever perfects the technique.

These ideas may seem far-out today. But we can at least contemplate them. What's intriguing are the fantastic things that will happen over the next 100 years that we cannot even conceive of.

So how do you, as an investor, prepare for what is to come? How can you position yourself to take advantage of the opportunities the new century will bring?

Here are some broad guidelines we suggest you adopt as your Millennium Investing Resolutions.

Resolution one: Be flexible. The times are changing at an incredibly rapid pace. At the Ninth General Assembly of the World Future Society, held in Washington, D.C., in July, 1999, Society vice-president Graham T. T. Molitor presented a chart based on the works of John and Magna McHale, two of America's leading futurists. It showed the elapsed time between the discovery or invention of various technical advances and their practical application. In the case of photography, it was 112 years. The telephone took 56 years to make the transition. By the time radio came along, scientists had reduced the gap to 35 years. Television took 12 years. Transistors reduced the time frame to three years. Solar batteries dropped it to two years. The pattern is clear.

This means that if you want to be on the leading edge of investing, you have to be prepared to make changes. That's not to say the classic buy-and-hold investor won't prosper. But it depends what he or she decides to hold. Shares in a leading carriage manufacturer might still have looked good in 1900. But twenty years later they would have been worthless.

"Times change." We all know the expression, and indeed they do. But the twenty-first century investor might want to modify it somewhat, to "Times change fast." Believe us, they will.

Resolution two: Be in the right place, with the right company. From our current vantage point, at the dawn of the new millennium, it's clear that certain sectors of the economy are almost guaranteed to prosper. We'll discuss some of them later. However, it is not enough to know that telecommunications, to cite one example, will be a sure-fire winner in the twenty-first century. You have to go to the next step and determine which companies in the telecommunications industry are going to emerge from the intense competitive battle as the big winners and the profit-spinners.

Experience shows us that even companies in seemingly can't-miss businesses can go under as a result of bad management, bad strategy, bad planning, bad luck, malfeasance, or any combination of the foregoing.

Consider the case of Livent. Here was a company that was at the forefront of the glitzy entertainment business, one of the sectors that is certain to do well in the years to come. It owned the rights to great shows like *Ragtime* and *Fosse*; it held valuable real estate in major cities; it was headed by one of the most dynamic personalities in

North American theatre. And then everything exploded. It may be years before we understand the true reasons why, with all the suits and counter-suits that have been launched. But the bottom line for investors is that the stock suddenly became worthless. A great industry with a bright future. But the wrong company.

There are two ways to protect yourself against this kind of financial disaster in the twenty-first century. One is to stick with the market leaders in the areas you identify as high priority — the biggest and the best in their lines of business, the Sonys and Microsofts. The second way is to take a diversified approach within your target sectors. Instead of buying one great company, buy a package of them. (We'll discuss ways to do that later.)

Resolution three: Don't put all your faith in demographics. One of the hot buttons for investors in the '90s was demographics. Understand the demographic trends and you'll know where to put your money, or so went the mantra. Authors became rich, publishing books and giving lectures on the topic.

Yes, demographics is an important consideration when you're looking forward. But it's not the *only* consideration. And don't lose sight of the fact that demographic patterns can change. Some experts are now predicting a new baby boom in the early part of the twenty-first century. What would that do to all the projections that are based on the assumption of a continually aging society?

Look at the sad tale of Loewen Group. How could you lose investing in the shares of a rapidly-expanding funeral home company at a time when the population is aging? More customers every year, which had to translate into more profits in a high-margin business. The stock couldn't help but go up.

But it didn't work out that way. The population may be aging, but life expectancy is increasing. As a result, people aren't dying off as quickly as expected. That has an obvious impact on the funeral business. Then Loewen got socked with some huge legal settlements that devastated the company's bottom line. Various take-over battles further drained resources. In 1999, the company was forced to file for creditor protection under Chapter 11. The stock, which in 1996 had gone as high as

$58.75 a share, was trading on the TSE at about $1 in September, 1999.

Demographics may have encouraged some people to believe that Loewen Group couldn't lose. But it did.

Resolution four: Don't assume new companies will drive out old ones. Another popular theory in the '90s was that new industries would drive out the old. The industrial-based economy was tottering and was about to be overtaken by the new knowledge-based economy.

There's nothing wrong with this theory, as long as investors don't take it to extremes. Yes, knowledge industries will probably offer greater profit potential going forward. But that doesn't mean old-line industries won't make money too.

The steel industry was big at the end of the nineteenth century. It will almost certainly still be big at the end of the twenty-first century. We'll still likely be using forest products to build homes and make paper (forget about the paperless society, it's not going to happen). Manufacturers will still build personal transportation vehicles, and suppliers will continue to make parts for them. We'll still need to mine base metals, like copper, lead, and zinc. The mines may be on the moon or Mars, but private industry will run them.

So don't put all your investing eggs in the glamour baskets of high tech. There will be plenty of money to be made from dull, old-line companies as well.

Resolution five: Stay diversified. All this leads to the last of our rules — maintain a diversified portfolio. Don't succumb to the temptation to invest heavily in one sector of the economy, such as the Internet, because you've decided it's the wave of the future. It may well be — but there will be many other great opportunities as well and you don't want to exclude them.

Diversification also extends to the asset classes you use. The twenty-first century won't be any different from the twentieth in that sense. Equities, fixed-income securities and cash will continue to have a place in all portfolios. Bull and bear market cycles will continue. Interest rates will still rise and fall, affecting bond prices. The basic rules of the economy are not going to change just because the calendar does. So don't get swept up in millennium euphoria and allow it to affect sound deci-sion-making.

Finally, diversification includes geography. Canada should prosper in the twenty-first century. But it will likely not prosper to the same degree as the United States, which has the huge advantage of being the home base of many of the world's leading companies in the most important growth sectors. It's sad but true — Canada will never have a Microsoft, or a Dell, or a General Electric. We simply don't have the population, or the capital base, or the market potential.

Here's another argument for geographic diversifica-tion. Canada will not experience anything like the growth rate of the developing world. We cannot hope to see our GDP expand at anything like the rate of China or India or Malaysia. Investing in those countries will continue to be a roller-coaster ride, as we saw in the late '90s. But, over time, a dollar invested in the Far East will almost certainly add more value than a dollar invested in Canada.

Winning Sectors

Now that we've laid out the ground rules, let's look at some of the economic sectors that are most likely to prosper in the coming century and discuss ways to profit from them.

Pharmaceuticals. It's difficult to find any reason why this sector should not be one of the big winners in the next century. With the baby boomers aging and life expectancy increasing, the demand for drugs, both prescription and over-the-counter, seems certain to rise. Moreover, pharmaceutical research continues to produce new products, creating demand where none existed before — just look at the Viagra phenomenon.

You could pick any major pharmaceutical company like Merck or Warner Lambert and almost certainly make money on their stock over time. But a safer route to go is simply to buy the industry. One of the most effec-tive ways that we have found to do this is through the Pharmaceutical Trust, which is offered annually by First Trust Canada. The Pharmaceutical Trust operates something like a mutual fund, except that it has a limited life-span (about five years) and does not actively trade stocks. The trust invests in a portfolio of about 20 of the world's largest pharmaceutical companies and holds them until maturity, at which time the assets are paid out. Management fees are very low and the profit potential is high. To the end of August, 1999, the first offering of this trust, the 1996 version, was showing a three-year average annual compound rate of return of 34.4 percent. The 1997 version had a one-year gain of 27 percent while the 1998 edition was up 36.3 percent in its first year. Those are impressive numbers but, given the prospects for the industry, we see no reason why this growth cannot continue in the years ahead.

Health care. The health care industry can be expected to prosper for the same reasons as the pharmaceutical industry. People can expect to live longer, but they will require increased care as they age. This will work to the advantage of companies like MDS Inc., which provides diagnostic services. Companies in the nursing home, laser surgery, hospital equipment and medical technology businesses should do well. The best opportunities will be in the U.S. because Canadian companies will be constrained by government budgets as long as health care remains 100 percent public.

There are several mutual funds that specialize in this field. The top performer recently is the Talvest Global Health Care Fund, which returned 51 percent for the year to August 31.

Financial services. Wealth management has become the new buzzword of the financial services industry as the twentieth century winds down. Everyone, from banks to insurance companies, wants a piece of this lucrative business. We expect the demand for professional money management and estate planning to grow rapidly as we move into the twenty-first century for two reasons: the increasing complexity of the financial world and the growing capital assets of baby boomers as they approach retirement age.

There are some funds that specialize in this sector, although they have not done well recently because of weakness in Canadian bank stocks over the summer of

1999. However, long-term, the AIC Advantage Fund, which focuses on financial institution stocks, has done very well for its investors. Over the decade to August 31, 1999, the fund produced an average annual return of better than 17 percent. That's indicative of the kind of potential this sector offers.

Computer technology. There is absolutely no doubt that computer technology is going to continue to dominate the investing scene in the twenty-first century. There is so much happening, on so many fronts, that the prospects are dazzling.

There are many ways to invest in this burgeoning industry. They include:

Hardware manufacturers: These are the companies that make the boxes, the key boards, the innards, the printers, the disk drives and all the other accoutrements that make up a modern computer system. We're talking about the IBMs, Dells, and Hewlitt-Packards of the world.

The beauty of these companies is the speed of obsolescence in the industry. The technology is advancing so quickly that a brand-new machine is outdated in a couple of years. This creates a steady market for new components, such as modems and expanded hard drives, as well as for whole new systems. Car makers have nothing on these guys.

Software developers: Here we get into the Microsofts of the world, the companies that produce the intelligence that makes your computer the useful tool that it is. Again, this is a terrific business because of the obsolescence factor. A new version of Windows guarantees millions of new sales. Games are becoming ever more sophisticated. Business applications are always being upgraded. It's a money machine.

Access companies: These are the firms that make their money by providing on line access to the Internet, along with a bunch of accompanying goodies in the form of special features. America Online is the best-known and most successful.

Content providers: This is a growing part of the business, consisting of companies whose main function is to create Web content for resale.

Advertising specialists: The growth of the Internet will inevitably lead to an expansion of online advertising. Companies like Double-Click are already profiting.

This list just scratches the surface. The computer technology industry is already huge, but it continues to expand like a supernova. You can invest by buying individual companies, but a better way may be to choose a mutual fund that will provide broader diversification. Our top choice at this time is the Green Line Science and Technology Fund, which had an incredible one-year rate of return of 115.5 percent to August 31, 1999 and a five-year average annual compound rate of return of 33.1 percent.

Entertainment. The entertainment industry was one of the dominant forces of the twentieth century. It figures to be equally so in the twenty-first. However, we expect it will evolve into some very different formats over time. By the middle of the century, we expect that all upscale homes will be built with an "entertainment room" that will feature wall-size screens, multi-dimensional speakers, and virtual reality equipment. You will "live" the entertainment experience, not just observe it or listen to it.

The companies that will prosper from these breathtaking advances will be those on the leading edge of both hardware and content development. One firm that immediately comes to mind is Sony, which has traditionally been in the vanguard of new electronic technology and is also actively involved on the content side, from movie production to compact disks.

At this time, there are no mutual funds in Canada that specifically target the entertainment industry in a meaningful way (there is one labour-sponsored venture capital fund but it is very small and not actively sold). But we expect that will change going forward, because this industry figures to be a big money-maker in the next century.

Telecommunications. The competition is fierce, especially in the domestic telephone market. But telecommunications companies are likely to offer great growth opportunities in the twenty-first century for two reasons:

- Rapidly increasing demand for data transmission. The Internet and other forms of data transmission offer tremendous possibilities to telecommunications firms. They're already investing billions of dollars to expand capacity in this area, with much more to come.
- Demand in developing countries. The emerging nations of the world are far behind the West and Japan in terms of basic telephone service, to say nothing of data transmission, satellite communications, etc. There is going to be a lot of catching up to do. Companies like Bell Canada International are already positioning themselves to take advantage of this.

There are several dedicated telecommunications mutual funds now available that offer investors an opportunity to invest in this area. We particularly like Spectrum United Global Telecommunications Fund, which had a five-year average annual compound rate of return of 22.7 percent to August 31, 1999.

Vacation properties. For a change of pace, let's give some thought to the outlook for vacation property in the next century. They aren't making any more of this stuff. Desirable mountain property and lake or ocean front land should steadily increase in value as the years pass, especially if the location is easily accessible from major centres.

However, we know from experience that this kind of real estate goes through boom and bust cycles. Back in the early '90s you could have bought lake front homes in Ontario's fashionable Muskoka district for sixty cents on the dollar. By the end of the decade, prices were going through the roof. One home on Lake Joseph that had been purchased for less than $300,000 a decade before was assessed at over $1 million.

The beauty of investing in vacation property is that you can enjoy it while the value is rising. Just don't make the mistake of buying at the top of a cycle or selling at the bottom.

CONCLUSION

There are many more profit possibilities in the next century. We haven't even touched on the potential of home security systems, cloning, agriculture, tourism, education, and more. Exciting times lie ahead, but they could be confusing times as well if you don't keep your perspective.

But if you stay with the basic guidelines we've outlined in this chapter, and follow the portfolio-building techniques and strategy advice still to come, you'll make out just fine.

THE OUTLOOK FOR
THE YEAR 2000

So the U.S. Federal Reserve decides to raise interest rates – the second quarter-point increase in 1999. Rumours at the time of writing suggested we might see a third hike. The Fed had adopted a neutral bias last August. At the time, all the moves were premised on the position that the U.S. economy was in overdrive.

NORTH AMERICAN OUTLOOK
It All Depends on Your Time Horizon

The increase in U.S. interest rates was billed as a preemptive strike against inflation. That from Fed governors who still believe that tight employment markets lead to higher wages, which leads to — gulp — inflation!

Not that there were any other signs of inflation. The consumer price index (CPI) was tame, as was the producer price index (PPI). (The PPI measures what manufacturers pay for goods and services that are then recast and sold at the retail level. It is seen as a forward-looking inflation indicator: According to theory, if prices are rising at the PPI level, it won't be long before those same increases show up in the CPI numbers.)

The principal problem last August was the employment numbers — if you can call it a problem when an economy has full employment. There was also concern that growth in the Pacific Basin could take some steam out of the U.S. economy.

But this is a Canadian book. You might ask, why are you paying so much attention to the U.S. economy? What about us? Unfortunately, our economy will always be driven to a large extent by what goes on south of the forty-ninth parallel. When the U.S. sneezes, we get a cold. When the U.S. is expanding, we benefit (although, in this last expansion, we have not kept pace with the U.S. experience). The bottom line is that what affects the U.S. market will have consequences here. And within the context of a global forecast, it's important to understand what is driving the biggest economy in the world.

A U.S. Sneeze, a Canadian Cold

The U.S. Federal Reserve has a dual weapon in the war against inflation: the Fed Funds Rate and the Discount Rate. The first one is the rate charged by banks when lending to one another; the second is the rate the Fed charges banks that are borrowing to prop up their reserves.

If the Fed thinks the economy may be overheating, it will raise one or both of these rates in the hopes of slowing demand. In other words, these rates reflect the bias of the Fed. Higher rates indicate a tightening bias, while lower rates mean an easing of monetary conditions. Commercial banks are expected to follow the lead of the Fed. (If they don't, the Fed can resort to other more drastic policies to produce the desired effect.)

The Bank of Canada has many of the same weapons at its disposal. However, for the most part, policies at the Bank of Canada are affected by policies at the U.S. Fed. Say, for example, the Fed raises rates by 100 basis points (one percent) over the course of a year, in an effort to slow down the U.S. economy.

Let's assume that the Canadian economy is expanding, but, typically for most North American recoveries, at a slower pace than the U.S. economy. The Bank of Canada may not want to raise interest rates, fearing that a decision to do so could have a severe impact on the Canadian recovery. However, if the Bank of Canada does not follow the lead of the Fed, the value of the Canadian dollar will suffer.

A lower Canadian dollar can have a dramatic impact on our economy. A lower dollar makes it more expensive to buy U.S. goods and services, for instance. That winter holiday in Florida will cost more, and in the long run, a lower dollar can be inflationary.

On the positive side, a lower loonie makes Canadian exports more attractive. Given the Free Trade Agreement, Canadian companies get to enjoy windfall profits at the expense of U.S. corporations competing in the same markets. But how long will that last before someone in Congress starts to complain? They will argue that Canada has an unfair advantage over U.S. companies in their congressional districts, because of a favourable exchange rate. In the end, Congress may jawbone the Bank of Canada into some sort of action, even though it may not make much sense in terms of domestic policy.

Interest Rate Debate

Our Year 2000 forecast begins and ends with Fed policy. There are pieces in the middle that will not require Fed intervention. But we need to understand what the Fed is looking at in order to make rational decisions about the future.

We suspect that the Fed will be preoccupied with the employment data through most of 2000. But the numbers they will look at are most likely not the ones you should be concentrating on.

Consider an example. In August, 1999, the Fed raised the discount rate and the Fed funds rate by 25 basis points. There were a couple of reports that made these rate hikes a foregone conclusion. The first was the July, 1999 employment data. The U.S. Commerce Department had released a report that U.S. companies added 310,000 jobs to their payrolls in July, 1999. It's not the raw number that carries the greatest weight, but rather the actual number versus the best estimates. The creation of 310,000 new jobs was well ahead of consensus estimates of 200,000 new jobs. This implied an over-heated economy.

From the Fed's perspective, with so many new jobs being created and with such low unemployment numbers — the U.S. economy had 4.3 percent unemployment at the time of that report — there was bound to be increased pressure on wages.

In fact, within the July jobs numbers were indications of wage pressure. Over the year ending July, 1999, average hourly earnings had risen about three percent. Even more suggestive were the quarterly numbers. According to the Commerce Department, the quarterly numbers suggested that U.S. wages were rising at a 3.8 percent clip, much higher than market estimates of 3.4 percent. In other words, if wages kept gaining at the same pace, they would rise 3.8 percent between July, 1999 and July, 2000.

But is it reasonable to assume that higher wages always lead to inflation? We're not so sure. First of all, you can't view employment data and wage increases in a vacuum. Higher wages by themselves are not inflationary — a point that U.S. Labor Secretary Alexis Herman was quick to make at the time he was releasing those figures.

Wages have to be viewed within the context of productivity. And at the time of writing, the actual year-over-year output per worker had risen 3.9 percent. So productivity was up even more than wages over the same period.

Let's consider these numbers within the context of your local widget company. Your company pays employees $10 an hour, and the employees produce 10 widgets an hour. So each widget costs your company one dollar to make.

Now suppose you raise the employees' rate of pay to $11 an hour. That's a 10 percent wage increase, which, on the surface, is inflationary. But what if that employee can now produce 12 widgets in the same hour? You've got a 20 percent increase in productivity. Your company's profit margin increases, because it now only costs 91.7 cents to produce each widget.

As long as productivity is able to keep pace with wage increases, then it's possible to have higher wages without inflation. This is a phenomenon we've seen throughout most of the 1990s.

Which Numbers Are Right?

So, knowing this, why did the Fed raise rates in August, 1999? It comes down to your time horizon. If you are a

Fed governor, and are gearing up for a preemptive interest rate hike, the quarter-to-quarter numbers, even the month-to-month numbers, are where you will focus. The Fed tends to look at the shorter term numbers, because they are trying to be proactive rather then reactive — that is, trying to make changes before the economy goes too far down the wrong road.

You'll look at statistics like the U.S. Labor Department's productivity-and-costs report, which covers a broad range of wages, salaries, and benefits, including stock options. And that number soared at a five percent annual rate in July 1999, the largest increase in more than 18 months. Any slowdown in productivity, and unit labour costs (determined by the cost per widget) will shoot up rapidly. Demand is already strong — and may increase, as the economies in the Asia Pacific Basin pick up steam. Labour markets are tight. If prices in the early stages of processing are beginning to tighten, companies may increase prices.

In that regard, the Fed may be on to something. We don't think that third quarter productivity will be any better than what was recorded in the second quarter. Remember, these are quarter-to-quarter comparisons, extrapolated to an annual rate.

We have concerns about the third quarter of 1999, and perhaps through the first quarter of 2000; productivity may have trouble keeping pace with wages. We say that because the number of hours an employee worked in the second quarter of 1999 was on the rise. A longer work week means overtime, and that translates into higher costs for the company.

Employees earning time-and-a-half need to produce 50 percent more to maintain the balance between productivity and wage increases. How many people do you know who produce 50 percent more when they are working overtime? The longer the work week, the greater the amount of overtime being paid, and the harder it is for companies to maintain their profit margins. And there lies the problem with an overheated economy.

But we think most of these concerns will abate by the end of the first quarter of 2000. And for long-term investors, which is what you ought to be if you are investing in mutual funds, the far horizon is more important to your financial health.

Over the longer term, we do think that productivity will continue to outpace wage increases. Of course, that means employees must be motivated to produce more.

Bonuses based on productivity are one motivator. Sixty percent of Fortune 500 companies offer such bonuses. Another way to increase production is through technological advances, which can help companies streamline their production processes and build better products cheaper. Spending on new technology accounts for more than 30 percent of U.S. gross domestic production, and has been a significant part of the current expansion.

What About Capacity?

Of course, we need to ask how much room the U.S. economy would have to expand, if it were truly overheating. Is there sufficient slack in the system for companies to ramp up production, if necessary? We measure that with a statistic known as capacity utilization.

In June, 1999 U.S. companies were running at 80.3 percent of their maximum capacity, down slightly from 80.4 percent in May. Both months were well below the 85 percent level that traditionally triggers capacity concerns. (Again, small percentage changes can have dramatic impacts on the overall economy.) We think the numbers leave sufficient room to ramp up production. That's important information for investors with a long time horizon.

What About Y2K?

One final point to consider is Y2K. You've heard a lot of talk about the new millennium. This is another time horizon to contend with, albeit one with a pre-determined expiration date.

We think Y2K may explain some of the distortion in the 1999 productivity numbers in 1999. And removal of the millennium bug may spark productivity increases in the year 2000.

The world spent billions to solve the Year 2000 issue. Yet despite the enormous costs associated with this nonproductive item, companies were still able, for the most part, to increase their profit margins without triggering inflation. How much better will these companies do when they can begin spending their technology budget on improving productivity?

The way we see it, the new millennium sets the stage for some intriguing prospects. We'll have survived the Y2K scare. The economies of the Asia Pacific Basin should continue to bloom. We think Japan will have found the necessary footing for a sustained recovery. North American companies will start spending on new technologies, which should keep productivity running ahead of wage settlements. The growth-without-inflation scenario will continue.

What It All Means

All these paths lead us back to the American consumer. Higher wages in a non-inflationary environment translate into disposable income. That income can be used to buy new products or make new investments. The former leads to higher profits, the latter to greater liquidity. In either case, it translates into higher stock value.

Of course consumption patterns create their own problems. Scary U.S. trade figures have given some economists reason to pause. In June, 1999, according to the U.S. Commerce Department, the United States imported $24.6 billion more than it exported. That one-month deficit was $4 billion higher than expectations, 16.3 percent above the May level, and 40 percent above the same period the previous year. And for the record, 1998's U.S. trade deficit had been an all-time high.

Again, a trend is more important — e.g., the 16.3 percent increase over the May number — than the raw numbers are. Economists fear that deficits can have negative repercussions for the U.S. dollar. Lester Thurow, a professor at the Massachusetts Institute of Technology and a heavy hitter on the U.S. scene believes that trade deficits can trigger "capital flight" similar to what hit South Korea and other troubled Asian countries in 1997.

If he's right, record U.S. trade deficits would further erode the value of the U.S. dollar, which in turn could drive down stock and bond prices as foreign investors dump their U.S. dollar-denominated holdings. But before you move your entire portfolio to cash, let's think about this from a real-world perspective.

Can you really compare the U.S. economy of 1999 with South Korea or the other Asia Pacific economies of 1997? In the real world, "capital flight" is the result of unstable economies and a weak political infrastructure. We are not expecting to see capital leave the world's biggest economy anytime soon.

And to be blunt, we don't have any real faith in the U.S. trade numbers at the best of times. First of all, when the numbers are released, they are two months old. And we're not convinced they are particularly accurate.

In the real world, the U.S. government collects a duty on imports, and therefore has a vested interest in accurately valuing these goods. However, charges are rarely levied on exports. So ask yourself, if there is no revenue being generated from the export side of the ledger, is it really likely that the government spends much time trying to value exports accurately?

Dennis Gartman, an independent analyst in Vienna, Virginia, raised this issue at a conference in November 1998. According to Gartman, the U.S. government takes a best-guess approach to many exports. For example, software exports and full-length movies are weighed and then assigned a value based on their weight. According to Gartman, the U.S. government values software and movies as plastic... worth two cents a pound.

That can be significant. Intellectual property makes up a large percentage of U.S. exports. And it may be that the value of these goods is being drastically understated by the U.S. Commerce Department — rendering trade figures useless.

Gartman believes that the only reliable numbers are those that directly affect government revenue. Accounting for tax revenue is a case in point. And those numbers tell a very different story.

During the first ten months of fiscal 1999 (the U.S. government's fiscal year ends on September 30), the government took in U.S. $69.11 billion more than it spent. That surplus is more than 60 percent ahead of the comparable period in 1998. In fact, by the end of fiscal year 1999, the U.S. government will record the largest surplus in history.

How is that possible, if we are to believe the trade numbers? The trade deficit implies that consumers are spending more on foreign goods, and the profits generated from those purchases are being shipped overseas. How is it, then, that American companies continue to report record profits, and why are U.S. tax revenues way ahead of expectations?

Summary

Perhaps, based on what we've learned, it's time for a long-term reality check. We think you can take the U.S. trade numbers with a grain of salt. They may occupy center stage at some point during the year 2000, but aside from any short-term impact a surprise deficit number may have, we won't be making decisions based on trade numbers.

We also think that productivity gains will outpace wage gains starting in the second quarter of 2000. If we're right, that implies longer-term growth without inflation. And the fact the Fed is raising rates now may itself provide oomph to the equity markets… longer term. Because, if our scenario plays out, you won't see any inflation. And that will eventually put the Fed in a position to cut interest rates sometime next year. Think what that could do for stock prices down the road.

If the fear of higher interest rates can cap the potential upside to the equity market, the idea that the Fed may eventually cut rates would make bonds less appealing than stocks. And that can do wonders for the equity markets.

Over the short term, the North American financial markets may drift. But in the process, we may be setting in motion the conditions for double-digit returns in 2000.

THE GLOBAL OUTLOOK

A basic principle of investing is that diversification is a good thing and that global diversification is even better! Global investing works because the world is a fragmented, segmented, unpredictable place. Since there are different forces at play, markets are constantly fluctuating. At any time, there will be some markets that are particularly strong and some that are weak.

If there was ever a market to which this principle applies, it's Canada. Over the past 15 years, the TSE 300 Composite Total Return Index has recorded an annual compound rate of return of 9.55 percent — at the lower end of the industrialized world. In contrast, the United States S&P 500 was up by 19.46 percent, while the Morgan Stanley Capital International World Composite Index (MSCIWCI) was up by 17.35 percent. Furthermore, both the S&P and the MSCIWCI had less volatility than the TSE 300.

A large portion of the variance in overall stock prices is due to the unique risk of each country, and can therefore be diversified away in a security portfolio. Most of the rewards of global investing consist of striking a good portfolio balance.

For the money you intend to commit to equity investments outside Canada, we recommend putting 25 percent in Europe; 25 percent in the United States; 30 percent in the Far East (20 percent in Japan, 10 percent in the rest of the Asia Pacific Basin); 15 percent in Latin America; and 5 percent in emerging markets, specifically India. You've already read our thoughts on the United States. Here is our take on the rest of the world.

The Story in Europe

Europe has been a good place for investors in the 1990s. Over the past five years, the 500-company, 14-country Morgan Stanley Capital International (MSCI) Europe Index returned over 21.3 percent a year.

This was the highest of all of the regions. Over that same time period, the MSCI Europe, Australia, and Far East Index, known as EAFE, gained 10.0 percent per year. In 1998, European markets led the way as well, with Germany, France and the United Kingdom registering gains of 17.7 percent, 31.7 percent, and 14.6 percent, respectively.

Furthermore, at the start of 1999, the European outlook appeared buoyant. January 1, 1999, or E-Day, was the culmination of years of planning for European monetary unification. The treaty, signed in Maastricht in 1992 by the then twelve members of the European Community, had set out the eligibility conditions for individual countries. Eleven of the 15 countries of the European Community agreed to the terms of the January 1, 1999, union. The 11-country "European zone" includes countries such as Italy and Portugal, which as recently as two years ago appeared to have no chance of meeting the stringent fiscal and monetary entry rules conditions, had tightened their economic policies and made the cut.

On January 1, conversion exchange rates were frozen and pegged to the new Euro, which is now used for paper transactions. The individual European currencies are still in use in day-to-day monetary transactions, although they will be phased out by 2002.

The benefits associated with a single currency and fixed exchange rates appeared enormous. European and multinational firms using different currencies will no longer need hedging transactions to manage foreign exchange risk. The new European community was expected to emerge as a powerful economic entity with approximately 30 percent of world output. It was expected that the Euro would rival the U.S. dollar in importance in global markets.

However, events haven't unfolded quite as expected. The bloom appears to be off the European rose; Europe has been one of the weakest investment sectors as of June, 1999.

European growth has been slowing, averaging an unimpressive 1.6 percent on an annualized basis, or about 40 percent of that of the U.S. Europe's chronic unemployment problems are on the rise — recently the average rate for Europe was 10.4 percent. Germany, the so-called leader of the Euro zone, is mired in a serious slump, with growth in 1999 expected to be around 1.5 percent at most. German unemployment is continuing to climb, and the government's decision in 1999 to curtail part-time jobs was greeted unenthusiastically.

Furthermore, the Euro (EU) has been on a sharp descent. It opened at U.S.$1.1711 on January 1, but has fallen as low as U.S.$1.0108 before rebounding. Overall it has depreciated by more than 10 percent against the U.S. dollar.

Since European growth has been running at a much slower pace than that of the United States, European short-term interest rates have fallen to half of those of the U.S. This alone would be bearish for the currency. To make matters worse, there is some confusion over how strict the rules of the monetary regime will be. For example, the Euro zone finance ministers allowed Italy to relax its budget targets, a unilateral action that was not supposed to be allowed. The European Central Bank (central bank of the Euro zone) was ceded all monetary powers under the economic union.

Will things turn around for the Euro? Much depends on the commitment of member nations to a European trading bloc. The EU and its currency are artificial creations of a pan-European bureaucracy with far from unanimous popular support. Such structures are historically difficult to maintain, especially in light of the European tendency toward nationalism.

There are huge potential benefits to a common free-trade bloc and a unified currency regime. But the EU and the Euro have many tests to face before they can match the powerhouse U.S. economy and the strength of the U.S. dollar. Eventually global forces will require the European economies to liberalize and gradually erode their fortress-like mentality. The EU should survive and prosper and eventually become a tough competitor for the U.S. dollar.

Asia

Countries and regions fall out of favour and are avoided by investors. The Far East was one of the strongest regions in the world in the 1990 through mid-1997 period, in terms of economic growth and stock market performance.

However, investors have generally shunned the Far East over the mid-1997 through mid-1999 period. In part, this reflected the financial crises associated with the "Asian flu." The economic and political events leading up to these problems started in Thailand in June of 1997, when the Thai currency collapsed.

The smaller Southeast Asia countries were hit one by one as their currencies in turn came under pressure, due to escalating deficits and weakening economies. The problems then spread to the stronger countries in the region, engulfing two of the economic powers, South Korea and Taiwan.

Then the currency problems struck Hong Kong in late October 1997; the Hong Kong stock market lost over 10 percent in one single-day plunge on October 23. Events spilled over into Europe and North America in a domino effect — and the term "Asian flu" was coined. Further, in August 1997, the "Volga virus" had hit, with the virtual collapse of the Russian economy. The "Volga virus" struck a global market already contaminated by the Asian flu, and the result was a severe quality crisis.

Asia became a fallen angel. However, conditions have finally started to turn. Asian economies are expected to grow at a rate of 2.3 percent in 1999, with rates accelerating after that. The Far East should be one of the strongest regions in the new millennium. Of the total money you commit to equity investments outside of Canada, we recommend that 20 percent be placed in Japan, and 10 percent in the rest of Asia.

Here's our take on some current situations.

Japan

Japan was the economic miracle of the post-war era. The Japanese economy was considered the model of the industrialized world, with controlled inflation, low interest rates, and a responsive labour and business sector. Productivity rates were the highest in the world. A major investment boom sent real estate and security prices to unprecedented heights.

Accordingly, when the global recession hit, it hit Japan the hardest; the country has suffered through its worst downturn since World War II. To make matters worse, Japan's long-standing export propensity remained intact. The yen continued to strengthen despite the recession. A deflationary spiral developed. First, bloated real estate prices plunged; then security prices collapsed. There was virtually no economic growth. Japan saw a host of bankruptcies.

Tokyo has been one of the world's worst markets in the 1990s. The country spent the decade in the throes of a nasty recession — by some definitions, a depression.

Although it took almost four years to produce results, a major initiative launched in the summer of 1995 has reversed the economic situation. The Bank of Japan, through a liquidity injection program, forced interest rates lower, encouraged investors to invest abroad and purposely sent the yen tumbling. Japan began to work its way out of its problems by exporting its surplus through the purchase of foreign bonds, resulting in a weakening yen.

Prime Minister Keizo Obuchi's government introduced a major stimulus package aimed primarily at reviving the moribund consumer-spending sector. The Japanese banks and government are still working on plans to deal with bad loans — estimates for them have run as high as 100 trillion yen on. In fact, we're already seeing changes in Japan's largest banks, through restructuring, mergers, or the formation of loose alliances.

The recovery is continuing. Japan's economy was predicted to contract in 1999. However, analysts are now projecting a 0.5 percent growth. This is hardly the stuff of expansion but it does represent further evidence that the nine-year recession is finally ending. The Tokyo Stock Exchange has been one of the world's leaders in 1999, with a gain of better than 30 percent to the end of June 1999.

The only fly in the ointment is the yen, which tends to rise as the economy expands. However, the upturn in U.S. interest rates may help keep the yen under control. The recovery is reaching the self-sustaining stage — the only worry is the pressure that could be placed on interest rates.

Taiwan

The Taiwan market had a terrible year in 1998. The after effects of the Asian flu, the confidence crisis associated with the Volga Virus, and then the technology stock collapse (Taiwan is big in this area) all took their toll. However, the Taipei Market was having a nice run in early 1999, fueled by lower interest rates and improved domestic spending.

After a short dip in January, it was almost straight up until early July. Then the Taiwan government officials pushed things too far and precipitated a China crisis. In July, Taiwan's president, Lee Teng-Hui, stated that China and Taiwan should deal with each other as separate states. Chinese officials viewed the statement as highly provocative, since China considers the island of Taiwan as merely a renegade area and has long wanted to reunite it with the mainland. On August 2, 1999, China announced a test launch of a new long-range missile. The war of words represents the worst crisis since 1996, when China's military, in a major saber-rattling display, lobbed missiles into the Taiwan Strait. Taiwan prices sold off as the skirmish continued.

Taiwan's economy remains healthy. Unlike those of most of the region, it grew in 1998, recording GNP growth of five percent. The government's economic support package of support for the ailing real estate market has been constructive. We like the prospects in Taiwan where interest rates have moved lower and domestic spending is improving.

Latin America

A region that usually reflects its own unique developments rather than the systematic pull of North America is Latin America. Latin America should represent a small but permanent element of your global portfolio.

The major Latin America investment markets are "the big four": Argentina, Brazil, Chile, and Mexico, plus Peru and Venezuela. These countries and their markets are still at the developing stages. The free market initiatives undertaken (including the abolition of price controls, removal of trade barriers, and privatization of telecommunications and utilities) have created a constructive investment climate. Latin America countries have been steadily removing foreign restriction barriers and allowing for freer flow of capital. On the development front, a young population (about 55 percent of the South American population is below 25 years of age), democratic reforms, and advances in managing the huge supplies of natural resources have been constructive.

But this is a difficult and sometimes perverse region. Two steps forward, one step (sometimes two or three steps) back. The politics remain questionable; political scandals surface with some regularity and intensity; and the underground economy and influence peddling are still an integral part of life.

In late 1994, the Mexico peso crisis sent shock waves through world financial markets. The so-called "Tequila crisis" led to a severe devaluation of the Mexico peso. The Mexican peso was under pressure from a number of forces, including a sharply escalating current account deficit. The Mexican government lifted its peg on the peso/U.S. dollar, effectively devaluing the currency. By early January 1995 the currency had depreciated by over 45 percent and a financial crisis was underway. The problems spread to other Latin America countries.

The situation looked very gloomy and it took over 18 months for the market to recover. But the Mexican government's tight money conditions, loans and guarantees programs, and domestic interest rates policies worked to counteract the problems. Since then the introduction of economic and currency stabilization programs have helped considerably, although Latin America remains one of the most volatile economic regions in the world.

Countries such as Argentina and Brazil did not sit back and passively wait for the same fate as Mexico. Instead, in the wake of the crisis, they toughened their stabilization plans, maintained the currencies and withstood severe recessions.

The Latin America region is very disease vulnerable and is still reeling from the aftershocks of the Asian flu, the Volga virus, and the Brazilian currency crisis in January 1999. Weak commodity-prices (particularly oil) were a problem for this commodity-dependent region.

But all that notwithstanding, take a long-term view of this region that is trading at low P/E's and low price/book values.

The outlook for Mexico is particularly strong. The economic reform program implemented in 1995 has been relatively successful. Confidence has been restored as investors have bought into the plan. The Zedillo government's free trade program, fiscal conservatism, and contained currency management have restored confidence in Mexico and Latin America in general, and investors are streaming back. The Bolsa Mexicana de Volores, Mexico's only stock exchange, has been one of the world's leading markets in 1999, recording better than 25 percent gains to the end of June.

Financial crises are not new to Mexico — in recent years they have come in six-year waves (the peso was devalued in 1976, 1982, 1988, and 1994!).

However, Mexico is only one component of Latin America. And most investors who want to put money in this region do so with mutual funds. Taken as a whole, the average Latin American fund had lost three percent in the first six months of 1999.

Chile is now a significant component of World Bank and Morgan Stanley Capital international emerging markets indexes. This means that global fund managers who maintain index strategies will maintain a permanent Chilean allocation.

Of the total money you commit to equity investments outside of Canada, we recommend putting 15 percent of that amount into Latin America.

Emerging Countries

Our choice of emerging countries for the new millennium: India.

The Bombay Stock Exchange (BSE) suffered through a horrible 1998, losing about 17 percent of its value, reflecting the generally weak performance of all emerging countries. Of course, India's nuclear bomb crisis didn't help things — the BSE lost 8 percent in the midst of the crisis.

India's massive economic reform movement is now in its tenth year and remains focused on privatization and deregulation and globalization. The Indian economy is revitalizing. GNP growth was 5.8 percent in 1998 and running at just under 6 percent in 1999. The inflation rate has fallen to 4.7 percent.

Unfortunately, India has done little to curb its enormous population growth. At its present rate of expansion,

India could outpace China (which is reining in growth) in the next century.

The government is also focusing on reforming its secondary markets and attempting to attract foreign investment. It wasn't so long ago that foreign investment was discouraged, even prohibited. Now the government is actively encouraging investment, and a number of new investment vehicles have been created.

Indian stock markets are underdeveloped and volatile. More often than not, the Bombay Stock Exchange is at either the top or the bottom of the global performance list. There often seems to be a scandal underway. But slowly but surely Bombay is cleaning up its act. The Securities Exchange Regulation Act is to be amended to allow derivatives trading — a step that should improve overall market liquidity.

India presents an intriguing long-term investing opportunity. For strategic asset allocation purposes, India should be an essential part of your international exposure. India's negative correlation with the rest of the world markets also makes it an excellent candidate for diversification.

Of the total money you commit to equity investments outside of Canada, we recommend putting five percent into India.

Following are six model asset mixes, reflecting our outlook for 2000. These mixes range in aggressiveness from the "Safety" portfolio to the "Growth" portfolio. They are divided into RRSP and non-registered listings, the non-registered mix is the ideal one in each case. See "Who's Afraid of the Foreign Content Rule?" for a complete explanation of changes to foreign-content rules.

MODEL ASSET MIXES FOR 2000

SAFETY								SCORE: UNDER 15
Equities			Income			Cash		
Min	Policy	Max	Min	Policy	Max	Min	Policy	Max
0%	10%	20%	60%	75%	90%	10%	15%	30%

YEAR 2000 EXTENDED ASSET MIX

	NON RRSP	RRSP
Canadian Equity	5.0%	5.0%
U.S. Equity	5.0%	5.0%
International Equity	5.0%	5.0%
Special Equity	0.0%	0.0%
Total Equity Assets	**15.0%**	**15.0%**
Dividend Funds	25.0%	25.0%
Domestic Bond	25.0%	35.0%
Global Bond	15.0%	0.0%
Total Income Assets	**65.0%**	**60.0%**
Money Market	20.0%	25.0%
Total Cash Assets	**20.0%**	**25.0%**

SAFETY / INCOME								SCORE: 15 - 24
Equities			Income			Cash		
Min	Policy	Max	Min	Policy	Max	Min	Policy	Max
10%	20%	30%	50%	65%	80%	10%	15%	25%

YEAR 2000 EXTENDED ASSET MIX

	NON RRSP	RRSP
Canadian Equity	7.0%	7.0%
U.S. Equity	9.0%	7.0%
International Equity	9.0%	9.0%
Special Equity	0.0%	0.0%
Total Equity Assets	**25.0%**	**25.0%**
Dividend Funds	20.0%	25.0%
Domestic Bond	20.0%	30.0%
Global Bond	15.0%	0.0%
Total Income Assets	**55.0%**	**55.0%**
Money Market	20.0%	20.0%
Total Cash Assets	**20.0%**	**20.0%**

INCOME / GROWTH								SCORE: 25 - 34
Equities			**Income**			**Cash**		
Min	Policy	Max	Min	Policy	Max	Min	Policy	Max
20%	35%	50%	30%	50%	70%	10%	15%	25%

YEAR 2000 EXTENDED ASSET MIX

	NON RRSP	RRSP
Canadian Equity	10.0%	20.0%
U.S. Equity	12.5%	10.0%
International Equity	12.5%	10.0%
Special Equity	5.0%	0.0%
Total Equity Assets	**40.0%**	**40.0%**
Dividend Funds	15.0%	20.0%
Domestic Bond	10.0%	20.0%
Global Bond	15.0%	0.0%
Total Income Assets	**40.0%**	**40.0%**
Money Market	20.0%	20.0%
Total Cash Assets	**20.0%**	**20.0%**

GROWTH / INCOME								SCORE: 35 - 44
Equities			**Income**			**Cash**		
Min	Policy	Max	Min	Policy	Max	Min	Policy	Max
30%	50%	70%	25%	40%	55%	5%	10%	15%

YEAR 2000 EXTENDED ASSET MIX

	NON RRSP	RRSP
Canadian Equity	12.5%	30.0%
U.S. Equity	20.0%	7.5%
International Equity	20.0%	7.5%
Special Equity	7.5%	5.0%
Total Equity Assets	**60.0%**	**50.0%**
Dividend Funds	15.0%	25.0%
Domestic Bond	5.0%	15.0%
Global Bond	10.0%	0.0%
Total Income Assets	**30.0%**	**40.0%**
Money Market	10.0%	10.0%
Total Cash Assets	**10.0%**	**10.0%**

GROWTH								SCORE: 45 - 54
	Equities			Income			Cash	
Min	Policy	Max	Min	Policy	Max	Min	Policy	Max
40%	60%	80%	20%	30%	40%	5%	10%	15%

YEAR 2000 EXTENDED ASSET MIX

	NON RRSP	RRSP
Canadian Equity	15.0%	30.0%
U.S. Equity	22.5%	7.5%
International Equity	22.5%	7.5%
Special Equity	10.0%	5.0%
Total Equity Assets	**70.0%**	**50.0%**
Dividend Funds	15.0%	35.0%
Domestic Bond	5.0%	10.0%
Global Bond	5.0%	0.0%
Total Income Assets	**25.0%**	**45.0%**
Money Market	5.0%	5.0%
Total Cash Assets	**5.0%**	**5.0%**

AGGRESSIVE GROWTH SCORE								SCORE: OVER 55
	Equities			Income			Cash	
Min	Policy	Max	Min	Policy	Max	Min	Policy	Max
50%	75%	100%	0%	20%	30%	0%	5%	10%

YEAR 2000 EXTENDED ASSET MIX

	NON RRSP	RRSP
Canadian Equity	20.0%	35.0%
U.S. Equity	27.5%	5.0%
International Equity	27.5%	5.0%
Special Equity	10.0%	10.0%
Total Equity Assets	**85.0%**	**55.0%**
Dividend Funds	5.0%	32.5%
Domestic Bond	5.0%	10.0%
Global Bond	2.5%	0.0%
Total Income Assets	**12.5%**	**42.5%**
Money Market	2.5%	2.5%
Total Cash Assets	**2.5%**	**2.5%**

THE FUNDLINE: YOUR PORTFOLIO BUILDING BLOCKS

We believe a balanced approach best suits the needs of the long-term investor. The problem is finding the right balance – probably the most elusive concept in the investment business.

INTRODUCING THE FUNDLINE

To balance a portfolio, you need to diversify your holdings. But there is a right way and a wrong way to diversify. Holding ten or twenty mutual funds without knowing what each fund brings to the portfolio is cumbersome. And holding that set of funds without a planning system in place is unlikely to serve you well.

First you need to understand what levels of diversification are available. And then, with the proper tools, you can allocate your capital to funds that bring specific elements of diversification to the overall portfolio. You'll eliminate redundant funds. A well-diversified portfolio adds value and balance over the long term.

There are four elements to mutual funds diversification:

- Asset class (i.e. fixed income, equity, cash)
- Geographic boundaries
- Fund objectives
- Investment style

How do you incorporate the four basic diversification techniques into a portfolio? With an easy-to-understand portfolio building tool.

EXTENDED ASSET MIX / OBJECTIVES / INVESTMENT STYLE

Fund Name	Fund Type	Sub-Type	MVA	Canadian Equity	U.S. Equity	Europe	Japan	Far East	Latin America	Special Equity	Dividend	Fixed Income	Global Fixed Income	Money Market	Short Term	Mid Term	Long Term	Foreign Currency	Sector Specific	Small-Cap	Mid-Cap	Large-Cap	Top Down	Bottom Up	Value Method	Sector Rotation	Momentum	Indexation
AGF Global Real Estate Equity	Spclty	GlobRE								●								●	●	●	●	●		●	●			
AGF International Group-American Growth	USEq	LgCap	95.0		●												●	●			●	●	●				●	
AGF International Group-Asian Growth	FgnEq	PacRim	94.8					●									●	●			●	●	●				●	
AGF International Group-Canada Class	CdnEq	Divers		●													●	●		●	●		●				●	
AGF International Group-China Focus	FgnEq	China	84.8				●	●									●	●				●	●				●	
AGF International Group-European Growth	FgnEq	Europe	87.1			●											●	●				●	●				●	
AGF International Group-Germany Class	FgnEq	German	104.8			●											●	●		●	●	●	●				●	
AGF International Group-Intl Stock	FgnEq	IntlEq				●	●	●									●	●				●	●				●	
AGF International Group-Japan Class	FgnEq	Japan	114.2				●										●	●				●	●				●	
AGF International Group-Short Term Inc	FixInc	IntMkt	66.0										●		●			●					●	●				
AGF International Group-Special U.S.	USEq	Divers	64.1		●												●	●		●	●	●	●				●	
AGF International Group-World Equity	FgnEq	Global	89.2		●	●											●	●				●	●				●	
AGF International Value	FgnEq	Global	99.5		●	●											●	●			●	●	●	●	●			
AGF RSP Global Bond	FixInc	GlbBnd	86.5									●	●			●								●		●		
AGF RSP International Equity Allocation	FgnEq	Global	87.9		●	●											●	●				●						●

Since a picture is worth a thousand words, we bring you the FundLine. It's a portfolio building tool that streamlines the selection process by displaying the factors that affect the construction of a portfolio.

Within the FundLine there are 25 boxes. At the back of the book, there are FundLines for more than 1500 mutual funds. Knowing which elements a fund offers helps us eliminate redundant funds. You don't need three value-oriented Canadian equity funds, for example, because they do essentially the same thing.

For optimal diversification, simply fill in as many boxes as possible. Ideally, you will fill in at least 20 of the 25 boxes along the FundLine.

THE CHANGING ROLE OF DIVERSIFICATION

The idea that you shouldn't put all your eggs in one basket is not new. What is new is how we define the eggs that go into our basket. It wasn't so long ago that the eggs were looked on as individual stocks. Buy a portfolio of, say, 15 to 20 good stocks in different industries and you can virtually eliminate company-specific risk.

Company-specific risk refers to risks unique to certain firms. For example, the profitability of a gold mining company is driven by changes in the price of gold. Changes to the minimum wage law affect fast-food companies like McDonald's. Energy prices affect all companies to some extent, but the impact depends on the industry: When oil prices rise, so do the profits of oil companies; but those profits hurt the transportation sector, like airline and trucking companies.

This is where diversification can help. If you hold two different stocks in your portfolio, say an oil company and a transportation company, presumably you lessen the risks associated with the price of oil.

But of course, that's only true to a point. Higher oil prices would also, presumably, lead to inflation and perhaps higher interest rates — not very appealing outcomes for any company.

Studies over the past twenty years have demonstrated conclusively that you can virtually eliminate company specific risk by purchasing a diversified portfolio of stocks from a number of different industries.

But company-specific risk, while important, is not the only risk factor affecting your stock portfolio. There is also market risk. History tells us that stocks will rise and fall with the tide. When the market is going down, most stocks fall with it. And when the market is rising, it generally takes most stocks up with it. Unfortunately, there is no effective way to eliminate market risk.

Until the mid-1980s, market risk was not considered a major issue. That changed dramatically on October 19, 1987. That was Black Monday, a one-day panic sell-off that saw the stock market fall more than 23 percent. Shell-shocked investors became painfully aware of just how important market risk was.

In the aftermath of the stock market crash, investors gravitated to asset allocation. As we mentioned in "Picking Good Funds Isn't Enough", asset allocation is diversifying your basket across asset classes. By the early 1990s financial advisors were building portfolios that looked like Table 5.1 — a typical Canadian portfolio with three distinct asset classes: stocks (represented by the TSE 300 composite index), bonds (represented by the Scotia Capital Markets Bond Universe), and cash (represented by 91-day Treasury bills).

Each asset class has had its day in the sun over the last fifteen years. The TSE 300 composite index was the best performer three times. Bonds have come out on top four times, and cash has won twice. Yesterday's winners may be tomorrow's losers.

At first glance, Table 5.1 seems to suggest that you should just buy bonds. However, that's a simplistic view. It's true that during the 1990s bonds were by far the best-performing asset. They beat stocks hands down, and with less risk. (In fact, an all-bond portfolio had better risk-adjusted returns than a portfolio that was divided with 50 percent in equities, 40 percent in bonds, and 10 percent in cash; see the far right column of Table 5.1.)

TABLE 5.1

YEAR	TSE 300	SCM BONDS UNIVERSE	T-BILLS	PORTFOLIO
1998	-1.6%	9.2%	4.7%	3.4%
1997	15.0%	9.6%	3.2%	11.7%
1996	28.3%	12.3%	4.8%	19.6%
1995	14.5%	20.7%	7.6%	16.3%
1994	-0.2%	-4.3%	5.4%	-1.3%
1993	32.5%	18.1%	5.5%	24.0%
1992	-1.4%	9.8%	7.1%	3.9%
1991	12.0%	22.1%	9.8%	15.8%
1990	-14.8%	7.5%	13.5%	-3.1%
Std Deviation	15.3%	8.0%	3.2%	9.6%
Value of $1000	2,068.26	2,642.46	1,808.34	2,292.66

Source: PalTrak

The problem, of course, is that what was best in the past will not necessarily be the best in the future. Over the long term, we would expect bonds to underperform stocks, if only because stocks are the riskier asset class. And, longer term, higher-risk assets should outperform lower-risk assets.

That notion was turned upside down in the early 1990s, as interest rates began to fall from double-digit levels. Falling interest rates caused bond prices to rise dramatically. But we have to ask whether rates are likely to decline from current levels as precipitously as they did in the early 1990s. (That's what would have to happen for bonds to continue outperforming in the future.) We're not sure that's a likely scenario going forward. So over the next ten years, bonds are not likely to deliver the same kinds of returns as they did earlier.

The Extended Asset Mix (Geographic Diversification)

There is another conclusion we could draw from Table 5.1. Canadian equities, as measured by the TSE 300 composite index, have not been stellar performers during the 1990s. You might even say that the Canadian stock market has been an underperformer for the last two decades — partly because Canada is still a resource-based economy and commodity prices fell until recently, squeezing the profit margins of the resources industry.

This leads us directly into the next level of our "eggs-in-different-baskets" discussion. We know that the concept of asset allocation really took flight in the late 1980s. And we have laid the basic foundation for why asset allocation is important. Now we move to the next level, extending the asset mix decision to include geographic diversification.

FIGURE 5.1

ASSET CLASS	EXTENDED ASSET MIX		
Equity	Cdn Equity	US Equity	Intl. Equity
Fixed Income	Domestic Bonds	Global Bonds	
Cash	Money Market	CSB's	GIC's
Real Estate	Real Estate Funds	Family Home	Inv. Properties

Despite Revenue Canada's attempts to hamstring Canadian investors with outdated foreign content restrictions on RRSPs, global diversification adds performance value and reduces risk. Global diversification means that you are participating in different economies that are usually at different stages in the business cycle.

The best examples of this are Japan and the United States. In the 1980s, Japan was the hotbed of market action. Remember when 600-square-foot apartments in Tokyo were fetching more than $1 million on the open market? The Nikkei 225 stock average was above 37,000, and big-name blue-chip utility companies like Nippon Telephone were trading at 70 times earnings. Analysts were telling us that these valuations were reasonable because you had to look at different accounting standards when valuing Japanese companies. On this side of the pond, it wasn't that the U.S. stock market was in the dumps. But investors were being lured by government bonds paying double-digit interest rates. And equity markets seemed to be overvalued while trading at just 20 times earnings.

For the last ten years, the Japanese economy has paid for its excesses. Wallowing in a deflationary environment, the Nikkei 225 average is less than half the level it was ten years ago. In fact, over the last ten years, the Japanese stock market has produced a negative return. A $1,000 investment made at the beginning of 1990 was worth $674.97 at the end of December 1998. During that time, U.S. stocks have more than quadrupled in value, meaning a $1,000 investment in the U.S. stock market at the beginning of 1990 was worth $4,401.88 at the end of 1998.

Japan and the United States, then, have tended to be at opposite ends of the spectrum for the last twenty years. And these are the two largest economies in the world. If your equity assets had been split 50/50 between U.S and Japanese stocks, your portfolio would have returned $1,917.22, despite the precipitous decline in the Japanese market.

Of course, global diversification goes beyond the United States and Japan. We have Europe, the Far East, and Latin America to provide other elements of geographic diversification for your portfolio. Table 5.2 provides a lot of information about the performance of different markets during the 1990s. The shaded areas represent the top-performing markets in each calendar year. Note that each of the geographic regions has been the best-performing market at some point.

The far right column shows the performance of a portfolio equally weighted (20 percent invested in each region) among the five geographic regions. At the bottom of the table we have calculated the annual standard deviation and value of a $1,000 investment for each geographic region. (Standard deviation tells us how volatile an investment in each geographic region was during the 1990s. The higher the standard deviation, the higher the risk.)

When you build a portfolio, the idea is to reduce volatility (standard deviation), without sacrificing all of your return. The portfolio approach, if implemented properly, should produce better risk-adjusted returns over time. And, if you look at the standard deviation number in the portfolio column (far right column in table 5.2), it is lower than all other standard deviations, with the exception of the U.S. stock market.

TABLE 5.2

YEAR	CANADA	U.S.	EUROPE	JAPAN	FAR EAST	PORTFOLIO
1998	-0.4%	24.3%	34.2%	14.7%	11.4%	21.4%
1997	15.0%	28.0%	29.3%	-25.2%	-25.2%	15.3%
1996	28.6%	26.4%	23.9%	-16.6%	-8.0%	17.2%
1995	14.5%	29.8%	19.1%	-3.8%	-1.3%	15.7%
1994	1.4%	8.2%	8.7%	28.7%	21.0%	11.1%
1993	30.0%	18.5%	34.4%	29.6%	39.1%	29.4%
1992	-2.6%	14.5%	5.5%	-15.5%	-12.0%	1.5%
1991	11.7%	19.9%	12.4%	8.2%	10.4%	12.9%
1990	-13.4%	-4.2%	-8.0%	-35.7%	-34.3%	-13.9%
Std Deviation	14.5%	10.9%	14.3%	23.4%	23.0%	12.4%
Value of $1000	2,094.67	4,401.88	4,081.03	674.97	812.87	2,695.42

Source: PalTrak

Finally, take a look at the bottom line of Table 5.2, which tells you how much $1,000 invested at the beginning of 1990 would have been worth at the end of 1998. That line speaks volumes about the truly remarkable performance of the U.S. equity markets in the 1990s, not only in terms of actual return but also in terms of risk. The U.S. market returned the most on your initial investment and did so with the least amount of risk. That's not what you would normally expect over prolonged periods of time.

You might ask why the risk level in the U.S. is lower than Canada, at least in terms of standard deviation. Remember we said that standard deviation measures the variability of the underlying fund over a period of time, variablility is defined as the up and down movememnt of the underlying fund. In the U.S. over the last three years, the direction has been mostly up. In terms of variability, there has been very little downward movement in the U.S. market, and since standard deviation really takes into account up and down movements, actual standard deviation has been lower, implying, statistically at least, lower risk.

Stepping beyond the U.S. stock market for a moment, let's consider the performance of our hypothetical portfolio during the same period (see far right column of Table 5.2). Remember, we simply built the portfolio using a buy-and-hold approach, investing 20 percent of our total investment capital into each market at the beginning of 1990. No changes were made to the portfolio in the interim; no rebalancing was involved.

The portfolio had the second-lowest standard deviation of the five geographic regions, and, despite the dismal performance in Japan and the Far East during the 1990s, actually produced the third-best return of the five geographic regions — without any ongoing management.

Take a look back at our graphic Fundline, which gives you information in an easy-to-read visual form. Under the Extended Asset Mix heading, we have subdivided the three main asset classes (fixed income, cash, and equity) into 11 broader categories.

For equity funds we bring in geographic diversification with boxes representing Canada, the United States, Europe, Japan, the Far East, and Latin America. In order for a fund to be awarded a bullet under any specific country heading, the fund manager has to have at least 15 percent of the fund's assets invested in that region.

We have also included a special equity class which represents sector-specific funds, including real estate, precious metals, resource, science and technology, and any other special-equity type of fund.

Fixed-income assets are also represented in the asset class section of the FundLine. In this case, we have subdivided the fixed-income component into dividend funds, domestic bond funds, and global bond funds. The final category is money market, which simply represents any cash assets in your portfolio.

Diversification by Fund Objectives

To this point we have touched on two levels of diversification: asset mix and geographic diversification. The next level considers fund objectives.

Fund objectives look at what part of the market a fund focuses on. For example, does the fund concentrate on small-, mid- or large-cap stocks, or a combination of all three? We've all heard that over the long term, small-cap stocks tend to outperform their larger-cap cousins — although, to hear investors talk, the 1990s will go down in history as the era of the large-cap stock. For the last five years the performance of large-cap stocks has dominated, especially in the U.S. market. (Interestingly, however, if you go back to the beginning of the 1990s, the performance of the average U.S. small-cap fund has actually been a little better than the performance of the average large cap fund — despite the fact that U.S. small caps were the best-performing group in only four of the nine years in the 1990s.)

Note also from Table 5.3 that mid-cap stocks haven't led the performance parade in any given year. They also had the highest standard deviation of the three fund objectives reviewed in Table 5.3. Perhaps that is telling us that U.S. mid-cap stocks are ready to shine and will soon have their day in the sun.

TABLE 5.3

YEAR	U.S. LARGE-CAP	U.S. MID-CAP	U.S. SMALL-CAP
1998	27.8%	26.0%	18.5%
1997	30.3%	28.9%	21.7%
1996	18.1%	17.6%	11.2%
1995	26.0%	25.0%	20.5%
1994	2.6%	0.6%	0.0%
1993	13.2%	16.1%	27.8%
1992	15.9%	16.7%	22.8%
1991	25.3%	26.1%	32.3%
1990	-4.6%	-9.9%	-0.3%
Std Deviation	11.9%	13.0%	11.4%
Value of $1000	3,987.24	3,697.27	4,000.23

Source: PalTrak (average U.S. funds in each category)

In order for an equity or balanced fund to register a bullet in one of the three market-cap boxes, the fund has to have at least 30 percent of its assets invested in that specific group.

You'll notice in many sector-specific funds, we have included bullets in the small-, mid- and large-cap boxes. This isn't surprising, when you consider the mandate of a sector fund. Usually, because specialty fund managers are limited to a specific sector, they tend to buy a lot of companies in that sector, including companies of different sizes, in their attempt to diversify as much as possible.

Bond Fund Objectives

Bond funds have their own specific objectives. For example, does the manager focus on bonds with short-, medium- or long-term maturities? A short-term bond fund is one with an average term to maturity of less than three years. Mid-term bond funds have an average term to maturity of three to ten years, and long-term funds invest mostly in bonds with longer than ten years to maturity.

Normally, bond fund managers move through the maturity spectrum as the economy progresses thurough the business cycle. That is, the manager may extend the maturity — buy longer-term bonds — on a belief that interest rates are about to fall, or buy short-term bonds believing interest rates will remain the same or rise.

It is not surprising, given our previous discussion about the performance of bond funds in the 1990s, that long-term bonds were the best performers during the decade. In seven out of the last nine years, the long end of the yield curve has produced the best returns. A bond fund with a longer average term to maturity will move more dramatically than a bond fund with a shorter average term to maturity. Since interest rates have been on a downward spiral throughout most of the 1990s, longer-term bonds have been the main beneficiaries. However, when rates are rising, bond funds with a shorter average term to maturity will outperform, just as they did in 1990 and 1994.

You'll see in Table 5.4 that long-term bonds also carried the highest risk of the three bond fund objectives. Again, this is what you would expect. Going forward, with interest rates so low, we're not convinced that long bonds are the best alternative. In fact, for the next few years, bonds may well play their traditional role of reducing risk within a portfolio, rather than adding oomph to the bottom line.

TABLE 5.4

YEAR	LONG BONDS	MID BONDS	SHORT BONDS
1998	12.8%	9.1%	6.7%
1997	18.5%	9.7%	4.9%
1996	14.2%	12.7%	10.8%
1995	26.3%	21.8%	15.5%
1994	-7.4%	-5.2%	-1.0%
1993	22.1%	18.9%	13.4%
1992	11.6%	9.3%	8.6%
1991	25.3%	23.6%	17.9%
1990	4.3%	7.6%	10.5%
Std Deviation	10.7%	8.8%	5.7%
Value of $1000	3,179.24	2,691.81	2,275.18

Source: PalTrak (Scotia Capital Markets Bond Indexes)

Returning to our bond fund objectives, some managers do not attempt to alter their average term to maturity, preferring instead to hold a fixed maturity through all phases of the business cycle. The lowest-risk bond funds tend to fix their maturities at the short end of the yield curve. Some indexed bond funds are structured at the midpoint along the yield curve. And some actively managed funds, like the Altamira Bond Fund, always have a longer-term bias. The Altamira Bond Fund never has an average term to maturity below six years.

Bullets in the FundLine are based on the average term to maturity of the bond fund. (If the average term to maturity is less than three years, a bullet is registered in the short-term box. If the average term to maturity is between three and ten years, a bullet is recorded in the mid-term box, and when the average term to maturity is greater than ten years, a bullet is recorded in the long-term box.)

Sector-Specific Fund Objectives

Sector-specific funds are the so-called specialty funds that invest in a specific area of the economy. Resource and precious metals funds fall into this category; so do some of the new sector funds, like health sciences, technology, and telecommunications.

Often you will find these funds at the top and bottom of the performance parade. They've been called "the best of funds and the worst of funds." If you are holding a sector-specific fund in your portfolio, it's important to know what elements of diversification, if any, that fund's manager brings to the table.

Currency Risk

The last fund objective category we want to talk about is currency risk. If you buy a U.S. equity fund, you are buying a fund that invests in foreign securities denominated in a foreign currency. Changes in the foreign currency relative to the Canadian dollar can have a major impact on your portfolio, either adding to or taking from the performance of your particular fund.

Performance Distortions

Index funds are designed to provide mirror image performance against a specific index. Most U.S. index funds, for example, are designed to track the performance of the S&P 500 composite index. But when you convert those returns back to Canadian dollars, the return you see isn't always the return you get.

As an example, consider TD Green Line's U.S. index fund. This is one of the longest-running U.S. equity index funds in Canada. Table 5.5 looks at the Canadian dollar return of the fund and the S&P 500 index over the last five years.

TABLE 5.5

	1 YEAR	2 YEAR	3 YEAR	4 YEAR	5 YEAR
Green Line U.S. Index	21.1%	29.0%	31.0%	29.1%	28.0%
S&P 500 Index Cdn $	22.8%	30.5%	32.4%	30.6%	29.5%

Not all index funds have done so well. Consider, for example, the Scotia Can-Am Stock Index fund, which has also been around for five years. This fund uses a combination of S&P 500 Stock Index futures contracts and Government of Canada T-Bills to obtain a return in Canadian dollars similar to the S&P 500 Index.

To accomplish this, the Scotia Can-Am Stock Index fund buys Government of Canada T-Bills and then pledges up to 10 percent of these assets to purchase, on margin, S&P 500 Index futures contracts. The fund will carry sufficient S&P 500 futures contracts so as to closely match the performance of the S&P 500 index on an unleveraged basis.

Since it will not use futures contracts for speculative trading or to create a portfolio that is leveraged, the fund will always set aside sufficient cash or cash equivalents to satisfy the obligations of the futures contracts. Therefore the RRSP equity index fund gives you dollar-for-dollar exposure to the U.S. equity market. But, since the bulk of the fund's assets are in Canadian dollar-denominated investments — i.e., Government of Canada Treasury Bills — this offering is not considered foreign content within an RRSP. You get foreign exposure without filling up your foreign content allowance.

So we have two funds with similar objectives and different approaches. In both cases the objective is to track the performance of the S&P 500 composite index. The Green Line fund buys the underlying stocks, while the Scotia Can-Am fund uses Treasury bills plus derivatives. Table 5.6 looks at the performance numbers over the same five-year period.

TABLE 5.6

	1 YEAR	2 YEAR	3 YEAR	4 YEAR	5 YEAR
Green Line U.S. Index	21.1%	29.0%	31.0%	29.1%	28.0%
Scotia Can-Am Stock Index	19.7%	22.5%	24.6%	24.5%	24.6%
S&P 500 Index Cdn $	22.8%	30.5%	32.4%	30.6%	29.5%

Notice the distortions. Over the last five years, the Scotia Can-Am Stock Index Fund has lagged the S&P 500 Index and the Green Line U.S. Index Fund. And not by a little. The difference was 3.4 percent compounded annually.

So what happened to cause the distortion? It's not that the Scotia Can-Am Stock Index Fund was badly managed. On the contrary, it was managed according to the prospectus. The difference in return is almost entirely due to currency translation. Over the past five years, the Canadian dollar has declined in value relative to the U.S. dollar. That's an advantage for the Green Line fund, which converts all of its assets to U.S. dollars and is 100 percent invested in U.S. stocks. It's a disadvantage for a fund that has most of its assets invested in Canadian dollar-denominated Treasury bills and that does not actively manage currency risk.

To avoid such distortions, buy an RRSP U.S. equity index fund that hedges its currency exposure — caused by having the bulk of its assets in Canadian Treasury bills — back into U.S. dollars. An example would be the CIBC U.S. Equity Index Fund, which uses currency futures and forward contracts to hedge currency exposure.

That doesn't mean you should avoid the Scotia Can-Am Stock Index fund, or any other RRSP Equity Index fund that does not hedge currency exposure. It may be, going forward, that you don't want to be hedged back into U.S. dollars. Table 5.7 looks at the first six months of 1999 (ending June 30). The Canadian dollar actually rallied against the U.S. dollar, which had a positive impact on the Scotia Can-Am Stock Index fund relative to the S&P 500 Index (Cdn$) and the Green Line U.S. Index Fund.

TABLE 5.7

	1999 TO JUNE 30TH
Green Line U.S. Index	6.9%
Scotia Can-Am Stock Index	10.5%
S&P 500 Index Cdn $	8.1%

Rather than trying to slant your decision-making towards a hedged or unhedged approach to currency management, the goal of this exercise is to make sure you understand what a specific fund's objectives are, and how the fund's management team will deliver on those objectives.

Diversification by Management Style

The final element of diversification only applies to mutual funds. We're talking about investment management style. How does the manager execute the fund's objectives?

Diversification by management style has gained more than its fair share of press over the last couple of years, especially since Synergy Asset Management came onto the scene. Synergy President Joe Canavan built a family of mutual funds on the concept of style diversification. He believes, as we do, that the market rewards different management styles at different points of the business cycle (see Table 5.8), and that a portfolio diversified by management style can help reduce risk over time.

TABLE 5.8

YEAR	VALUE	GROWTH	INDEXATION*
1998	-2.6 %	-4.3 %	-1.6 %
1997	15.0 %	22.0 %	15.0 %
1996	32.9 %	29.6 %	28.3 %
1995	18.1 %	11.4 %	14.5 %
1994	-8.2 %	-3.1 %	-0.2 %

. . .

1993	35.1 %	48.8 %	32.5 %
1992	20.5 %	-2.5 %	-1.4 %
1991	23.0 %	13.2 %	12.0 %
1990	-12.1 %	-9.0 %	-14.8 %
Std Deviation	17.3 %	19.1 %	15.3 %
Value of $1000	2,840.60	2,441.07	2,068.26

* Indexation is represented by the TSE 300 composite

Source: PalTrak (Average Canadian equity funds using specific styles)

Most investors view investment styles from two perspectives: value and growth. However, we think two styles is too narrow a focus. We have taken the two basic styles and redefined growth as momentum and/or sector rotation. Further, we want to know whether the manager or management team practices a top-down or bottom-up view of the market.

We've also included indexation as a management style. Index funds are unique and have quite different objectives. Rather than trying to outperform a benchmark index, the index fund simply attempts to mirror the underlying index. Because of that, tracking error and timing are more critical issues. (Tracking error measures the degree by which the underlying fund's return deviates from the return of the benchmark index.)

Investment Objectives and Styles

Scanning through mutual fund literature, there is a lot of discussion about how managers will fulfill their obligations to provide the unitholders with above-average returns. Most fund managers will spend a lot of time explaining the rationale behind their particular approach, telling you why their approach is worth consideration in your portfolio. But few will explain the difference in styles, and why those differences are significant.

We're not here to defend any particular management style. Quite frankly, we are not convinced that, over the long haul, one approach is any better than another. However, as seen in Table 5.8, the different investment styles can be rewarded at different stages of the business cycle.

Over the long-term, any management style will provide good risk-adjusted returns. That's because the mutual fund industry is good at weeding out sub-standard managers. Managers who are not able to fulfill their long-term objectives are eventually replaced with people who can.

Over the long-term, most funds end up in the same place. The managers simply take different roads to get there. For example, value managers usually attempt to match the market returns when prices are rising. When prices are falling, value managers try to ensure that their portfolio doesn't decline as much as the market. Presumably this means a smoother ride along the road to financial freedom.

Momentum managers, on the other hand, will try to outperform the market on the upside, and match the market returns on the downside — which, some would argue, is a riskier strategy. However, in defense of these managers, the market goes up about four years to every one year of decline.

With that in mind, we see six basic management styles:

- Top-down
- Bottom-up
- Value
- Momentum
- Sector rotation
- Indexation

The six basic management styles fit equity fund managers well. But when you use them to scrutinize a bond manager, they provide a different perspective.

Obviously, when we assign investment styles to a bond fund manager, our definitions are much different from what they would be for an equity fund manager. So we define all six of the management styles by looking at them first from the perspective of an equity fund manager, and second from the perspective of a bond fund manager.

Determining what type of investment management style is being used with each fund is not a straightforward exercise. Some fund companies tell you what you want to hear. When value managers are hot, that's the mandate for their funds; when growth managers are hot, they will follow a growth-oriented style like momentum or sector rotation.

However, we think the best managers are the ones who stick with the style that got them there. We try to look at each fund objectively, we read the marketing material supplied by the fund companies, and we attempt to decipher the investment style that is having the most influence over the fund's performance. There is as much art as there is science to our approach. And in some cases, we may have categorized a fund incorrectly. But, on a macro scale, we believe a process system that may have some imperfections is better than no process at all.

EQUITY FUND MANAGEMENT STYLES

Top-Down Approach

A top-down manager begins with an overview of the economy. Are we headed for a period of slow growth with no inflation, or rapid growth with high inflation? Perhaps the economy is descending into a recession, which will impair earnings and push up the unemployment numbers. Or maybe we are moving into a period of expansion, which will boost sales and lift earnings.

The top-down investment management team will weigh the potential scenarios and assign a probability ranking to each of them. The managers then focus on industries that are expected to profit under a specific macro-economic scenario. And within those industries, management seeks out the companies that look most promising.

Bottom-Up

A bottom-up manager is also interested in the outlook for the economy. It doesn't do much good to invest in stocks if we are about to enter a major recession that will hinder the profits of all companies. But rather than using the macro-economic scenario to determine investment choices, many bottom-up managers will use it to determine what percentage of the portfolio to hold in cash.

A true bottom-up philosophy seeks out companies that are undervalued and that have exciting long-term potential. The best company is one the manager can buy and never sell. Some bottom-up managers will focus on specific industries, and then choose stocks that look particularly interesting at the time. The technology industry is an example of just such a philosophy in today's market.

Value

Most value managers follow the traditions of Benjamin Graham, David Dodd, and Warren Buffett. Graham, and Dodd, the authors of *Graham and Dodd's Security Analysis*, are viewed by many as the architects of value investing. Warren Buffett is a strong follower of their philosophy.

Value investing is a defensive approach, as these managers usually seek out long-term investments in out-of-favour companies. Stocks being overlooked by the general investing public are their bread and butter. Ideally, a value investor buys shares in a company that has a strong balance sheet and solid earnings growth at a time when its value on the stock market is less than its break-up value. Most value investors use a bottom-up selection process, and prefer to buy and never sell.

Momentum

Most momentum managers follow trends. They are particularly drawn to companies that have been able to grow their earnings faster than the overall market has. Momentum managers also look at chart patterns, to see if a particular stock is trending higher. They often buy a number of stocks in a specific industry, or a basket of stocks representing a cross section of the market, on the basis of a breakout or a change in a particular technical pattern.

Momentum managers believe that when a stock, or industry, or the market, moves in a particular direction (representing strong momentum), its path of least resistance will be in that same direction. Buy and sell signals are based on the degree of momentum and on changes in that momentum.

Generally, momentum managers are a bit more aggressive. Their funds are usually higher-risk, and the returns reflect that. There can be increased costs associated with momentum investing, because you are more apt to buy and sell over shorter periods of time. That's a generalization, though; some stocks, like Microsoft, Intel, and AOL, have been able to grow earnings faster than the market for years.

Sector Rotation

A sector rotator normally focuses on specific industries within the overall market. Generally, a manager following this philosophy uses a top-down approach. The idea is to follow the ups and downs of the economy, moving from one industry to another at different stages of the business cycle.

During the expansion phase of the business cycle, sector rotators usually seek cyclical companies (often just called "cyclicals"), like the auto industry, transportation stocks, and consumer durables. (Consumer durables include things like washing machines, kitchen appliances, and so on — big-ticket items that are not purchased on a regular basis.) These are industries that tend to profit during upturns in the economy and suffer the most during an economic slowdown.

During periods of economic contractions, a sector rotator will move in to defensive industries like pharmaceuticals and healthcare — sectors where profit margins are not tied as closely to changes in the business cycle.

Indexation

The goal of an index fund manager is to track the benchmark index. Canadian index funds typically track either the TSE 35 Index, the TSE 100 Index, or the TSE 300 Index. In the next year, you'll begin to see Canadian equity funds tied to the new TSE/S&P 60 Index.

An index meaures the performance of a cross section of stocks or bonds in specific markets. The idea is to provide the investor with a snapshot as to how the "market" is performing at a point in time.

U.S. index funds typically track the S&P 500 Index, although we are beginning to see some new U.S. index funds that track the Dow Jones Industrial Average and the NASDAQ 100 Index. There is even one U.S. index fund — the CIBC U.S. Equity Index Fund — that tracks the Wilshire 5000 Index. The Wilshire 5000 is the largest index in terms of component stocks. It is designed to track the performance of 5000 U.S. companies, which presumably cover a cross-section of the U.S. economy.

You would think index fund managers have the easiest job: simply buy the stocks that are in the index. However, that's easier said than done. The trick is to buy the stocks in the correct weight, so as to minimize tracking error. The best index fund managers have the lowest tracking error with the underlying index. The strong selling point of the index fund is its low management fees, since there are no buy and sell decisions to make.

Summary

As you might expect, equity managers may employ a number of investment styles when running a portfolio. For example, some equity managers follow a top-down bias focusing on sector rotation for the core of the portfolio. That same manager may take a small percentage of the portfolio and employ some good old bottom-up, value techniques to select specific stocks to hold for long periods.

BOND FUND MANAGEMENT STYLES

The performance of high-grade bond funds is driven by interest rates. We emphasize the "high-grade" trademark to distinguish bond funds that invest in government or high-grade corporate bonds from the significantly different "high-yield bond funds," which invest in junk bonds.

A high-yield bond fund manager will invest in bonds issued by companies that may or may not be able to repay the principal at the end of the term. There is a risk of default, which adds another dimension to what drives performance. This risk also defines differences in management styles for bond funds.

We expect a bond fund's net asset value will move inversely to a change in the level of interest rates. If interest rates are rising, the net asset value of the bond fund will decline; if interest rates are falling, the fund's net asset value will rise.

Knowing that a teeter-totter relationship exists is only the first step. What we need to do is determine just how much impact a change in interest rates will have on the net asset value of the bond fund. In other words, how long is this teeter-totter?

For that, investors should look at the bond fund's average term to maturity. The longer the term to maturity, the more volatile the fund will be.

We know that domestic bond fund managers attempt to beat the average or benchmark index. While domestic bond fund managers all have the same goal — to beat their peers — they try to accomplish it using different management styles. From our perspective, the top-down or bottom-up styles associated with equity funds also apply to bond funds. However, the rest of the management styles have different definitions when it comes to managing a bond portfolio.

Top-Down

Most bond fund managers use a top-down approach. They attempt to predict the direction of interest rates, and set their average term to maturity to take advantage of rate shifts. Predicting interest rates is a top-down job which includes an analysis of such macro-economic forces as inflation, jobs, and GDP growth. Interestingly, a top-down manager would also be sensitive to another macro-economic condition, currency fluctuations, and might buy or sell foreign pay bonds to take advantage of any weakness or strength in the Canadian dollar.

Bottom-Up

Few bond fund managers employ a bottom-up style. Those who do normally manage high-yield funds and look for opportunities among corporate or provincial bonds. The idea is to find opportunities at different points along the yield curve, where returns are greater than the perceived risk. Finding the "hump" along the yield curve before other managers jump on the bandwagon is the goal.

Value

Bond fund managers who practice a value style generally work from the premise that the portfolio should maintain a consistent average term to maturity and credit quality. In other words, the manager might purchase only medium-term high-grade corporate bonds, or only long-term high-grade government bonds. The idea is to buy undervalued bonds for yield and capital appreciation within the context of a specific term to maturity and credit quality.

Momentum

Most top-down bond fund managers follow a style known as interest rate anticipation. In the FundLine, we define this as market timing (see section on "Package Deals"). Predicting changes in the shape of the yield curve, and then altering the average term to maturity to profit from those changes, is the goal of market timers. From our work, we note that most domestic bond fund managers follow a management style defined as top-down/market timing.

Sector Rotation

We normally associate this style with equity managers. And, to be fair, the term "sector rotation" may be somewhat misleading when applied to bond fund managers. However, we think of sector rotation as a style that analyses sector, coupon and credit analysis, or, if you prefer the more generic term, "spread trading." The goal is to examine current yields spreads between bonds in different sectors: What is the spread between Government of

Canada five-year bonds and, say, Province of Ontario five-year bonds? The manager compares these spreads with historical spreads in similar interest rate environments, and then seeks out the most attractive sectors, coupons and credit ratings. This is an active management style that generally begins from a bottom-up point of view.

Indexation

We offer a more liberal interpretation when it comes to defining whether or not a bond fund manager is operating an indexed portfolio. Obviously, for a pure indexed bond fund, like the Green Line Canadian Government Bond Fund, which tracks the Scotia Capital Markets Government Bond Index, the distinction is clear.

However, there are cases in which bond fund managers always maintain the average term to maturity of their portfolio within close proximity to their benchmark index. For example, if we looked at a long-term bond fund that always maintained its average term to maturity within one year of the Scotia Capital Markets Long Bond Index, we would consider that a long-term bond fund with an indexed management style. (Note that in the FundLine we have a slot to define whether the bond fund's average term to maturity is short-, medium- or long-term). Similarly, a fund like the Green Line Short Term Income Fund is, for all intents, indexed to the Scotia Capital Markets Short Term Bond Index, or some other short-term barometer. It is our opinion, because the manager has so little room to move, that this is an indexed management style.

SUMMING UP

All these elements may seem complex at first, but if you think about them you'll see how they fit together like the pieces in a puzzle. Individually, each FundLine component may not seem very important in your investing strategy. But by putting them together, you'll create a cohesive portfolio that should produce good returns under any market conditions.

THE SECRET WEAPON: MVA

When looking at mutual funds, investors first search periodic returns. That's not surprising, since returns are the most visible aspect of a mutual fund's performance, and past returns are easy to quantify.

MANAGER VALUE ADDED – RATING FUND MANAGERS
The Search for Performance

The idea that fund XYZ returned 10 percent in 1998, 25 percent in 1997, and 15 percent in 1996 is straightforward. With that return data, it is easy to calculate potential returns: $1,000 invested in fund XYZ at the beginning of 1996 would have been worth $1,581 at the end of 1998.

What seems to get lost in this hype is the disclaimer attached to these numbers: "Past performance is not necessarily indicative of future results." We think there needs to be some balance between the raw performance numbers and the risks associated with getting those numbers.

The first question is whether the search for better-than-average risk-adjusted returns is worth the effort. Obviously, we think it is, because we believe that over long periods, top-performing funds add value. And the numbers bear that out.

For example, $1,000 invested in a hypothetical median-performing balanced portfolio made up of 25 percent Canadian equity funds, 10 percent U.S. equity funds, 15 percent international equity funds, 40 percent Canadian bond funds, and 10 percent Canadian money market funds (which, for the record,

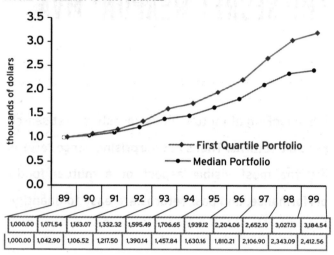

FIGURE 6.1 – MEDIAN VS FIRST QUARTILE

	89	90	91	92	93	94	95	96	97	98	99
First Quartile	1,000.00	1,071.54	1,163.07	1,332.32	1,595.49	1,706.65	1,939.12	2,204.06	2,652.10	3,027.13	3,184.54
Median	1,000.00	1,042.90	1,106.52	1,217.50	1,390.14	1,457.84	1,630.16	1,810.21	2,106.90	2,343.09	2,412.56

is the asset mix for the FPX Balanced Index; see the section on Index Portfolios) would have returned 9.2 percent compounded annually over the last ten years (ending June 30/99). Ten years at 9.2 percent turns $1,000 into $2,412.56 (see Figure 6.1). Not bad for a passive, median-performing portfolio.

But look what happens if you are able to buy funds that, over the long term, are better-than-average performers. If you had been able to find and hold funds that were first-quartile performers over that ten-year period, your portfolio would have returned 12.3 percent compounded annually, taking your $1,000 investment to $3,184.54 (Figure 6.1).

Obviously, finding above-average performers is not easy. Using our hypothetical first-quartile portfolio, you would be faced with choosing among 610 Canadian equity funds, 217 U.S. equity funds, 89 International equity funds, 219 Canadian bond funds, and 158 Canadian money market funds. Separating the wheat from the chaff is easy if you are looking at past performance. It is much harder when you are trying to find funds that will outperform in the future.

For the record, then, we think that past performance is important, but only to a point. Make it one consideration in the fund selection process, not the only consideration.

UNDERSTANDING HOW WE SELECT FUNDS

Over the last year (to June 30, 1999), the AGF International Group-American Growth Class returned 30.2 percent, making it one of the top-performing mutual funds available to Canadian investors. The two- and three-year compound annual returns were equally impressive: 37.3 percent and 36.6 percent, respectively. Not surprisingly, such stellar returns have attracted a lot of new investors. Over the last year, the fund's assets have risen by 136.7 percent, and now total more than $1.5 billion.

Should you buy this fund? It depends. If your decision to buy hangs on the performance numbers, and you don't fully understand how that fund fits in your portfolio, then the answer is no. Buying on that basis is rainbow-chasing. It means you're ignoring the risks. The AGF International Group-American Growth Class has a three-year annual standard deviation (or risk) of 20.6 percent, which is much higher than the 15.4 percent for the median U.S. equity fund. The higher the annual standard deviation number, the greater the potential variance in the fund's return over any given year. In short, higher standard deviation means higher risk. The AGF American Growth Fund tends to buy growth stocks, which, on average, tend to be more volatile than, say, value stocks. A growth stock example is Microsoft; a value example is an electric utility company. And while we would concede that higher risks beget higher returns, you need to know if you are the type of investor who can withstand the risks associated with those returns.

If, on the other hand, you own a Canadian equity fund, a Canadian bond fund, and some money market investments, then maybe the decision to hold a higher standard deviation fund is appropriate.

This brings us to the heart of our investment philosophy, and to our step-by-step approach to building the right portfolios:

- Set your financial objectives and understand your risk tolerances. In short, define your investment personality.
- Establish an appropriate asset mix (decide what percentage of your assets should be invested in money market funds; what percentage in fixed-income funds;

and what percentage in equity funds), based on your investment personality.

- Extend your asset mix to include geographic diversification. Earmark appropriate percentages of your assets for Canadian equity funds, U.S. equity funds, international equity funds, bond funds, and money market funds; decide what percentage should be allocated to investment products that go beyond mutual funds.

- Enhance your diversification by choosing offerings with different objectives (e.g., small cap versus large cap) and investment management styles (top-down versus bottom-up; momentum; sector rotation versus value).

- Seek out the best managers in each category. Now, finally, performance becomes an issue, because you have clearly defined the role each fund will play in your portfolio.

So in a nutshell, it comes down to a selection process. Understanding what role each fund plays for you is more important than the specific performance numbers of that fund.

Look at it this way. Suppose you liked the prospects for General Motors, because the company was gaining market share and improving profit margins. The basis of your rosy forecast for General Motors comes down to an analysis of past trends — market share and profit margins. Now think about this: Is that any different from analyzing the historical returns of a mutual fund, and then, based on that analysis, concluding that that fund will be a strong performer in the future?

That's where the selection process comes into play. Would you buy shares of General Motors if you already owned shares of Ford and Daimler-Chrysler? Maybe! On the one hand, you already own two of the three North American car makers. If General Motors is gaining market share, it is likely to come at the expense of Ford and Daimler-Chrysler. Thus General Motors brings nothing to the table in terms of diversification.

On the other hand, if you think the outlook for General Motors is better than the outlook for Ford and Daimler-Chrysler, there is a compelling argument for buying the stock. But in terms of your overall portfolio, wouldn't it make more sense to sell the shares of Ford and Daimler-Chrysler first, and then use the proceeds to buy General Motors?

Mutual fund portfolios are no different. First we must see the role a specific mutual fund plays within the context of the overall portfolio. In other words, what elements of diversification does it bring to the table? Only after that do we analyze the historical returns of the mutual fund, just as we would analyze profit margins, earnings, and market share for a stock. And in both cases, we need to recognize the shortfalls of the analysis. This, in no small way, explains the "past performance" caveat in the fund's marketing material.

The bottom line is that periodic returns are the most visible and least predictable aspect of a mutual fund, just as earnings and profit margins are for a company. We are not here to diminish their importance, only to suggest that performance numbers, and the management who generated those numbers, are less important than proper diversification.

Knowing How to Measure

The search for a tool to measure the value added by a mutual fund manager is one of the great challenges in the mutual fund industry. Finding the right measure is like trying to find the Holy Grail.

Imagine that you are General Motors' chairman of the board. Your job is, first, to manufacture quality cars cost-effectively, and, second, to market those cars through the GM distribution network.

To evaluate your performance we need to see if you are meeting those dual objectives. For example, the company's profit margin (the difference between what it costs to manufacture a car and what you get when you sell the car) will tell us how cost-effective your manufacturing plants are. The key is the trend in profit margins — are they increasing or decreasing? At the same time, analyzing whether the company is gaining or losing market share tells us how well you are maintaining the distribution network. Both of these factors can be quantified mathematically.

Of course, simply knowing what your profit margins are tells us nothing about value. Only if we compare those margins against a relative benchmark can we assess whether the margins are good or bad.

Obviously, we cannot evaluate performance by comparing the profit margins of your company to, say, the profit margins of Microsoft. We would be comparing apples to oranges. For performance evaluations to be relevant, we need to compare the efficiency – i.e., profit margins – of your manufacturing plants with the margins of the automobile manufacturing industry.

The same is true of the distribution network. We cannot compare the volume of traffic and the one-on-one contact in a car dealership with the traffic flow and self-service model of a Wal-Mart. We would compare the company's numbers with those of its industry.

And some aspects of your job are simply not quantifiable. For example, in your position as chairman of the board, you are also responsible — at least on a macro scale —— for making sure your customers are satisfied, and that your employees are happy and remain loyal. Both of these issues can have a dramatic impact in the future, yet neither can be quantified today. So any measurement of value has its limits.

How, then, do we search for value among mutual fund managers? We begin by looking at a mutual fund as a company. The fund's prospectus defines the company's objectives, and the portfolio manager is the person responsible for guiding the company within the context of those objectives. The prospectus is a unique document, in that it acts as a sort of job description for the portfolio manager.

Finding the Right Benchmark

Suppose you are holding a Canadian equity fund in your portfolio. The objective, as defined by the fund's prospectus, is to invest in Canadian stocks. The manager invested within those guidelines and the fund returned 18 percent last year. Is that good or bad?

Against GICs that returned four percent over the same period, the fund's return was sensational. But that is not a fair comparison; it's like comparing General Motors' profit margins with Microsoft's. One has nothing to do with the other. Similarly, you can't compare a Canadian equity fund with a balanced portfolio that is divided equally between stocks, bonds, and cash, or with the yield on risk-free Treasury bills, or any other single barometer.

In the case of our Canadian equity fund, we need to look at the returns on the Canadian stock market over a similar period. If Canadian stocks, on average, returned 25 percent, the 18 percent returned by our fund pales by comparison. Had Canadian stocks returned 15 percent, we would guess the fund manager had added value.

So what makes a reasonable benchmark? Most important is that categories and benchmarks reflect what managers do, rather than what they say they do! A benchmark, then, should be:

Investable: The benchmark should represent a passive alternative to a fund manager. You should be able to actually buy the benchmark or a proxy for it.

Unambiguous: The TSE 300 Composite Index is an unambiguous benchmark. Its composition is published, and investors know what comprises it and how its value is determined.

Measurable: The benchmark should be calculated and published periodically and subject to precise calculations.

Appropriate: The benchmark should match the objectives of the mutual fund. A Canadian equity fund that specializes in small-cap stocks should be compared to a Canadian small-cap index. Similarly, a U.S. equity fund that invests in a diversified portfolio of U.S. stocks should be compared to a broad-based U.S. stock index.

A model that rates mutual fund managers has to evaluate the managers' returns against the performance of a passive portfolio. To justify paying the manager of a Canadian equity fund, you would like to have that manager outperform the TSE 300 (large-/mid-cap benchmark), the TSE 100 (large-/mid-cap benchmark), the new S&P/TSE 60 (large-cap benchmark), the TSE 35 (blue chip/large-cap benchmark), or the Nesbitt Burns Small Cap Index (small-cap benchmark).

FIGURE 6.2 - AGF 20/20 AGGRESSIVE GROWTH FUND

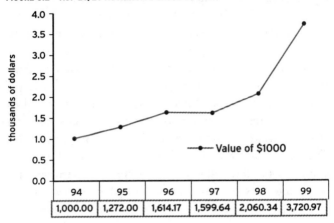

94	95	96	97	98	99
1,000.00	1,272.00	1,614.17	1,599.64	2,060.34	3,720.97

FIGURE 6.3 - UNIVERSAL JAPAN FUND

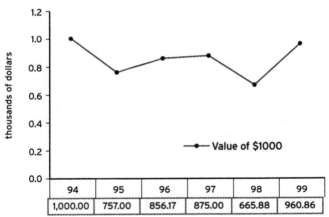

94	95	96	97	98	99
1,000.00	757.00	856.17	875.00	665.88	960.86

FIGURE 6.4 - IVY CANADIAN FUND

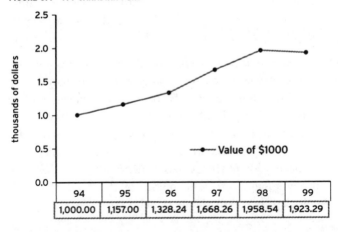

94	95	96	97	98	99
1,000.00	1,157.00	1,328.24	1,668.26	1,958.54	1,923.29

THE QUEST FOR VALUE

Now let's look at three different funds with very different performance records.

The first on our list is the 20/20 Aggressive Growth Fund, which has been managed by Richard Driehaus since June 1993. Based on the data from Figure 6.2, the AGF 20/20 Aggressive Growth Fund returned 30 percent compounded annually over the five years to June 30/99. That's enough to turn a $1,000 investment made at the beginning of June 1994 into $3,710.93 by the end of June 1999. Looking at these performance numbers, few investors would have been disappointed. Indeed, we suspect that most investors would vote Driehaus into the Managers' Hall of Fame.

Mind you, not all mutual funds had such spectacular returns. For example, the Universal Japan Fund has been lucky to break even over the last five years. In fact, over the last five years, this fund, managed by Campbell Gunn of Mackenzie Financial, has produced a compounded annual return of -0.8 percent. That's right; a negative five-year return! A $1,000 investment made at the beginning of June 1994 would have been worth $960.86 by the end of June 1999 (see Figure 6.3).

Finally we will look at the Ivy Canadian Fund. Managed by Jerry Javasky of Mackenzie, the fund has been a steady performer. Over the last five years, it has returned 14 percent, compounded annually. A $1,000 investment made at the beginning of June 1994 would have grown to $1,923.29 by the end of June 1999 (see Figure 6.4).

Three very different funds, with three very different performance records. If we were to look only at past returns of one fund relative to the others, then Driehaus would win hands down. In fact, we could argue that Driehaus added value, Javasky was okay, and Gunn should be looking for new employment.

Of course, we are painting this picture with too broad a brush. The fact is that, at this stage, we have no way of evaluating any of the managers, because we have no benchmark against which to measure their performance. Comparing Driehaus's U.S. equity fund against Gunn's

FIGURE 6.5

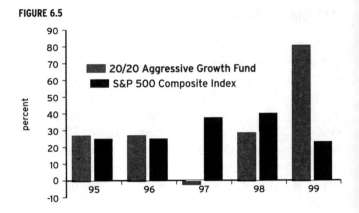

Japan fund or Javasky's Canadian equity fund is another apples-to-oranges comparison. The managers' job descriptions cannot be compared.

What we really want to know is how much of the stellar performance posted by Driehaus was the result of his shrewd stock-picking ability, and how much was the result of simply investing based on the objectives as defined by the prospectus. Remember, this is a U.S. stock fund, and he was expected to invest in the U.S. market.

To make a fair comparison, then, we need to evaluate him against a reasonable benchmark. This will be the Standard and Poor's (S&P) 500 Composite Total Return Index[1] (adjusted for Canadian dollars).

Most investors think of the 20/20 Aggressive Fund as a small to mid-size fund. And it is, to a point. However, looking at the numbers at the end of June 1999, we see that the average market cap (average share price multiplied by the number of shares outstanding) of the stocks held in the 20/20 Fund is U.S. $13 billion. That average market cap is not too far removed from the market cap of the companies in the S&P 500 Composite Index; and is certainly higher than, for instance, those in the Russell 2000 Index, which otherwise we might consider a better proxy for the 20/20 Aggressive Fund. For our example,

---

[1] The Standard and Poor's 500 Total Return Index tracks the performance of 500 of the largest companies that trade in the U.S., and is adjusted back to Canadian dollars. The total return component assumes all dividends paid by the companies are re-invested back into additional shares.

then, the S&P 500 Composite Index is a reasonable benchmark for judging the fund manager.

Looking at the same period returns — from the beginning of June 1994 to the end of June 1999 — the S&P 500 Composite Total Return Index returned 29.5 percent compounded annually, or just slightly less than the five-year returns posted by the AGF 20/20 Aggressive Growth Fund. In Figure 6.5 we show the annual returns for both.

Richard Driehaus underperformed the S&P 500 in two of the five years. The period from June 1996 to June 1997 is particularly interesting: he achieved -0.9 percent, while the S&P 500 composite index was up 36.3 percent.

If you had simply purchased the S&P 500 Index over the five years, you would never have had a losing year. And your $1,000 investment would have risen to $3,638.98, less than $100 below what Driehaus' fund earned over the same time frame, with substantially less pain along the way.

That's what we mean when we talk about standard deviation. A fund with a higher standard deviation is usually a fund that has a greater chance of having a losing year. In this case, the AGF 20/20 Aggressive Growth Fund has a three-year standard deviation of 29.2 percent, compared with 14.4 percent standard deviation for the Standard and Poor's 500 Composite Index.

So we concede that Dreihaus earned a slightly better return than the benchmark index. But he did so by assuming twice as much risk. Risk is not a bad thing, but we have to ask how it constitutes value added. We believe it is more than an ability to outperform. It is all about risk-adjusted performance relative to a benchmark.

This is more than an academic exercise. MVA addresses a very simple question. Are you better off buying the fund or the underlying benchmark index? (Assuming, of course, you can buy the index.) In this case, you can, using Standard and Poor's 500 Depository Receipts (symbol SPY, traded on the American Stock Exchange). SPY has an annual MER of 0.18 percent, and it promises to mirror the performance of the Standard and Poor's 500 Composite Index.

Figure 6.6 compares the performance of the Universal Japan Fund to the Salomon Japan Equity Index, our

FIGURE 6.6

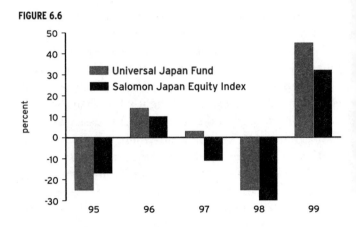

benchmark for Japanese equity funds. Campbell Gunn managed to beat that index in four out of our five years. He was not as bad a manager as you might have first thought. While the numbers leave a lot to be desired, they are the result of poor performance in the Japanese stock market. And, like it or not, the Universal Japan Fund's mandate is to be invested in Japan at all times.

To knock Gunn's numbers without recognizing that the fund's prospectus obligated him to invest in an underperforming market would be unfair. (Think of our General Motors example. Can we penalize the chairman because the company's profits are down, without considering why they're down? It's one thing if profits have fallen because of generally poor car sales. It's quite another if your sales are down because you have lost market share to Ford and Daimler-Chrysler.)

If we want to devise a model to evaluate a manager, then the model must only look at those factors the manager could control. The only control Gunn had was his ability to make better-than-average investments in the Japanese market. And looking at the numbers, we believe he did that. So while a $1,000 investment in his fund five years ago might have fallen to a disappointing $960.86, it is still well ahead of the $748.26 you would have gotten by investing in the Salomon Japan Equity Index.

One final point about Gunn's risk-adjusted performance. The three-year annual standard deviation of his fund was 24.2 percent, compared with 24.1 percent for the benchmark index. So he was able to generate better-

FIGURE 6.7

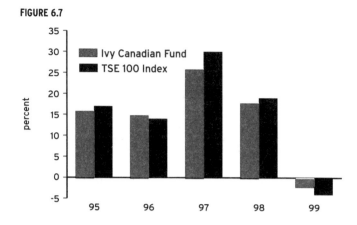

than-benchmark performance with the same level of risk. That's much different from our previous example of equal performance at twice the level of risk.

Finally, let's review the numbers for the Ivy Canadian Fund. Figure 6.7 shows its annual returns relative to the TSE 100 index. At first glance, you can see how closely the Ivy Canadian fund correlates to the benchmark index.

What you might not see is Ivy's consistency. For example, in the last year, the Ivy Canadian Fund returned 1.8 percent, compared with 4.1 percent for the benchmark index. This doesn't surprise those investors who follow Javasky's conservative value style. He makes no apologies that his goal is to protect your principal, even if it costs something on the performance side.

Over the last five years, a $1,000 investment in the Ivy Canadian Fund would have returned $1,923.29 at the end of June 1999. The same $1,000 invested in the TSE 100 index would have returned $1,950.11. (TSE Index Participation 100 Shares (TIPS 100) trade on the Toronto Stock Exchange under the symbol HIP.)

The performance of the two investments is virtually identical. However, in this case, Javasky was able to produce those performance numbers with a 10.6 percent annual three-year standard deviation, compared with 19.5 percent for the benchmark index. In this case, we believe that Javasky added value because he produced nearly identical returns with about half the risk.

MVA: Not the Only Consideration

You may be asking yourself whether we are suggesting that you only buy funds if the manager has added value. Looking at the three examples just cited, you would purchase the Universal Japan Fund and the Ivy Canadian Fund. Presumably, you would avoid the AGF 20/20 Aggressive Growth Fund. Clearly, such a strategy would be harmful to your pocketbook.

Remember, MVA simply scores portfolio managers on their ability to do better than a passive benchmark on a risk-adjusted basis. The benchmark acts as the fund manager's job description. Managers can get 100+ MVA ratings in a couple of ways: by outperforming the benchmark with the same degree of risk; or by matching the benchmark's performance, with less risk. In some cases, managers take on greater risk than their benchmark indexes and yet produce far better returns. And sometimes managers who underperform their benchmarks can still get 100+ MVAs, because the risk in their funds is so much lower than the risk in the index.

If you buy a fund simply because of the manager's rating, then you are as guilty as if you were buying solely on the basis of past performance. Screening funds on the basis of MVA ratings alone is still rainbow-chasing. It's just a different rainbow.

The fact is, if you don't think Japan should be part of your portfolio, then don't buy a Japan equity fund, regardless of how well the fund is managed. Similarly, don't avoid a U.S. equity fund just because you can't find one in which the manager has added value. On the other hand, if your asset mix has a place set aside for a Japan fund, then look for one in which the manager has added value. What's important is to follow the portfolio building blocks from start to finish.

BRINGING RISK INTO THE DISCUSSION

While most investors understand that a trade-off between risk and return exists, few know how to quantify that relationship. We know, for example, that an investment in pork belly futures could double or triple in a short period of time. We also know that speculating in commodity futures carries great risk, and we could lose our entire portfolio, and then some, in an equally short time.

On the other hand, we know that an investment in Canada Savings Bonds is, in terms of the principal investment, a risk-free exercise. We will receive a fixed rate of interest on our investment and our principal will be repaid in full when the CSBs are redeemed. The decision to buy or not to buy is driven by a subconscious assessment of the trade-off between risk and return, a trade-off that can only be made with certainty when looking at extreme situations.

Still, risk is an important consideration as we attempt to evaluate a mutual fund manager. It is one thing to assess whether a manager performed well relative to a benchmark; it is quite another to look at risk-adjusted returns relative to a benchmark.

Do managers add value if they can match a benchmark with less risk? Well, the Ivy Canadian Fund had returns just slightly below the benchmark — but the fund's returns were much more consistent. We think there is value in not having periods when you lose money. It would be unfair to characterize as average a fund manager who was able to equal the performance of the benchmark index, with less risk.

We define risk as the volatility of returns of the underlying fund, and we quantify risk mathematically, using, as you have seen, standard deviation. Without getting caught up in a litany of mathematical mumbo jumbo, annual standard deviation statistically quantifies the percentage return that the fund can vary from one year to the next. The higher the annual standard deviation, the more volatile and, by definition, the more risky, the fund is.

Of course, we believe that investors really define risk as the potential for loss over any given time period. Figure 6.8 looks at the "rolling" 24-month returns of our Ivy Canadian Fund. Put another way, this graph looks at all of the possible 24-month holding periods since the fund's inception. It asks three questions:

1. What was the best compound annual return over any 24-month period? (22.27 percent.)

FIGURE 6.8

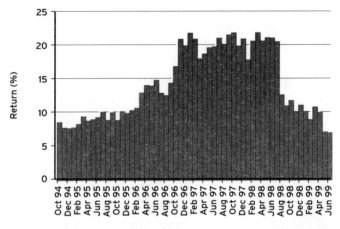

	TOTAL CHANGE	ANN CMPD RATE	$ 10,000 INVESTED	24 MONTHS ENDING
Best	49.49%	22.27%	$14,949.21	Oct 97
Worst	15.25%	7.36%	$11,525.18	Jun 99
Average	31.46%	14.65%	$13,145.65	n/a

Source: Portfolio Analytics

2. What was the worst compound annual return over any 24-month period? (7.36 percent.)
3. What was the average compound annual return over any 24-month period? (14.65 percent.)

Never a loss over any 24-month period has to be worth something.

The rolling return graph provides a foundation for investors to make rational decisions about risk. You simply pick your time horizon — 24 months, in this case — and ask yourself, could I withstand the worst-case scenario over any period?

Manager Value Added (MVA)

The total return of a mutual fund's investment portfolio can be affected by three factors:

1. Where the portfolio is invested, as defined by the fund's prospectus. Is this fund mandated to hold

Canadian equities, U.S. equity, bonds, real estate, gold, etc? We can evaluate what return we should expect in a given sector by looking at the returns earned on the comparable benchmark.

2. The degree of risk the manager is assuming. A basic investment tenet states "higher risk begets higher returns." We would expect, by definition, a high-risk Canadian equities fund to generate greater returns than the TSE 300 Composite Index. The point is, how much of the excess returns generated by the Canadian equity fund were the result of the higher level of risk assumed by the manager, and how much were the result of the shrewd stock-picking ability of the manager?

3. The ability of the manager. The best scenario is a fund manager who manages to generate higher returns than the benchmark index, and does so with less risk.

Manager Value Added (MVA) is a mathematical model that quantifies the risk-adjusted return of the fund with the risk-adjusted return of the comparable benchmark over the previous three years. The goal is to evaluate how much the manager contributed to the returns in the portfolio. In other words, of the three factors cited above, how much of the portfolio's return was the result of factor 3?

MVA is an index that ranks managers on their ability to add value while keeping risk to a minimum. With the MVA index, all managers start with a base value of 100. Managers who score above 100 have added value over the last three years, while managers who score less than 100 have not added value.

Performance Measures Uses and Abuses

Performance measures can be used to evaluate performance during both bull and bear markets. However, determining the appropriate benchmark and selecting an appropriate time frame is not a simple matter. Studies have shown that high-performing funds in one year are sometimes the big losers the next year.

Taking that analysis one step further, some funds outperform the averages in strong markets, but underperform when markets are weak. And more often than not, mutual funds on average do not outperform a randomly selected portfolio of securities. A key criterion in selecting a good fund is consistency of performance. How well does the fund perform in bad markets? In good markets? As a result, the fund's beta, variance, and reward-to-risk measures are all-important tools.

You should also examine the tenure of the fund's manager and whether the person who managed the fund's portfolio when it produced big gains is still at the helm. Often, good managers are lured into a better-paying competitor's camp; poor managers usually find themselves out of a job. In other instances, the portfolio is run by a management team. That can be a plus, because at least it provides a degree of consistency.

At all costs, avoid selecting funds strictly on the basis of recent quarterly or annual performance numbers cited in the financial press. The star performers this quarter or year may well be the laggards next period.

SOME FINAL THOUGHTS

We believe that the MVA index is an excellent model for rating fund managers. But, as with any rating model, it is not intended to be a guide for future performance. We believe portfolios ought to be approached from the top down. Rather than selecting funds on the basis of any measurement standard, you should first look at how these funds fit within the context of your long-range objectives and risk tolerances.

The MVA index ranks funds on the basis of return per unit of risk over the past three-year period. Obviously, we have to be careful not to infringe on our real-world view that no ideal time period for measuring funds exists. However, since our model requires reasonable risk measurements, we were drawn to the three-year standard deviation numbers widely available in PalTrak. This is a mutual fund subscription data service, investors and advisors can purchase it from Portfolio Analytics in Toronto.

Quantity was also a factor. In the current PalTrak data base, there are more than 1,300 funds with three-year track records, versus about 900 funds with at least a five-year track record. By using the three-year numbers, we are able to rank more funds without, in our opinion, sacrificing the validity of the index. Because we are also using the annual three-year standard deviation as our risk measure, the three-year time period appears to be a reasonable compromise.

If this approach seems complicated — well, it can be. But, fortunately, the calculations are not something you have to do yourself. The MVA indexes are calculated monthly by Portfolio Analytics (phone: 1-800-531-4725; in Toronto, 416-489-7074; and via e-mail, paltrak@pal.com).

PUTTING THE PIECES TOGETHER

In case you ever wondered what your financial advisor does – or should be doing – by now you probably have a much clearer idea. Investment planning, or portfolio building (call it what you will), is a multi-step process that begins with an understanding of your investment personality. The results of that discussion should have led you to an asset mix decision or policy statement.

Within the policy statement there should be a range of possibilities and enough elasticity to allow some fine-tuning, based on your advisor's view of the future. (Or our view, if you are a do-it-yourselfer and you want to match up with our Year 2000 forecast. See "Outlook for the Year 2000.")

Remember, the FundLine will build your four levels of diversification, the MVA will help you find the best mutual funds in each category. (Our *2000 Buyer's Guide to Mutual Funds* will further assist you on that point.) That combination should provide you with a well-diversified portfolio of top-ranked funds.

Whether you choose to use an advisor or not is personal. Either way, you now have all the necessary portfolio building blocks. Use them yourself, or use them to review the advice of your consultant.

MEET THE CHAPMANS

The job now is to show you how to put the pieces together in the form of a portfolio that's right for you. With that in mind, allow us to introduce the Chapmans. Jack and Barbara are both 45 years old. Jack is in middle management at a mid-size Canadian insurance company; Barbara is a trainer at an air-traffic control simulator.

They own their own home, although there is about $100,000 remaining on the mortgage. They are always conscious of the fact that you never really own anything as long as you owe money on it.

Jack enjoys his work. Having spent ten years with the company, he has moved up the ladder, and plays a small but important role within the corporate structure. The salary is good — about $60,000 per year. Jack has an excellent health plan. (It is an insurance company, after all.)

Barbara also likes her job of training pilots. She has been in and out of the workforce over the last seventeen years, sometimes taking extended periods off. Now she makes about $40,000 a year.

Jack is part of a company-funded retirement program, which will provide a stipend when he retires. This is not a pension one could live on comfortably; it is meant as a supplement to other plans Jack and Barbara will build over the course of their working careers. The company has provided employees with financial planning seminars. And Jack has attended more than his share, even though he is still 20 years away from retirement. Age 65 is about the earliest Jack can realistically retire.

The Chapmans have three children — Christopher, Loa, and Machaela. Christopher is the oldest. He is 16 and taking driver's education. The sooner he can get his license, the sooner he can date. This suits Jack just fine; he never really dated until he could drive either. However, from a financial planning perspective, the Chapmans are concerned about the cost of insuring Chris.

Fortunately, Christopher is a disciplined driver, perhaps as a result of his enthusiasm for martial arts. He holds a first *dan* black belt in tae kwan do, and hopes to test for his second *dan* early in the new year.

Loa, 13 years old, is working hard at being a dancer. She takes ballet, acrobatics, jazz, and tap — more than enough classes, in Barbara's opinion. Barbara's the one who has to drive Loa to all her classes, which take up three nights a week during the school year. Christopher will soon come in handy as a substitute bus driver.

Still, Jack and Barbara feel that Loa's dance lessons are time well spent — that dancing builds stamina and character. Barbara was a pretty fair ballet student in her own right.

Machaela is only six. She was the pleasant surprise in the Chapman family, and is filled with personality beyond her years. Jack and Barbara could not have planned for a more complete package. In fact, they weren't planning for any package.

From a financial perspective, however, having a third child has changed some long-term plans for the Chapman family. When Machaela is in university — assuming she goes — Jack and Barbara will be in their sixties. That's not a bad thing, but any thoughts of early retirement are now on the back burner. Unless their investment portfolio does better than expected, both plan to work until they are 65.

The goal now is to build a decent retirement nest egg after taking care of the children's education needs. The Chapmans have already put registered education savings plans in place for all three children. The objective now is to establish an asset mix for their long-term investment account.

Most of the investment funds are outside an RRSP. This has its pros and cons. On the positive side, foreign content is not an issue. On the negative side, there is tax to be paid on the investment returns — so it's paramount that any funds used in this process be tax efficient, and that income, if any, be tax advantaged.

Jack and Barbara have some RRSP catch-up room from previous years, so most of the investment portfolio could be switched to an RRSP over the next two to three years.

The Chapmans want to fine-tune their long-term investment plan. This uncertainty has gone on too long. It is clearly time to make some decisions.

The Chapmans' Questionnaire

Jack and Barbara have decided to answer the questions as a family, taking into account both incomes and assuming the assets are jointly owned. The first question relates to their net worth.

Question 1

Rating your Net Worth

Is your approximate net worth:

Less than $25,000?	1
Between $25,000 and $50,000?	3
Between $50,001 and $100,000?	5
Between $100,001 and $250, 000?	7
Greater than $250,000?	10
NET WORTH SCORE:	7

The Chapmans scored a 7 on their net worth question. Their investment portfolio is valued at $100,000. Their house has a value of $275,000, but with a $100,000 mortgage outstanding. If Jack and Barbara had decided to include the house in their net worth statement, then they would have received the highest score possible on this question.

The choice not to include the family home as an investment asset was a joint decision. Neither Jack nor Barbara ever considered the house an investment. Rather, it was a place to live and raise a family. They never intended to sell it, nor were they relying on it for their future retirement needs. Ideally, they would like to remain in the same home after retirement, and live off their pensions and the accumulated value of the investment portfolio.

This issue leads us directly to the next question: What rate of return do the Chapmans need in order to meet their retirement objective? We know that Jack will receive a small pension from his company. It may be sufficient to provide the necessities, but not enough for the extras. Jack and Barbara want the extras.

They expect his company-sponsored pension to provide an income equal to about 30 percent of Jack's best five years. Using today's numbers, if Jack were 65, a fully funded plan would provide him with a pension income of $18,000 per year. Barbara's pension will provide about 20 percent of what she earned during her best five years. If Barbara retired at 65, she would receive about a fifth of her $40,000 annual salary, or around $8,000 per year.

Both Jack and Barbara feel that their retirement income should be at least 70 percent of their current income. Their combined income is $100,000. If they were to retire at 65, based on that income level, they can expect their pensions to pay them about $26,000 per year. Add in the Canada Pension, and, if they are lucky, the Old Age Security, and their income might total $35,000 at retirement. Not enough! (Put another way, they would expect their pensions and government benefits to provide an income equal to about 35 percent of their best five years.)

Their investment portfolio needs to make up the difference. Assuming they would like to earn $70,000 at retirement, the investment portfolio needs to be large enough to pay out about $35,000 in income.

If the Chapmans were not planning to add more funds to their investment portfolio over the next twenty years, what rate of return would be required to make certain they can draw $35,000 to age 85? (That's twenty years of income after they retire, and we are assuming that they have a zero balance at age 85.)

If there is no inflation over the next 40 years — taking into account 20 years to accumulate the portfolio and 20 years of withdrawals from the portfolio — then the Chapmans need to earn 6.8 percent on their investments after tax.

At the end of 20 years, their $100,000 portfolio would be worth $375,479. Assuming the portfolio still earns 6.8 percent after retirement, and the Chapmans begin systematically withdrawing $35,000 a year, the portfolio will last another 20 years. When they are 85 there will be no assets remaining in the portfolio.

But wait a minute. It looks good in theory... but in the real world? There are two problems with this approach. First, because the portfolio is outside an RRSP, tax has to be paid on the returns. Second, we have not adjusted the returns for inflation.

The former could be fixed by simply opting for the RRSP strategy rather than the non-registered route. The inflation question affects their portfolio, whether it's inside or outside an RRSP. We trust you see why this is such a tricky calculation.

So let's revisit the required rate of return for a moment. Prudence dictates that we factor in some inflation over the next 40 years. (Though inflation is somewhat muted while they are working, because their wages should keep pace. That means a better pension at retirement.)

Still, to be safe, you should include inflation in the discussion. You want a consistent number that can be used in the long-term calculations. The Chapmans decide on a three percent inflation factor.

Second, how will the Chapmans deal with the tax problem? All those capital gains, dividends, and interest income will trigger tax. Let's assume that the Chapmans are in a 40 percent tax bracket. Imagining the most tax efficient structure for their non-registered portfolio, they will still need to earn about 14.4 percent before tax.

If you were investing in the U.S. over the last few years, you might say, "Piece of cake!" But in reality, a 14.4 percent return is a tall order for long-term investors. The long-term average return on a 100 percent equity portfolio is about 11 percent a year. To assume you are going to build a balanced portfolio that generates a return of 14.4 percent compounded annually is simply not realistic.

So there needs to be some additional fine-tuning. Remember, we said that the Chapmans had not intended to add anything to their investment portfolio. Perhaps they need to rethink that. For example, if the Chapmans were to add $6,000 each year to their portfolio ($500 per month), their required rate of return for a non-registered portfolio is 10.91 percent. That's still a very aggressive target, but possible.

But before we embark on that aggressive a portfolio, let's ask what tax does to the long-term rate of return. What happens to the calculation if the Chapmans opt for the RRSP portfolio, deferring tax from the accumulation phase into the withdrawal phase?

Their required rate of annual return drops to about 9.8 percent. And that's assuming the Chapmans make no additional contributions to the RRSP.

Jack and Barbara decide to look at what happens if they contribute $3,000 a year to their RRSP. They discover that they have unused room in their RRSP to shelter most of their investment portfolio over the next three years. Now the required rate of return falls to 8.7 percent — which seems reasonable for a long-term balanced portfolio. Wonderful how a questionnaire can bring clarity to a complex situation.

The 8.7 percent figure gives the Chapmans a score of 10 on their "required rate of return" question. Here's the chart for you to do your own calculations.

Question 2
Financial Goals

Having determined your financial goals (i.e. retirement, saving for a home, children's education) we must assess the rate of return required to attain these goals. Is your required rate of return:

Less than 6%?	1
Between 6% and 9%?	5
Greater than 9% but no more than 12%?	10
Greater than 12%	15
FINANCIAL GOALS SCORE:	5

The Risk Profile

The next part of the questionnaire involves a series of questions related to risk. How comfortable are the Chapmans with fluctuations in their investment portfolio? It probably depends on when you ask the question. (And whom you ask!)

The fact is, questions that relate to risk are subjective. No matter how hard you try, it is difficult to know exactly where you stand on hypothetical questions. Would you be able to stay calm during a serious correction? Would you sell in a panic? The real answer to that question is "I don't know!" The truth is, you can only know after having lived through a major stock market correction.

But as with all investor profiles, the questions need to be asked. We simply do what the Chapmans do; we do the best we can.

The answers to the risk profile are as follows:

Question 3

Liquidity

How important is it that you have cash available for emergencies or investment opportunities?

It is extremely important.	1
It is important	2
It is slightly important.	4
It isn't important at all	5
Liquidity Score:	4

Question 4

Safety

After one year of investing, how much would the value of your long-term investment capital have to decline before you would sell it and take a loss?

I would sell if my investment declined by 5%.	1
I would sell if my investment declined by 15%.	2
I would sell if my investment declined by 25%.	3
I would sell if my investment declined by 50%.	4
I would not sell my investment.	5
Safety Score:	3

Question 5

Current Income

How important is it that you receive an income stream from your investments over the period of your investment horizon?

It is extremely important.	1
It is important.	2
It is only slightly important.	3
It isn't important at all.	4
Current Income Score:	4

Question 6

Future Gains:

How would you describe your reaction to financial news that may have a detrimental effect on your investments?

I would be very anxious and likely to sell my investments.	1
I would be fearful and consider selling my investments.	2
I would be uncomfortable but would hold my investments.	3
I would remain calm and definitely hold my investments.	4
Future Gains Score:	2

Question 7

Portfolio Variablility

How important is it that you never experience a loss in your portfolio during a given time period?

It is extremely important.	1
Is is important.	2
It is only slightly important.	3
It isn't important at all.	4
Portfolio Variability Score:	2

Question 8

Performance Review

Which performance numbers most concern you?

Monthly performance numbers.	1
Quarterly performance numbers.	2
Annual performance numbers.	3

Question 9

Speculation

Within the past five years, how often have you invested money in speculative investments?

I have never invested speculatively.	1
I have invested speculatively once.	2
I have invested speculatively twice.	3
I have invested speculatively three or more times.	4
Speculation Score:	2

Question 10

Investment Time Horizon

How long do you plan to hold your investments?

Less than two years?	0
Between two and five years?	3
More than five and less than ten years?	6
Ten to twenty years?	10
More than twenty years?	15
Investment Time Horizon Score:	10

The Chapmans' Personal Investor Profile

CATEGORY	INFORMATION FOUND WHERE?	TOTAL SCORE
Net Worth	Question 1	7
Financial Objectives	Question 2	10
Risk Assessment Profile	Questions 3 – 8	16
Time Horizon	Question 9	10
Total Score (A + B + C + D)		43

Based on the Chapmans' answers in the investor profile, they fall into the Growth/Income category, which leads to the following policy statement:

GROWTH / INCOME								SCORE: 35 - 44
Equities			Fixed Income			Cash		
Min	Policy	Max	Min	Policy	Max	Min	Policy	Max
30%	50%	70%	25%	40%	55%	5%	10%	15%

Based on the forecast from Chapter 3, we recommend extending the RRSP asset mix as follows:

Extended Asset Mix

	RRSP
Canadian Equity	30.0%
U.S. Equity	7.5%
International Equity	7.5%
Special Equity	5.0%
Total Equity Assets	50.0%

. . .

Dividend Funds	25.0%
Domestic Bond	15.0%
Global Bond	0.0%
Total Income Assets	**40.0%**
Money Market	10.0%
Total Cash Assets	**10.0%**

FUND SELECTION

Having arrived at an extended asset mix, the next step is security selection. Which funds do the Chapmans want in their RRSP portfolio? This is where we draw on the FundLine and the MVA. The FundLine helps us determine which elements of diversification each fund brings to the table, while the MVA helps us select above-average managers.

Before we go any further, we wanted to take a moment to address a frequently asked question about MVA. We've often been asked why we created an MVA index with an actual score. Why not simply give funds our $$$$ rating?

Because we wanted to introduce MVA as a statistical tool, to be used within the context of an overall portfolio. The idea is to build a portfolio where the average weighted MVA (i.e., MVA multiplied by the weight of that fund within the portfolio) is above 100. So within the portfolio you can have individual funds that have MVAs below 100 — especially if those funds bring the right elements of diversification to the portfolio.

Canadian Equity Funds

With that in mind, let's walk the Chapmans through the portfolio process step by step. We'll begin with Canadian equity funds, a 30 percent allocation within the portfolio. The Chapmans narrow their selection to four Canadian equity funds, all with excellent MVA ratings.

They decide to invest 15 percent of their portfolio in the AIC Diversified Canada fund for two reasons: 1) the fund provides exposure to large-cap stocks, and 2) it has about 18 percent of its assets in large-cap U.S. compa-

FUND NAME	MVA
Fidelity Canadian Growth Company	123.6
Saxon Small Cap	122.8
AIC Diversified Canada	118.3
Ivy Canadian	111.5

nies. By using this fund they gain some exposure to the U.S. market with a fully RRSP-eligible fund.

Another 15 percent is invested in the Fidelity Canadian Growth Company Fund. Again there were two reasons for choosing this fund. First, the Fidelity fund provides exposure to both small- and mid-size Canadian companies; second, the MVA was in the fifth percentile (the top five percent of all Canadian equity funds) of all Canadian equity funds.

One of the funds that beat Fidelity in the MVA rank was the Chou RRSP Fund. In fact it was the number one MVA fund with a rating of 145.6. The Chou RRSP Fund would also have been a good choice. However, the Chou funds are only available in Ontario, and the Chou RRSP Fund has a $3,500 minimum initial purchase. Our desire was to use examples that all Canadians could purchase, so we will focus on funds that have small minimum investments and are available across Canada.

The first two pieces of the portfolio are in place. The AIC Diversified Canada Fund gives the portfolio an average weighted MVA of 17.75 (MVA of 118.3 x 15 percent portfolio weight = 17.75). The Fidelity Canadian Growth Company Fund adds 18.54 to the weighted average MVA (123.6 x 15 percent portfolio weight = 18.54).

U.S. Equity Funds

The next step in the construction process is to invest 7.5 percent of the portfolio's assets in U.S. equity funds. The following funds are possibilities:

Green Line U.S. Index 102.7

Investors U.S. Growth 101.6

AIM American Premier 101.0

In this case the Chapmans choose the Green Line U.S. Index Fund. This is a no-load fund with a low MER (currently 63 basis points, or 0.63 percent). This fund is designed to mirror the performance of the S&P 500 Composite Index, or as the prospectus says, a "recognized U.S. Index," the current "Recognized Index" being the S&P 500 Total Return Index. As an index fund, the only box that can be filled under management style is indexation. But that does provide another level of diversification.

The MVA is 102.7, so on a weighted average basis, the Green Line U.S. Index Fund adds 7.70 points to the weighted average MVA of the portfolio (MVA 102.7 x 7.5 percent portfolio weight = 7.70 weighted average MVA).

When it comes to the MVA on the Green Line U.S. Index Fund, some explanation is in order. Recall that the MVA rates fund managers on their ability to beat the performance of the benchmark on a risk-adjusted basis. Managers can score an MVA above 100 in a number of ways. The fund returns could be higher than the benchmark index with the same level of risk. The fund returns could be the same as the benchmark index, but with less risk. In both cases, the manager would end up with an MVA above 100.

But here's the question. How does a fund produce an MVA above 100 when the fund is designed to track the benchmark index? Same return, same level of risk — but with an MER. That's right; the index fund has to produce its returns after accounting for the MER. In all measuring periods, the return of the index fund should be the same as the benchmark index less the MER.

There are a couple of explanations for the MVA on the Green Line U.S. Index Fund. The first has to do with the portfolio itself. The Green Line U.S. Index fund is designed to track the S&P 500 Composite Total Return Index. But it doesn't always hold all 500 stocks in the index. Rather, the managers engage in some complex statistical analysis and try to mirror the underlying benchmark index with a portfolio that may not include all the stocks in the benchmark index.

The other consideration is currency effect. Note the diamond in the currency effect box under Fund Objectives. The benchmark index is the S&P 500 Composite Index valued in Canadian dollars. The Green Line U.S. Index Fund does not hedge currency risk. That has been an advantage over the last couple of years, because the U.S. dollar has strengthened against the Canadian dollar.

International Equity Funds

Having completed the Canadian and U.S. equity fund selections, the next step is to find a reasonable international equity fund. Perhaps a fund that invests in Europe, another that invests in Japan, and still another that has some exposure to Latin America. Here are some possibilities:

BPI Global Opportunities 120.8

AGF Intl Group-Japan Class 114.2

Dynamic Far East 113.0

Atlas Latin American Value 81.1

In this case, the Chapmans decide to use all four funds. They decide to invest two percent in the BPI Global Opportunities Fund, which can invest anywhere around the globe. They invest half a percent in both the AGF International Group Japan Class and the Dynamic Far East Fund.

The remaining 1.5 percent earmarked for this part of the portfolio is allocated to the Atlas Latin American Value fund. Although this fund's MVA is below 100, it was the highest MVA available for a dedicated Latin America fund.

Specialty Equity

The portfolio allows for five percent of its assets to be invested in a specialty fund. These are funds that focus on specific sectors. They are not as diversified as a more broadly-based equity fund, which means that they are higher-risk. But it also means that they can provide some real oomph to your bottom line.

In the forecast chapter, we felt that science and technology would provide the necessary tools to drive productivity higher. And to us, that means that science and technology funds will be one of the strongest segments of the economy going forward.

The Chapmans narrow their specialty list to the following two science and technology funds.

Altamira Science & Technology   94.2

CIBC Global Technology   91.8

Both choices would work well in this portfolio. Both are no-load funds and both funds have reasonable MERs. The choice is based solely on the MVA rating. In this case, the Chapmans choose the Altamira Science and Technology Fund.

Construction in Progress

Before going further with the portfolio, let's see how the Chapmans have done with the first half. In Table 7.1, we see that the Chapmans have a weighted average MVA of 56.87 with half the portfolio invested.

TABLE 7.1 – EQUITY ASSETS

FUND NAME	PCT	MVA	WEIGHTED MVA
Fidelity Canadian Growth Company	15.0%	123.6	18.54
AIC Diversified Canada	15.0%	118.3	17.75
Green Line U.S. Index	7.5%	102.7	7.70
BPI Global Opportunities	2.0%	120.8	2.42
AGF International Group-Japan Class	2.0%	114.2	2.28
Dynamic Far East	2.0%	113.0	2.26
Atlas Latin American Value	1.5%	81.1	1.22
Altamira Science & Technology	5.0%	94.2	4.71
Totals:	50.0%	56.87	

The next issue: How well is the equity component diversified? The accompanying portfolio line demonstrates the elements of diversification that are in place now.

CHAPMANS' PORTFOLIO LINE

Extended Asset Mix											Objectives								Investment Style					
Canadian Equity	U.S. Equity	Europe	Japan	Far East	Latin America	Special Equity	Dividend	Fixed Income	Global Fixed Income	Money Market	Short Term	Mid Term	Long Term	Foreign Currency	Sector Specific	Small-Cap	Mid-Cap	Large-Cap	Top Down	Bottom Up	Value Method	Sector Rotation	Momentum	Indexation
◆	◆	◆	◆	◆	◆	◆								◆	◆	◆	◆	◆	◆	◆	◆	◆	◆	◆

As you can see, we are well on our way to filling in the majority of boxes along the FundLine. Now we move onto the income component of the portfolio.

Income Investments

The income component of the portfolio is made up of domestic bond funds and dividend funds. We are suggesting dividend funds as an income substitute. Although there is no tax advantage to having a dividend fund inside an RRSP, we think there is growth potential from some of the stocks in the dividend fund portfolio.

Plus, with interest rates at current levels, we think there is a greater likelihood that rates will rise rather than fall in the year 2000, at least through the first quarter. As such, we're not impressed with the near-term prospects for bond funds.

With that in mind, the Chapmans pick two domestic bond funds, two dividend funds, and one Canadian money market fund.

Fund	Value
Altamira Bond	104.0
C.I. Canadian Bond	102.5
Spectrum United Dividend	116.7
BPI Dividend Income	116.0
Perigee T-Plus	100.7

These domestic bond funds were chosen because they were currently invested at different points along the yield curve. The Altamira Bond Fund is one of the more aggressive bond funds in Canada. The average term to maturity does not go below six years. Currently the fund has one of the longest average terms to maturity of any Canadian bond fund.

The C.I. Canadian Bond Fund carries a bit less risk. Currently it is on the midpoint of the yield curve, with an average term to maturity that is less than ten years. Both managers have done excellent jobs, having beaten their benchmark indexes on a risk-adjusted basis. That's quite an accomplishment for bond fund managers, who have very little room to maneuver their portfolios. The Chapmans decide to invest 7.5 percent of their portfolio in each of the two Canadian bond funds.

The two dividend funds were chosen because of their MVAs. Spectrum United tends to hold more preferred shares than the BPI Dividend Income Fund. The BPI fund tends to hold a sizeable portion of the portfolio in common shares that pay high dividends. That may give some oomph to the portfolio's bottom line later in the year 2000. As well, the BPI Dividend Income Fund has one of the lowest MERs among dividend funds. The Chapmans allocate 12.5 percent of their portfolio to each dividend fund.

Finally, the choice of the Perigee T-Bill Fund is based solely on the MVA. This fund invests in Government of Canada T-bills, and represents the cash component of the portfolio. A 10 percent weight is given to this fund.

Based on these numbers, the income and cash assets break down as follows:

TABLE 7.2 – INCOME AND CASH ASSETS

FUND NAME	PCT	MVA	WEIGHTED MVA
Altamira Bond	7.5%	104.0	7.80
CI Canadian Bond	7.5%	102.5	7.69
Spectrum United Dividend	12.5%	116.7	14.59
BPI Dividend Income	12.5%	116.0	14.50
Perigee T-Plus	10.0%	100.7	10.07
Total Income and Cash Assets	50.0%		54.65

Adding this component of the portfolio brings the following elements of diversification into play.

Construction Completed

The Chapmans have now completed their portfolio. There are 13 funds in the portfolio, with an average weighted MVA of 111.52. The Chapmans were able to fill in 24 out of 25 boxes along the FundLine. (The only missing box is Global Fixed Income.)

The Chapmans have constructed a well-balanced portfolio with above-average managers. The complete portfolio is listed below (see table 7.3), along with the average weighted MVA and the completed FundLine.

TABLE 7.3 – CHAPMANS' COMPLETED PORTFOLIO

FUND NAME	PCT	MVA	WEIGHTED MVA
Fidelity Canadian Growth Company	15.0%	123.6	18.54
AIC Diversified Canada	15.0%	118.3	17.75
Green Line U.S. Index	7.5%	102.7	7.70
BPI Global Opportunities	2.0%	120.8	2.42
AGF International Group-Japan Class	2.0%	114.2	2.28
Dynamic Far East	2.0%	113.0	2.26
Atlas Latin American Value	1.5%	81.1	1.22
Altamira Science & Technology	5.0%	94.2	4.71
Altamira Bond	7.5%	104.0	7.80
C.I. Canadian Bond	7.5%	102.5	7.69
Spectrum United Dividend	12.5%	116.7	14.59
BPI Dividend Income	12.5%	116.0	14.50
Perigee T-Plus	10.0%	100.7	10.07
Totals for Chapman Portfolio	100.0%	111.52	

Extended Asset Mix											Objectives								Investment Style					
Canadian Equity	U.S. Equity	Europe	Japan	Far East	Latin America	Special Equity	Dividend	Fixed Income	Global Fixed Income	Money Market	Short Term	Mid Term	Long Term	Foreign Currency	Sector Specific	Small-Cap	Mid-Cap	Large-Cap	Top Down	Bottom Up	Value Method	Sector Rotation	Momentum	Indexation
◆	◆	◆	◆	◆	◆	◆	◆	◆		◆	◆	◆	◆	◆	◆	◆	◆	◆	◆	◆	◆	◆	◆	◆

HOW TO JUDGE PERFORMANCE

Now that the portfolio has been built, what's next? That's where financial advisors provide ongoing assistance, helping you navigate through the ebbs and flows of the business cycle.

Personally, we think the next logical step is to find a way to manage your expectations. The approach we use is to build a benchmark that represents your current asset mix. In the same way we have benchmarks for fund managers, you should have a benchmark for your mutual fund portfolio.

Follow the same guidelines that we used in the section on "The Secret Weapon: MVA.". Most important, the benchmark should be appropriate to your specific circumstances.

Whether it is the convenience or the advantage of having professional management expertise, the Chapmans have decided to use mutual funds. So it won't help them manage expectations if they create a benchmark that includes, say, the TSE 300 Composite Index, the S&P 500 Composite Index, some international benchmark, the Scotia Capital Markets Bond Universe, and Treasury bills. For one thing, the Chapmans can't buy the Scotia Capital Markets Bond Universe, and they have no way of replicating an international index.

They need a mutual fund benchmark. Constructing one is not as difficult as you might think. Remember, we think that a well-structured portfolio made up of above-average funds ought to outperform the median funds in each category.

To create a reasonable benchmark, you can track another portfolio that includes only the median performing funds in each category. It might look like Table 7.4.

TABLE 7.4

CHAPMAN BENCHMARK	PCT
Median Canadian Equity Fund	30.0%
Median U.S. Equity Fund	7.5%
Median International Fund	7.5%
Median Specialty Fund	5.0%
Median Canadian Bond Fund	15.0%
Median Canadian Dividend Fund	25.0%
Median Cdn Money Market Fund	10.0%
Totals	100.0%

The idea with benchmarking is to compare the performance of your homemade portfolio with the performance of the median funds in the benchmark. If you've constructed the portfolio correctly, your homemade portfolio should always outperform the benchmark.

WINNING REGISTERED PORTFOLIOS

By now, you should have a pretty good idea of how to go about building mutual fund portfolios using the FundLine and our MVA scores. Now let's apply the process to certain specific needs and show you how to create a personal portfolio that's exactly tailored to your requirements.

Let's begin with a situation that faces many Canadian investors — building an RRSP portfolio that is going to provide the right combination of growth potential with a relatively low risk level. We believe the risk aspect is extremely important in this case, because this is money you are putting aside for your later years. You should not be taking undue chances with it; rather your goal should be steady, sustained growth over a long period of time.

We won't lead you through the questionnaire process again. By now, you should have a good understanding of how it works. Instead, we will take two specific RRSP cases and show you how they lead to a different portfolio approach.

To begin, here's a reminder of how the FundLine boxes are distributed.

Extended Asset Mix	Objectives	Investment Style

Canadian Equity	U.S. Equity	Europe	Japan	Far East	Latin America	Special Equity	Dividend	Fixed Income	Global Fixed Income	Money Market	Short Term	Mid Term	Long Term	Foreign Currency	Sector Specific	Small-Cap	Mid-Cap	Large-Cap	Top Down	Bottom Up	Value Method	Sector Rotation	Momentum	Indexation
◆	◆	◆	◆	◆	◆	◆	◆	◆	◆	◆	◆	◆	◆	◆	◆	◆	◆	◆	◆	◆	◆	◆	◆	◆

PORTFOLIO #1 – AN AGGRESSIVE RRSP

First we'll look at the case of Michelle Ward. She is in her early thirties and has a position as an assistant sales manager in a small auto parts manufacturing company. She does not have a company pension plan, so her RRSP will be her primary source of retirement income as matters currently stand. Therefore, she makes the maximum annual contribution to her plan and is anxious to make sure it is invested in the most effective way possible.

After carefully completing the questionnaire, she ends up with a score of 56 points. That puts her into our Aggressive Growth category. At first glance, this may seem to be inconsistent with an RRSP portfolio, but a review of the questionnaire weightings provides an explanation. Michelle has a long time horizon (15 points) and wants to achieve an average annual return of 10 to 11 percent (also 15 points). She also scores maximum points because of not needing immediate cash flow, not requiring the RRSP money for emergencies, being willing to actively oversee her investments, and her willingness to stay with her investment choices over the long haul.

Here's the basic portfolio profile she is looking at:

AGGRESSIVE GROWTH								SCORE: 55+
Equities			Fixed Income			Cash		
Min	Policy	Max	Min	Policy	Max	Min	Policy	Max
50%	75%	100%	0%	20%	30%	0%	5%	10%

Considering our comments on the investing climate at this time, and taking the foreign content rules into account, we recommend the following adjustments to Michelle's asset mix:

EXTENDED ASSET MIX

	RRSP
Canadian Equity	35.0%
U.S. Equity	5.0%
International Equity	5.0%
Special Equity	10.0%
Total Equity Assets	**55.0%**

. . .

Dividend Funds	22.5%
Domestic Bond	20.0%
Global Bond	0.0%
Total Income Assets	**42.5%**
Money Market	2.5%
Total Cash Assets	**2.5%**

The selection of specific funds for Michelle's portfolio will be made on this basis. However, there is an important point to keep in mind here. We are following the 20 percent foreign content rule to the letter in this portfolio, but the introduction of new RRSP-eligible clone funds in 1999 will no longer make this necessary going forward. You will find more details on how these funds work in the section on "Who's Afraid of the Foreign Content Rule."

Now let's use the FundLine and MVA scores to build an RRSP portfolio for Michelle. Remember, we want a portfolio that fills in as many of our diversification boxes as possible and where the average weighted MVA is above 100.

Equity Funds

Canadian equity funds have been given a 35 percent allocation in this case. Since this is an RRSP, the largest part of those holdings should be in diversified and large-cap funds. We are also looking for some other important features. First, in this case, we want funds that achieve a high MVA more through superior performance than as a result of lower risk. Remember that MVA is determined by two factors: performance against a benchmark index and standard deviation (a measure of their risk). For a long-term aggressive portfolio, superior performance gets priority. Second, given our positive view of the U.S. equity markets, we want Canadian stock funds that have at least 15 percent U.S. content.

Here are two funds that pop out as being worthy of Michelle's consideration:

AIC Diversified Canada   118.3

Universal Canadian Growth

To these, we want to add a small-to-mid cap Canadian equity fund to provide greater portfolio diversification. One that looks very attractive on our first run-through is the GBC Canadian Growth Fund. There's just one slight problem with it: a $100,000 minimum initial investment requirement. Michelle will undoubtedly have that kind of money some day, but she doesn't now. So we need an alternative. Here's our choice:

Fidelity Canadian Growth Company   123.6

We only have room for a five percent U.S. equity weighting in this portfolio, so we'll choose a core index fund that will produce returns consistent with the movement of the S&P 500 Index. Our selection is the Green Line U.S. Index Fund.

Green Line U.S. Index Fund   102.7

For our global selections, we want one core fund that will provide Michelle with broad diversification. But she would also like to have a small portion of her RRSP invested in one of the world's hottest areas at this time. Since we are very positive about the outlook for Asia in the year 2000, we recommend a Far East Fund for her.

AIC World Equity   105.7

Scudder Pacific   108.1

Finally, Michelle has a very long time horizon. She's going to see an incredible expansion of infrastructure in the less-developed parts of the world over the next 30 years or so. She would like her RRSP to hold a high-growth fund that is well positioned to profit from these events. What better field than telecommunications? There are several good funds of this type now available, but most don't have the three-year record needed for an MVA score. One that does is the Spectrum United Global Telecommunications Fund.

Spectrum United Global Telecommunications Fund   95.8

That completes the equity side of Michelle Ward's RRSP portfolio. But there is still a little more work to do.

Income Funds

Because of Michelle's investor profile and the many years remaining before she will need the money, we decided to give her some growth potential in the income side of her portfolio as well. A good dividend income fund that invests mainly in high-yielding common stocks is the best way to achieve that. The Bissett Dividend Income Fund would be a fine choice here; however, the $10,000 initial investment requirement makes it too rich for Michelle at this stage. Maybe later. In the meantime, the Royal Dividend Fund is an excellent alternative.

Royal Dividend Fund   112.0

To this, we'll add a fund that is more oriented to fixed-income securities but which tends to produce a better rate of return than the average bond fund because its assets are more broadly diversified: the AGF Canadian High Income Fund.

AGF Canadian High Income Fund   110.2

The result here is two income funds that carry higher risk than usual for funds of this type, but which also offer the potential to generate much better than average returns. To illustrate, the Royal Dividend Fund averaged better than 20 percent annually over the three years to June 30, 1999.

Cash Funds

Finally, Michelle's portfolio will have a small 2.5 percent cash position — low because of the aggressive nature of her RRSP. There are many funds that would fit nicely here. We'll use a popular no-load fund from Green Line.

Green Line Canadian Money Market Fund   96.6

RRSP Aggressive Portfolio summarized

Here's how Michelle's RRSP portfolio looks now that our selections have been completed:

PCT	AGGRESSIVE GROWTH RRSP PORTFOLIO	WT. MVA	MVA
15.0%	AIC Diversified Canada	17.75	118.3
10.0%	Universal Canadian Growth	10.97	109.7
10.0%	GBC Canadian Growth	12.01	120.1
5.0%	Green Line U.S. Index	5.14	102.7
2.5%	AIC World Equity	2.64	105.7
2.5%	Scudder Pacific	2.70	108.1
10.0%	Spectrum United Global Telecommunications	9.58	95.8
22.5%	Royal Dividend	25.20	112.0
20.0%	AGF Canadian High Income	22.04	110.2
2.5%	Green Line Canadian Money Market	2.42	96.6
100.0%	Portfolio MVA	110.44	

As you can see, Michelle has a well-diversified aggressive portfolio, with a high weighted MVA. Here's what her FundLine summary looks like.

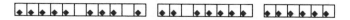

A few boxes are not filled. There is no Latin American position, the fund has no global bonds, and we don't have a fund that is heavily invested in long-term bonds. However, given our current view of the markets and the nature of this portfolio, we don't see any of these as serious omissions. This portfolio should do a first-rate job for

Michelle over the long term and ensure that she has a very healthy RRSP when the time comes to make use of it.

PORTFOLIO #2 – A CONSERVATIVE RRSP

As you approach retirement, your RRSP strategy should begin to change. You no longer have a long time horizon of 20 or 30 years. You want to protect the capital you've built over time, but you don't want to sacrifice your growth potential entirely.

Charles White is in exactly this position. He's 58 years old and expects to retire sometime in the next five years. He has been self-employed for most of his life, working as a freelance book and magazine editor. So his RRSP will be his main source of income when he stops work, although he expects to supplement it by taking the occasional contract job.

He has dutifully contributed $3,000 a year to his RRSP for the past 30 years and invested it conservatively but wisely. His average annual compound rate of return over that time was eight percent, so his RRSP is now worth about $340,000 (it's amazing how a relatively small annual investment can grow over time if invested well). He wants to make changes in his RRSP to reduce the overall risk level and completes our questionnaire accordingly. His score comes out at 34, right at the top of the Income/Growth Portfolio range — although he's nearing retirement, his score is relatively high because of the net worth he's built through his RRSP.

Here's the portfolio profile that fits his score:

INCOME / GROWTH								SCORE: 25-34
Equities			Fixed Income			Cash		
Min	Policy	Max	Min	Policy	Max	Min	Policy	Max
20%	35%	50%	30%	50%	70%	10%	15%	25%

We'll make some slight adjustments from our policy numbers here to reflect the fact that Charles is already in a good financial position and to strengthen his cash position somewhat. Here is the portfolio asset mix we'll work with in this case:

EXTENDED ASSET MIX

	RRSP
Canadian Equity	20.0%
U.S. Equity	10.0%
International Equity	10.0%
Special Equity	0.0%
Total Equity Assets	**40.0%**
Dividend Funds	10.0%
Domestic Bond	30.0%
Global Bond	0.0%
Total Income Assets	**40.0%**
Money Market	20.0%
Total Cash Assets	**20.0%**

Now to the fund selection.

Equity Funds

We will change the emphasis in the equity fund selection process. In Michelle Ward's case, we looked for funds that achieved high MVA scores more on the basis of performance than because they displayed relatively low risk. Now we'll reverse our priorities. Charles wants his RRSP to keep growing, but he wants his risk exposure lowered. So we'll look for equity funds that achieve those goals, starting with a core Canadian equity holding.

Ivy Canadian 111.5

Ivy Canadian, a Mackenzie Financial fund, is known by professionals as one of the most conservatively managed funds of its type in the country. The manager is Jerry Javasky, and his approach is to buy sound core stocks and to hold large amounts of cash during periods of market uncertainty to cushion the impact of any correction. He has been very successful with this juggling act; Ivy Canadian is now the largest domestic equity fund in Canada. It fits perfectly into Charles White's revamped portfolio.

To balance Ivy Canadian, we'll add a Canadian small-cap fund, but one which is less volatile (and therefore less risky) than most funds of this type. We have one that is well suited to these needs, the Saxon Small Cap Fund.

Saxon Small Cap   122.8

This fund has produced some fine results (average annual return for the five years to June 30/99 was almost 15 percent) while doing a good job of protecting investors' assets.

Because this is an RRSP portfolio, we will limit the foreign content to 20 percent even though, as we noted earlier, the new generation of RRSP-eligible clones offers us a way around this limit. For example, our choice for the U.S. equity fund we'll include is one that is now available in an RRSP-eligible version if you prefer to go that route. However, the management expense ratio of the clone will be somewhat higher than that of the parent fund, which will result in a slightly lower MVA score.

BPI American Equity Value   99.3

The BPI American Equity Value Fund has been an outstanding performer in the U.S. Equity category in recent years. Over the five years to June 30/99, it gained an average of 28.9 percent a year while never recording a loss over any given 12-month period. That's a remarkable record.

We'll complement the BPI fund with a conservatively managed international fund and also give Charles some exposure to the recovering Japanese market.

Templeton International Stock   105.6

This fund can invest around the world except in North America. So we aren't duplicating the asset base of the BPI fund in any way. Templeton International Stock is one of the best funds of its type, employing the value investing principles of the legendary Sir John

Templeton. Average annual compound rate of return over the five years to June 30/99 was 13.4 percent.

AGF Japan Class 114.2

We like the prospects for Japan at this time so we will put a small portion of this portfolio into the well-run AGF Japan Class. Despite the volatility of the Japanese stock market in recent years, this fund's low-risk style allowed investors to ride out the storm with minimal damage and left them well positioned to profit from the recovery. The fund gained 28 percent in the first half of 1999 alone.

Income Funds

In Michelle Ward's RRSP, we added a growth component to this section of her portfolio. Here we will take an approach that is better suited to the needs of Charles White. We will include a dividend fund once again, but this time we will select a fund that invests less in common stock and more in lower-risk preferred shares — the Spectrum United Dividend Fund.

Spectrum United Dividend 116.7

This fund doesn't offer anything like the capital gains potential of Royal Dividend. But it provides much better cash flow, which Charles will need when the time comes to start drawing income, and is much less volatile.

We will supplement this with two outstanding fixed income funds: the AGF High Income Fund, which we were already introduced to in Michelle's portfolio, and the C.I. Canadian Bond Fund.

AGF High Income 110.2

C.I. Canadian Bond 102.5

The C.I. fund is one that, in our view, doesn't get enough attention. It is managed by John Zechner. He has made it into one of the country's top-performing bond funds. It has easily beaten the average for its category the majority of the time and is a top-quartile performer over its life. The three-year average annual return of 9.6 percent to June 30, 1999, is made even more attractive by the fund's better than average bond risk. Holdings comprise mainly Government of Canada bonds, with the remainder in high-quality corporate and provincial debt. This is a very sound choice for a portfolio of this type.

Cash Funds

Finally, we included a 20 percent cash position in this portfolio. This represents a sizeable chunk of the assets, almost $70,000, so we want to make sure this money goes into a fund with a low MER and a high MVA. Here's our choice:

Perigee T-Plus   100.7

You need a $5,000 minimum investment to get into this fund, but that won't be any problem for Charles. What he gets for his money is a very low management expense ratio and a fund that invests mainly in Treasury bills, but with some corporate notes also in the mix to provide higher yields.

RRSP Conservative Portfolio summarized

Putting everything together, here is the portfolio we created for Charles White:

PCT	INCOME GROWTH RRSP PORTFOLIO	WT. MVA	MVA
10.0%	Ivy Canadian	11.15	111.5
10.0%	Saxon Small Cap	12.28	122.8
10.0%	BPI American Equity Value	9.93	99.3
5.0%	Templeton International Stock	5.28	105.6
5.0%	AGF International Group-Japan Class	5.71	114.2
10.0%	Spectrum United Dividend	11.67	116.7

. . .

10.0%	AGF Canadian High Income	11.02	110.2
20.0%	C.I. Canadian Bond	20.50	102.5
20.0%	Perigee T-Plus	20.14	100.7
100.0%	Portfolio MVA	107.68	

The FundLine result is this:

◆◆◆◆◆◆ | | ◆◆ | ◆ | ◆◆ | ◆ | ◆◆◆ | ◆◆◆◆◆◆

Again, there are a few gaps. But what we're missing are funds that tend to be higher risk and therefore not suitable for this portfolio: Latin America, global bonds, long-term bonds, and sector-specific funds. The portfolio we've ended up with should continue to provide above-average returns until the time Charles is ready to retire, while keeping his risk within comfortable bounds.

PORTFOLIO #3 – REGISTERED RETIREMENT INCOME FUND (RRIF)

So far we've looked at two RRSP scenarios. The next logical step is to move to the post-RRSP stage, the point where the plan is converted to a RRIF. This conversion must take place no later than the end of the calendar year in which you turn 69. You don't necessarily have to go the RRIF route — you could choose an annuity or just withdraw the cash if the plan isn't locked in. However, we strongly recommend a RRIF for most people because of the flexibility and tax advantages it offers.

A RRIF differs from an RRSP in two fundamental ways: you cannot make any contributions to a RRIF and you must withdraw a minimum amount each year, based on a federal government formula (you can take out more than the minimum if you want). Whereas with an RRSP long-term growth is the main investment objective, in a RRIF cash flow and safety of principal become the priorities. The securities in the plan should throw off enough income to meet your withdrawal requirements. They should also be selected with an eye to exposing the portfolio to as little market volatility as possible, while still maintaining reasonable growth potential — after all, you may be relying on the RRIF for income for the next 20 or 30 years.

For this portfolio example, we'll use the case of Barbara Bream. She is 64 years old and has just retired from a nursing career. You'd think she would have a pretty good pension in this situation, but she changed jobs several times during her working years and spent a long period in private practice. So her total pension credits are actually quite small. Her RRIF is very important to her future financial well-being.

It's a good-sized plan, now worth about $275,000 in total assets. That may seem like a lot but, given her dependence on this money, it really isn't. She needs to manage it as effectively as possible.

Barbara completes the questionnaire, putting emphasis on safety and income in her responses. She ends up with a score of 23 points, which puts her into our Safety/Income category. Here's the profile:

SAFETY / INCOME								SCORE: 15-24
Equities			**Fixed Income**			**Cash**		
Min	Policy	Max	Min	Policy	Max	Min	Policy	Max
10%	20%	30%	50%	65%	80%	10%	15%	25%

Because Barbara is still quite young in retirement terms, we'll make a couple of small modifications to the policy positions. We'll increase the equities segment to 25 percent to provide more growth potential (we don't want to run down the assets of the RRIF too quickly). And we'll add to her cash position to reflect the potential of higher interest rates, which would hurt bond prices but increase money market fund returns. Here is the asset mix we will work with:

EXTENDED ASSET MIX

	RRIF
Canadian Equity	7.0%
U.S. Equity	9.0%
International Equity	9.0%
Special Equity	0.0%
Total Equity Assets	**25.0%**

. . .

Dividend Funds	25.0%
Domestic Bond	30.0%
Global Bond	0.0%
Total Income Assets	**55.0%**
Money Market	20.0%
Total Cash Assets	**20.0%**

Now let's choose some mutual funds that fulfill her needs.

Equity Funds

Although we've allowed for 25 percent equity content in this portfolio, we have only allocated seven percent to Canadian stocks. That's because we see the Canadian market as potentially more volatile than the U.S. and international markets, while offering less long-term return potential. For our Canadian equity fund, we want one that has a proven low-risk record. Here's what we choose:

Spectrum United Canadian Investment 109.2

This fund concentrates on Canadian blue chip stocks. It is run by Kim Shannon and Gaelen Morphet of Mercury Asset Management (a Merrill Lynch subsidiary) and has a reputation for producing decent returns with minimal risk. The five-year average annual compound rate of return to June 30/99, was just under 15 percent.

Because of the strength of the U.S. stock market, we want to focus Barbara's equity holdings on that country. Here again, our goal is to find a fund that combines good returns with a first-class safety record. Our choice is a fund many Canadians are unfamiliar with, AIM American Premier.

AIM American Premier 101.0

This fund has gone through a number of managers and style changes over time. But since coming under the control of AIM Funds Management in 1996, it has developed into a first-rate offering. The safety record since AIM took charge is perfect — never a losing 12-month period over that time. As for profits, the fund averaged better than 30 percent a year over the 36 months to June 30/99.

We decide to round out the rest of Barbara's equity positions with a global fund and a Japan fund, to give her some exposure to the resurgence in that part of the world. Here are our choices:

Atlas Global Value   93.4

Fidelity Japanese Growth   110.2

The Atlas Global Value Fund is something of an anomaly. It is oriented towards smaller companies, yet has a very fine safety record in the overall Global Equity category. Performance has been steadily improving under manager Anthony Rawlinson of Global Value Investment, and the fund produced an average annual return of almost 17 percent over the three years to June 30/99.

The Fidelity fund is one of our favourite Japanese equity offerings (AGF being the other).

Fixed-Income Funds

The funds chosen for this segment of Barbara's portfolio have to perform the twin functions of generating income without exposing her to undue risk. Our first selection is what we call a "true" dividend fund.

BPI Dividend Income   116.0

The fund offers a portfolio of preferred shares and dividend-paying common stocks that generates excellent cash flow through monthly payments — very important for Barbara. But it also offers some capital gains potential as a bonus. In fact, the total return (distributions plus capital gains) has consistently been above average for the Canadian Dividend category since Eric Bushell took over as manager in 1995. The safety record is very good, thus fulfilling another of Barbara's concerns.

For our second income-producing fund, we selected something a little different — one of the new breed of Canadian high income balanced funds. These invest in a variety of securities, including royalty trusts, REITs, preferred shares and bonds, with the goal of producing above-average cash flow. Here's the fund we picked:

Guardian Monthly High Income Classic   100.0

This fund hasn't been in existence for three years, so we are assigning it an MVA of 100 for purposes of this portfolio-building exercise. The risk level here is somewhat higher than you will find in most fixed-income funds, because of the inclusion of royalty trusts in the portfolio. However, the cash flow is excellent, which is very important in the context of a RRIF. In calendar 1998, this fund yielded 7.4 percent on a cash flow basis, using the net asset value at the start of year as a base. Distributions are paid monthly.

To further enhance the income potential of this RRIF, we'll include a fund we've already seen in the conservative RRSP portfolio, AGF High Income Fund.

AGF High Income   110.2

To offset the higher risk of the Guardian fund, we round out Barbara Bream's RRIF with two ultra-conservative fixed-income funds.

Scudder Canadian Short-Term Bond   101.8

Ivy Mortgage   96.8

These are both defensive funds, which means that they are exposed to very little risk in a rising interest rate environment. The cash flow they generate will be less than Barbara will receive from the other three fixed-income funds, but it will supplement that income nicely while these funds reduce her overall risk profile.

Cash Funds

Finally, we will round out this RRIF portfolio with a high-performance money market fund, which will provide a combination of cash reserve, modest income, and safety. Since she will be investing about $60,000 in this fund, we'll choose the Bissett Money Market Fund for her. It has a $10,000 minimum but that isn't a problem in her case. The fund offers a low MER and very good returns for its type. Plus, it's no load.

Bissett Money Market   99.8

RRIF Portfolio summarized

Putting it all together, here's the RRIF Portfolio we've constructed for Barbara Bream.

PCT	SAFETY/INCOME RRIF PORTFOLIO	WT. MVA	MVA
7.0%	Spectrum United Canadian Investment	7.64	109.2
9.0%	AIM American Premier	9.09	101.0
4.5%	Atlas Global Value *	4.20	93.4
4.5%	Fidelity Japanese Growth	4.96	110.2
15.0%	BPI Dividend Income **	17.40	116.0
10.0%	Guardian Monthly High Income Classic ***	10.00	100.0
10.0%	AGF Canadian High Income	11.02	110.2
10.0%	Scudder Canadian Short-Term Bond	10.18	101.8
10.0%	Ivy Mortgage	9.68	96.8
20.0%	Bissett Money Market	19.96	99.8
100.0%	Portfolio MVA	104.14	

* Provides exposure to Europe and Far East

** Pays Monthly Income

*** Pays regular monthly income from a portfolio of income trust units. Without a three-year record, MVA is assumed to be 100 for purposes of building portfolio.

FundLine summary:

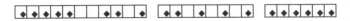

Gaps in the FundLine include Latin America, special equity, global bonds, long-term bonds, sector-specific funds, and mid-cap funds. None of these are significant in the context of a RRIF. However, if Barbara had expressed a desire to have some U.S. dollar exposure in her plan because she expected to some winters in the sun belt, we would have added a foreign bond fund with strong U.S. currency exposure.

PORTFOLIO #4 – REGISTERED EDUCATION SAVINGS PLAN (RESP)

Emma and Mark Brown have just had a joyous event — the birth of their first child, a handsome son whom they have named Robert. The baby is only three months old, but the parents are already thinking about the future. Both are university graduates, and both had to incur substantial student debt to pay for the cost of earning their degrees. They don't want their son to face that kind of financial burden when his turn comes.

So they've decided to open a registered education savings plan (RESP) for Robert, attracted in part by the new federal government program that contributes up to $400 a year in grants to such plans. They've opted for a self-directed mutual fund plan, which gives them plenty of investing scope.

Robert is of course too young to complete our question-naire, so Emma and Mark do it on his behalf. They arrive at a score of 44, having put their emphasis on a relatively high return (10 to 11 percent annually) and the child's relatively long investment horizon (15-20 years). That puts young Robert's RESP into our Growth/Income category.

The parents have made one key decision. They want to invest the government grant money in low-risk securities. If for any reason Robert does not go to college, that grant money will have to be repaid to Ottawa down the road. They want to be sure that, whatever happens with the rest of the investments, the money will be available should that eventuality ever arise.

Here's what the base profile of this portfolio will look like:

GROWTH / INCOME								SCORE: 35-44
Equities			Fixed Income			Cash		
Min	Policy	Max	Min	Policy	Max	Min	Policy	Max
30%	50%	70%	25%	40%	55%	5%	10%	15%

We'll stay with the Policy figures for this one, since there is no particular need for any rebalancing. Here's how we will distribute the assets.

EXTENDED ASSET MIX

	RESP
Canadian Equity	20.0%
U.S. Equity	15.0%
International Equity	10.0%
Special Equity	5.0%
Total Equity Assets	**50.0%**
Dividend Funds	30.0%
Domestic Bond	10.0%
Global Bond	5.0%
Total Income Assets	**45.0%**
Money Market	5.0%
Total Cash Assets	**5.0%**

As you can see, U.S. and international holdings account for well over 20 percent of the assets of this portfolio. However, this does not present a problem. For some strange reason, the 20 percent foreign content limitation does not apply to RESPs. So Mark and Emma could invest the entire portfolio outside Canada if they so chose. They prefer to keep some of the assets at home, however. Let's see how it all comes together.

Equity Funds

Mark and Emma look ahead to what they hope will be a bright world in the twenty-first century for their son to grow up in. They decide to focus on forward-looking funds with a growth orientation in their portfolio mix. So we select two Canadian stock funds that fill this bill very nicely: the Saxon Small Cap Fund, which we already introduced in one of our RRSP portfolios, and the Talvest Millennium Next Generation Fund, which seeks out stocks in companies that are expected to prosper in the next century.

Saxon Small Cap   122.8

Talvest Millennium Next Generation   113.6

We already know about the fine record of the Saxon fund. The Talvest entry holds an assortment of small- and medium-sized companies, including many found on the TSE 300. For its foreign exposure, the fund holds nearly a quarter of its portfolio in Diamonds Trust Series Units, which track the Dow Jones Industrial Average, and S&P 500 Depository Receipts, which track the S&P 500 Index. So this is not a typical small- to mid-cap fund. The strategy is paying off, as returns have been well above average. Over the five years to June 30/99, this fund returned an average of 19.5 percent annually, double the average of its peer group. This one could really boost young Robert's returns.

Of course, we want to include a strong U.S. position in this portfolio. AIM American Premier Fund, which we introduced earlier, fits the bill nicely.

AIM American Premier   101.0

For the international segment, we'll give young Robert some units in the fine Templeton International Stock Fund, and provide some extra exposure to Japan by including the CIBC Japanese Equity Fund, one of the top performers in its category over the past three years.

Templeton International Stock   105.6

CIBC Japanese Equity   112.4

We decided to add a sector fund to the RESP mix as well, one that is in tune with one of the main themes of the new millennium. Our choice is the CIBC Global Technology Fund.

CIBC Global Technology   91.8

The risk level of this fund is a little higher than average, but it's been shooting out the lights in performance terms, which would delight Robert if he were old enough to understand the implications. In the year to June 30/99, the fund gained an amazing 64.8 percent and it boasts a three-year average annual compound rate of return to that date of 35.6 percent.

The net result of these choices is a high-performance equity section which should provide excellent ongoing growth in Robert's RESP.

Fixed-Income Funds

We'll balance off some of the equity risk on the fixed income side by choosing the Spectrum United Dividend Fund as our main dividend entry. Readers will recall this fund from our second RRSP portfolio. It is a conservative, well-managed fund that will provide the RESP with steady income for reinvestment and modest growth potential, with limited risk.

Spectrum United Dividend   116.7

We will also add a position in the Dynamic Dividend Growth Fund. This is a different type of dividend fund from that offered by Spectrum United. Here the emphasis is on blue-chip growth stocks, with dividend income a secondary concern.

Dynamic Dividend Growth 106.5

Now we need to address the concerns of Mark and Emma about the possibility of having to repay the federal government grants at some point in the future. So we'll select two fixed income funds that offer decent return potential, without undue risk. One is the AGF Canadian High Income Fund, which we have already used in other portfolios. The other is the Fidelity North American Income Fund.

AGF High Income 110.2

Fidelity North American Income 98.8

The Fidelity fund offers Robert some foreign bond exposure, especially to the U.S. dollar. Its performance has been steadily improving after an initial setback when the Mexican peso collapsed.

Cash Funds

We don't want to hold much cash in this portfolio because of its long time horizon and emphasis on growth. A five percent position in the Beutel Goodman Money Market Fund will do the job nicely.

Beutel Goodman Money Market 98.0

RESP Portfolio summarized

Here's how the final RESP Portfolio for baby Robert Brown works out:

PCT	SAMPLE RESP PORTFOLIO	WT. MVA	MVA
10.0%	Saxon Small Cap	12.28	122.8
10.0%	Talvest Millennium Next Generation	11.36	113.6
15.0%	AIM American Premier	15.15	101.0
6.5%	Templeton International Stock	6.86	105.6
3.5%	CIBC Japanese Equity	3.93	112.4
5.0%	CIBC Global Technology	4.59	91.8
20.0%	Spectrum United Dividend	23.34	116.7
10.0%	Dynamic Dividend Growth	10.65	106.5
10.0%	AGF Canadian High Income	11.02	110.2
5.0%	Fidelity North American Income	4.94	98.8
5.0%	Beutel Goodman Money Market	4.90	98.0
100.0%	Portfolio MVA	109.03	

The result is an RESP with very strong growth potential, decent income for reinvesting purposes, and protection for the government grant assets, as desired by the parents. The FundLine profile looks like this:

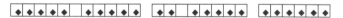

Most of the investment bases have been covered. There is no significant Latin American exposure, and we've avoided long-term bonds at this time because of our concerns about the outlook for interest rates over the next year. Apart from that, Robert's portfolio provides the fullest possible diversity.

BUILDING YOUR OWN PORTFOLIO

Your personal registered portfolio may match up quite well with one of the samples we've created here, in which case you may wish to emulate it. However, be aware that there will be several funds besides those we've highlighted here that will do as good a job for you in a specific context. So you may prefer to make some substitutions.

If your personal needs are somewhat different from those of our fictional characters, we recommend you use

SUCCESSFUL NO-LOAD PORTFOLIOS

By now, you should have a clear idea of how to go about building any type of mutual fund portfolio you wish. However, until this point we have made our selections from the entire fund universe. But often people don't have that freedom. They concentrate their investments with just one or two companies, so their choices are limited. What do you do in that situation?

Essentially, the same thing. You determine your investment profile and then make your selections from the funds offered by the particular company, using the same principles we have outlined. You may have some difficulty achieving an average MVA of 100+ if the particular fund company doesn't offer many high-scoring funds. But you should certainly be able to fill in most of the FundLine boxes. If you can't, we suggest you move to a different fund company; the one you're working with doesn't offer enough selection.

In this chapter, we will focus on building successful portfolios using three top no-load firms. They are:

Royal Funds. This is the largest no-load fund organization in Canada, so it is a logical choice to represent the bank groups.

Altamira Funds. Although some of the Altamira funds have slipped recently, this is still a very popular company with investors, who like the ease of telephone ordering.

Phillips, Hager & North. This high-end company is a good choice for investors who can meet the minimum investment requirements. It has more top-rated $$$$ funds (see *Gordon Pape's 2000 Buyer's Guide to Mutual Funds*) than any other firm.

For each company, we will build two portfolios. The first will be a Safety Portfolio, designed for investors who wish to keep their risk to an absolute minimum. The second is a Growth Portfolio, where the emphasis is placed on long-term above-average gains and the risk profile will be somewhat higher. For all portfolios we will use the Policy figures that apply for each profile. So the Safety Portfolios will be basically divided this way:

SAFETY PORTFOLIOS

Equities	10%
Fixed income	75%
Cash	15%

The Growth Portfolios will use this basic asset mix:

GROWTH PORTFOLIOS

Equities	60%
Fixed income	30%
Cash	10%

The extended asset mix in each case may vary, depending on what options each company has available.

We'll assume that each portfolio has $25,000 in assets, and that these are not registered plans. Let's get started.

ROYAL SAFETY PORTFOLIO

For the Royal Safety Portfolio, we will use this extended asset mix:

EXTENDED ASSET MIX

	ROYAL SAFETY
Canadian Equity	5.0%
U.S. Equity	2.5%
International Equity	2.5%
Special Equity	0.0%
Total Equity Assets	**10.0%**
Dividend Funds	25.0%
Domestic Bond	45.0%
Global Bond	5.0%
Total Income Assets	**75.0%**
Money Market	15.0%
Total Cash Assets	**15.0%**

Our first selection here will be the core Canadian equity fund. Royal has several domestic stock funds available, but only one really meets our requirements for this low-risk portfolio: the Royal Canadian Equity Fund. It offers a blue-chip portfolio with a reasonable track record and a middle-of-the-road risk rating. Here is its FundLine profile:

Royal Canadian Equity — 98.4

◆ ☐ ☐ ☐ ☐ ☐ ☐ ☐ ☐ ☐ ☐ ☐ ☐ ☐ ☐ ☐ ☐ ◆ ◆ ☐ ☐ ◆ ☐ ◆ ☐

Our other equity funds will have to provide exposure to all other parts of the world. Since Royal doesn't offer a true global fund, we will have to use two separate funds to achieve this goal: the Royal U.S. Equity Fund and the Royal International Equity Fund. The U.S. fund generates average returns for its category (three-year average annual compound rate of return of 23.3 percent to June 30/99). However, it has a very good risk profile, which will suit our safety-conscious investor just fine. The International Equity Fund also has a very good risk record, although its returns are somewhat below average.

Here are the FundLine profiles:

Royal U.S. Equity 89.7

Royal International Equity 100.0

At this point we should comment that, while these funds aren't bad, they would not rank high on our list if we were able to select from the entire universe. You now begin to see the problems that arise when you limit yourself to one company.

Fixed-Income funds

These represent the core holdings in this portfolio, and fortunately Royal offers a good selection from which to choose. We'll begin with the Royal Dividend Fund, which represents 25 percent of the assets in this portfolio. This is a very well managed fund that invests primarily in high-yielding blue-chip stocks, such as banks and utilities. It usually produces very good returns and averaged 17.5 percent annually for the five years to June 30/99. The risk level is somewhat higher than we would like in this Safety Portfolio, but since this is the only dividend fund Royal offers we don't have a lot of choice.

Royal Dividend 112.0

On the bond side, our core holding will be the Royal Bond Fund. This is a very good performer with above-average returns over time. The average annual compound rate of return for the five years to June 30/99 was 9.8 percent, well above par for its peer group. The main drawback of this fund is a below-normal safety record, which pulls down the MVA. Our weighting for domestic bond funds is 45 percent; we will give this fund a 25 percent allocation.

To offset the risk, we will allocate 20 percent of the portfolio to the Royal Mortgage Fund. The returns from this fund are less impressive and are slightly below average for the Mortgage category generally. But the safety profile is excellent; over the past five years this fund has never experienced a losing 12-month period.

Finally, in our bond fund section, we will give a five percent portfolio weighting to the Royal Global Bond Fund. This is not one of Royal's strongest entries, as the low MVA indicates. Returns have been above average for the Foreign Bond category, but the safety record leaves something to be desired.

Here are the FundLines for our bond and mortgage funds.

Royal Bond   93.0

Royal Mortgage   92.7

Royal Global Bond   80.8

Cash funds

The cash weighting in this portfolio is 15 percent, again a reflection of the strong safety orientation. We will divide this position among two money market funds from the Royal group. The Royal Canadian Money Market Fund will get a ten percent weighting and we will add a five percent position in the Royal U.S.$ Money Market Fund to provide currency diversification. Here are the appropriate FundLines:

Royal Canadian Money Market   93.3

Royal U.S.$ Money Market   95.1

Royal Safety Portfolio summarized

Here is how our Safety Portfolio looks now that all the selections are complete:

PCT	ROYAL SAFETY PORTFOLIO	WT. MVA	MVA
5.0%	Canadian Equity	4.92	98.4
2.5%	U.S. Equity	2.24	89.7
2.5%	International Equity	2.50	100.0
25.0%	Dividend	28.00	112.0
25.0%	Bond	23.25	93.0
20.0%	Mortgage	18.54	92.7
5.0%	Global Bond	4.04	80.8
10.0%	Canadian Money Market	9.33	93.3
5.0%	U.S.$ Money Market	4.76	95.1
100.0%	Portfolio MVA	97.58	

The overall FundLine profile looks like this:

As you can see, we could not achieve our goal of a portfolio MVA of more than 100 in this case. There were simply not enough high-rated funds in the Royal family that fit the Safety Portfolio parameters. We did do a pretty good job of diversification, however, considering the limitations of this portfolio. The Japan, Latin America, and Specialty Equity boxes are empty, but in a safety-oriented fund that's all right. We also don't have any small-cap or sector funds — again, not a problem in a Safety Portfolio.

Now let's see how we do with a Royal Growth Portfolio.

ROYAL GROWTH PORTFOLIO

As usual, we'll begin the portfolio building process by deciding on an extended asset mix. Here is the model we will use:

EXTENDED ASSET MIX

	ROYAL GROWTH
Canadian Equity	15.0%
U.S. Equity	20.0%
	. . .

International Equity	15.0%
Special Equity	10.0%
Total Equity Assets	**60.0%**
Dividend Funds	15.0%
Domestic Bond	15.0%
Global Bond	0.0%
Total Income Assets	**30.0%**
Money Market	10.0%
Total Cash Assets	**10.0%**

Equity funds

This is a growth-oriented portfolio so we have a lot more scope for building our equity positions. The emphasis in our fund selection will be on performance rather than safety — we're willing to accept more risk in exchange for the prospect of better returns.

Canadian equities will make up 15 percent of our holdings. We allocate two-thirds of that to the core Royal Canadian Equity Fund and put the rest into the Royal Canadian Growth Fund. The latter has a small cap orientation, although it may invest in mid-cap and large-cap funds as well. It has not been a particularly strong performer, but we feel it's important to have some small cap exposure in a Growth Portfolio like this.

Here are the profiles:

Royal Canadian Equity   **98.4**

Royal Canadian Growth   **102.1**

We have given a 20 percent weighting to U.S. equity funds in this portfolio because of the long-term strength of the American market. We aren't happy devoting that full weighting to the U.S. Equity Fund, but we don't like the ultra-conservative Zweig Strategic Growth Fund in this context. So we will put half the U.S. weighting into the new Royal U.S. Index Fund, which tracks the S&P

500 Total Returns Index. Since the fund has not been in operation for the three years necessary to calculate an MVA, we will give it a 100 score for calculation purposes.

Here are the profiles of our two U.S. selections:

Royal U.S. Equity   89.7

Royal U.S. Index   100.0

Our international component allows for a 15 percent weighting. We'll put two-thirds of that into the Royal International Fund, which was introduced as part of the Safety Portfolio. The rest will go into the Royal Japanese Stock Fund, which will increase our exposure to a part of the world that is in a turnaround situation. This fund has been showing steady improvement recently and gained almost 30 percent in the year ending June 30/99. The safety rating is very good for the Japanese Equity category.

Royal International Equity   100.0

Royal Japanese Stock   104.1

Finally, we have room in this section for some special equity funds. Our first selection will be the Royal Energy Fund. This one specializes in oil and gas stocks, an area which is quite strong at the present time. It is a cyclical fund so it isn't one we would be likely to hold in this portfolio forever. But it has been on a run recently (gain of 24.4 percent in the first six months of '99) and is very well managed by Gordon Zive.

Royal Energy Fund   105.1

Our second selection is the Royal Life Science and Technology Fund. This is a high-performance entry that has averaged almost 21 percent annually over the past three years, and has a good safety profile as well. Its numbers are not as good as some of the others in its category, which explains the relatively low MVA, but it is the only fund of this type that Royal offers and we feel it should be part of a Growth Portfolio.

Royal Life Science and Technology   85.7

Fixed-income funds

No surprises here. We'll divide this position between the Royal Dividend Fund and the Royal Bond Fund, both of which were included in the Safety Portfolio.

Royal Dividend   112.0

Royal Bond   93.0

Cash funds

Cash holdings represent only ten percent of this portfolio. We'll split them evenly between the same two money market funds we used in the safety portfolio.

Royal Canadian Money Market   93.3

Royal U.S.$ Money Market   95.1

Royal Growth Portfolio summarized

Here's the end result of our Royal Growth Portfolio:

PCT	ROYAL GROWTH PORTFOLIO	WT. MVA	MVA
10.0%	Canadian Equity	9.84	98.4
5.0%	Canadian Growth	5.11	102.1
10.0%	U.S. Equity	8.97	89.7
10.0%	U.S. Index	10.00	100.0
10.0%	International Equity	10.00	100.0
5.0%	Japanese Stock	5.21	104.1
5.0%	Energy	5.26	105.1

. . .

5.0%	Life Science & Technology	4.29	85.7
15.0%	Dividend	16.80	112.0
15.0%	Bond	13.95	93.0
5.0%	Canadian Money Market	4.67	93.3
5.0%	U.S.$ Money Market	4.76	95.1
100.0%	Portfolio MVA	98.83	

The final FundLine profile looks like this:

Again, we have not been able to achieve the goal of a portfolio MVA in excess of 100, but we have come closer than we were able to do with the Safety Portfolio. We also have managed to create a portfolio here that is more diversified than the Safety Portfolio was.

ALTAMIRA SAFETY PORTFOLIO

Apart from the banks, there are only a handful of companies that offer no-load funds with minimal initial investment requirements. The largest and best-known of these is Altamira. The company became the darling of small investors in the early '90s, offering a combination of easy access (all you had to do was pick up the phone), good service, and great returns. But the firm hit a rough patch in the latter part of the decade, plagued with a messy ownership dispute that ended up in court, declining returns on key funds, and the departure of two well-known managers, Frank Mersch and Will Sutherland. There is now a new management team in charge and the firm is working hard to rebuild its image and attract new customers. Let's see how successful we are in using our portfolio-building techniques with their funds. Again, we will start with a Safety Portfolio, using this extended asset mix:

EXTENDED ASSET MIX

	ALTAMIRA SAFETY
Canadian Equity	5.0%
U.S. Equity	2.5%
International Equity	2.5%
Special Equity	0.0%
Total Equity Assets	**10.0%**
Dividend Funds	15.0%
Domestic Bond	55.0%
Global Bond	5.0%
Total Income Assets	**75.0%**
Money Market	15.0%
Total Cash Assets	**15.0%**

Equity funds

Altamira offers a number of Canadian stock funds from which to choose. The largest and best known is Altamira Equity, which produced great returns in the early '90s under the direction of Frank Mersch. However, that fund is now in a rebuilding process and looks a little too aggressive for a Safety Portfolio. Therefore, we will choose Altamira Capital Growth for our Canadian stock position. This fund specializes in large-cap stocks and while it doesn't have a particularly attractive safety profile, it's a lot better than that of Altamira Equity where, over the three years to June 30/99, investors had a 44 percent chance of being down after any given 12-month period. Capital Growth has also produced much higher gains over the past three years, averaging 12.7 percent annually compared to 5.3 percent for Equity.

Altamira Capital Growth   97.5

Our choice for a U.S. equity fund ends up at the Altamira U.S. Larger Company Fund by default. The companion Select American Fund has a small-cap fund emphasis and is a chronic underperformer. Altamira has three new index funds that track various U.S. indexes, but it's too soon to get a handle on their effectiveness.

Altamira U.S. Larger Company   88.5

The choice of an international fund presents something of a problem. Altamira does not offer any "pure" fund of this type — one that invests in all parts of the world except North America — except for their new Precision International RSP Index Fund. This fund has a very short track record and no MVA score, but it is our only choice. We'll assign it a neutral 100 MVA for computing purposes.

Altamira Precision International RSP Index   100.0

Fixed-income funds

We reduced the dividend percentage in this portfolio compared to that in the Royal Safety Portfolio. Reason: the risk factor of Altamira Dividend is much higher than we like in this context, and recent returns have not been impressive, although the fund shows above-average numbers over five years. Altamira's bond funds are more to our liking, however, so we have added to their percentages while reducing the dividend component to 15 percent.

Altamira Dividend   101.6

On the bond side, we have a number of attractive choices. Altamira Bond was the top-performing fund of its type in the '90s, under the direction of Robert Marcus. However, it specializes in long bonds, which makes it higher-risk by nature. Since this is a Safety Portfolio, we will therefore give this fund a 15 percent weighting.

Altamira Bond   104.0

The company's middle-of-the-road bond fund is Altamira Income, which has been a steady performer over many years. It tends to track the Scotia Capital Markets Universe Bond Index and does not make any big bets on interest rate movements. It will serve very nicely as a core fund for this portfolio, and we will give it a 25 percent weighting.

Altamira Income   95.4

Next we will add a short-term bond fund to this portfolio, to offset the higher risk inherent in Altamira Bond. The Altamira Short Term Government Bond Fund will perform this job very nicely. Returns are modest during times of low interest rates, but that's offset by a high degree of safety. We'll give this fund a 15 percent weighting.

Altamira Short Term Government Bond   93.4

We aren't excited by either of the company's foreign bond offerings. The Global Bond Fund has a very poor safety rating for a fund of this type. However, it partially compensates for that with above-average returns. The Short Term Global Income Fund is a very weak performer. Global Bond gets the reluctant nod, with a five percent weighting.

Altamira Global Bond   78.3

Cash funds

Not a lot of choice here. We'll put this money into the Altamira T-Bill Fund. It's too new to have an MVA score, so we'll assign a 100 rating to it.

Altamira T-Bill   100.0

Altamira Safety Portfolio summarized

Here's where we come out with this portfolio:

PCT	ALTAMIRA SAFETY PORTFOLIO	WT. MVA	MVA
5.0%	Capital Growth	4.88	97.5
2.5%	U.S. Larger Company	2.21	88.5
2.5%	Precision International RSP Index	2.50	100.0
15.0%	Dividend	15.24	101.6
15.0%	Bond	15.60	104.0
25.0%	Income	23.85	95.4
15.0%	Short Term Government Bond	14.01	93.4
5.0%	Global Bond	3.92	78.3
15.0%	T-Bill	15.00	100.0
100.0%	Portfolio MVA	97.20	

Our FundLine profile looks like this:

| ◆ | ◆ | ◆ | ◆ | ◆ | | | ◆ | ◆ | ◆ | ◆ | | ◆ | ◆ | ◆ | ◆ | | | | ◆ | | ◆ | ◆ | ◆ | ◆ | ◆ | ◆ |

The relatively low MVA score of this portfolio is an indication of the type of performance problems Altamira has been experiencing. Hopefully, some of the new funds will pull up these averages going forward.

ALTAMIRA GROWTH PORTFOLIO

Moving now to an Altamira Growth Portfolio, we'll look first at the extended asset mix we will apply in this case.

EXTENDED ASSET MIX

	ALTAMIRA GROWTH
Canadian Equity	15.0%
U.S. Equity	15.0%
International Equity	20.0%
Special Equity	10.0%
Total Equity Assets	**60.0%**
Dividend Funds	10.0%
Domestic Bond	20.0%
Global Bond	0.0%
Total Income Assets	**30.0%**

...

Money Market	10.0%
Total Cash Assets	10.0%

Equity funds

We have a 15 percent Canadian equity weighting in this portfolio. Since the goal in this case is growth, we will distribute that among three funds, each with a five percent position. The Capital Growth Fund, which we introduced in the Safety Portfolio, will be one. Here are the other two:

Altamira North American Recovery Fund. This fund invests in the shares of smaller North American companies (mainly in Canada, as it is fully RRSP-eligible) that are deemed to be undervalued or in a turnaround situation by the manager, David Taylor. It has been an above-average performer, with an average annual compound rate of return of 10.2 percent over the three years to June 30/99. Risk is average.

Altamira Special Growth Fund. This is a traditional small-to-mid-cap fund. The mandate calls for the manager, Alex Sasso, to look for stocks with a market cap of less than $500 million, using a bottom-up approach. To minimize risk, the fund does not hold more than 20 percent of its assets in one industry. Returns haven't been great, but showed significant improvement in the first half of 1999. Average risk.

Altamira Capital Growth — 97.5

Altamira North American Recovery — 96.8

Altamira Special Growth — 105.1

Our U.S. equity weighting for this portfolio is 15 percent. We've given a higher priority to international funds (20 percent) as we feel that Altamira has greater strength in that area.

For the U.S. fund, we will put the entire position into the U.S. Larger Company Fund. We don't like doing that in a growth-oriented portfolio, but Altamira's small-cap U.S. entry is very weak. The new Precision U.S. Midcap Index Fund intrigues us, but is so recent we don't yet have FundLine specs available for it, much less an MVA.

Altamira U.S. Larger Company   88.5

For the international funds, a 20 percent weighting here gives us a lot more flexibility than we had in the Safety Portfolio. Since the company doesn't have a true international fund, other than the RSP Index Fund we used in the Safety Portfolio, we'll use three other funds to achieve this goal. They are:

Altamira European Equity Fund. This has been a pretty good performer, with an average annual compound rate of return of 16.6 percent for the five years to June 30/99. Risk is less than average for a fund of this type. The European markets slowed up in the first half of '99 and we don't expect them to do as well as the Far East in the next year. But Europe is a key part of any well-balanced portfolio, so this fund gets a ten percent weighting.

Altamira Asia Pacific Fund. The other ten percent of the international equity weighting will be invested in the Far East. Half will go into this fund, which invests in all countries of the region, including Japan. It's been hot recently, gaining 51 percent in the year ending June 30/99. Risk level is average.

Altamira Japanese Opportunity Fund. The focus here is small-to-mid-cap Japanese companies, which makes it one of the few funds of its type in Canada. It's been almost as hot as the Asia Pacific Fund lately, gaining 46.9 percent in the past year. The risk level is surprisingly low in the context of Japanese equity funds as a group.

Altamira European Equity   92.6

Altamira Asia Pacific   93.5

Altamira Japanese Opportunity   105.0

We have allocated ten percent of this portfolio to specialty funds. Half of that will be invested in the excellent Altamira Science & Technology Fund. This is another Altamira entry that has been on fire recently, gaining more than 70 percent in the year to June 30/99. The three-year average annual compound rate of return to that date was 38.3 percent.

The other half of this allocation will go to the new Altamira e-business Fund, which specializes in Internet-related stocks. This fund is too new for an MVA rating, but we feel we must find a place for it in the Growth Portfolio (it gained 57 percent in the first half of 1999). So we'll assign a neutral rating of 100 for now.

Altamira Science & Technology   94.2

Altamira e-business   100.0

Fixed-income funds

Our portfolio weighting here totals 30 percent. Of that, one-third will go into the Altamira Dividend Fund, which was also included in the Safety Portfolio. On the bond side, we will choose two of the company's more aggressively managed bond funds: Altamira Bond, which was also part of the Safety Portfolio, and Altamira High Yield Bond Fund. The latter specializes in high-yielding bonds (sometimes called junk bonds) issued by corporations and foreign governments. Although the fund is officially classified as a Canadian bond fund for RRSP purposes, it also provides some exposure to foreign bond markets and currencies. Returns have been good; the fund averaged 10.5 percent annually over the three years to June 30/99.

Altamira Dividend   101.6

Altamira Bond   104.0

Altamira High Yield Bond   94.8

Cash funds

Cash assets represent only ten percent of this portfolio. Here again, we will use the T-Bill Fund with an imputed MVA of 100.

Altamira T-Bill   100.0

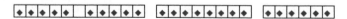

Altamira Growth Portfolio summarized

Here is how the Altamira Growth Portfolio looks in its final version:

PCT	ALTAMIRA GROWTH PORTFOLIO	WT. MVA	MVA
5.0%	Capital Growth	4.88	97.5
5.0%	North American Recovery	4.84	96.8
5.0%	Special Equity	5.26	105.1
15.0%	U.S. Larger Company	13.28	88.5
10.0%	European Equity	9.26	92.6
5.0%	Asia Pacific	4.68	93.5
5.0%	Japanese Opportunity	5.25	105.0
5.0%	Science & Technology	4.71	94.2
5.0%	e-business	5.00	100.0
10.0%	Dividend	10.16	101.6
10.0%	Bond	10.40	104.0
10.0%	High Yield Bond	9.48	94.8
10.0%	T-Bill	10.00	100.0
100.0%	Portfolio MVA	97.18	

FundLine profile:

The portfolio MVA here is again on the low side. However, we have achieved excellent diversification and completed all but one of our FundLine boxes.

PHILLIPS, HAGER & NORTH SAFETY PORTFOLIO

For our final no-load company, we chose one of the high-end firms that requires a fairly substantial initial investment to open an account. There are a number of quality companies of this kind, including Bissett, GBC, Leith Wheeler, Optima Strategy, ABC, and Mawer. For our portfolio-building process, we'll use Vancouver-based Phillips, Hager & North, which has become one of the most popular firms of this type.

PH&N, as it is known, is one of this country's top money management firms and in fact was named Mutual Fund Company of the Decade in *Gordon Pape's 2000 Buyer's Guide to Mutual Funds.* Investors like PH&N for its conservative style, low management fees, consistency, and above-average performance. The minimum initial investment for a non-registered account with PH&N is $25,000.

Here is the extended asset mix we'll use for the PH&N Safety Portfolio.

EXTENDED ASSET MIX

	PH&N SAFETY
Canadian Equity	5.0%
U.S. Equity	2.5%
International Equity	2.5%
Special Equity	0.0%
Total Equity Assets	**10.0%**
Dividend Funds	25.0%
Domestic Bond	50.0%
Global Bond	0.0%
Total Income Assets	**75.0%**
Money Market	15.0%
Total Cash Assets	**15.0%**

Equity funds

For this portfolio, we will use the Canadian Equity Plus fund for our five percent Canadian stock weighting. This fund holds some foreign content, as opposed to the Canadian Equity Fund, which is purely domestic. As a result, Equity Plus produces slightly better returns than its stablemate, and has a better safety profile. Average annual compound rate of return for the five years to June 30/99 was 13.9 percent.

PH&N Canadian Equity Plus   100.9

We have two choices for a U.S. stock fund; however, the PH&N North American Equity Fund is not one of the company's better performers. So we will go with their U.S. Equity Fund. It has an excellent long-term record, with an average annual gain of 18.2 percent over the decade to June 30/99. Recent performance has been weak, though, because the fund focuses on mid-cap stocks, which were out of favour in the late '90s. That's why the MVA score of this fund, which is based on the most recent three years, is not as high as you might expect. The safety record of this fund is better than average.

PH&N U.S. Equity   90.6

The company offers a true international fund, PH&N Euro-Pacific Equity. Until now, it has used a top-down approach, choosing the most promising countries in Europe and Asia and then buying the key indexes of each. However, PH&N is in the process of refining this approach to include bottom-up stock selection as well. Returns have tended to be slightly below average for the International Equity category. Risk is about average.

PH&N Euro-Pacific Equity   95.8

Fixed-income funds

We have some excellent funds to work with here. There is not a lot of choice but what there is just happens to be first-rate.

The dividend component of this portfolio, which is 25 percent of the asset mix, will be well filled by the PH&N Dividend Income Fund. The risk level here is slightly higher than we like for a Safety Portfolio because the fund invests mainly in common stock. But the results are terrific: over three, five, and ten years this was the number-one-performing dividend fund in Canada.

Average annual compound rate of return over the decade to June 30/99 was 13.4 percent.

PH&N Dividend Income 115.9

Our first bond fund selection is the PH&N Bond Fund, which receives a 30 percent weighting. This is one of the leading performers in its category, with a ten-year average annual return of 10.3 percent. It's a no-nonsense, middle-of-the-road fund that doesn't make any big bets. As a result, it has an excellent safety record to go along with its good returns.

The second bond fund we'll include is the PH&N Short-Term Bond and Mortgage Fund, which receives a 20 percent weighting. This is an ideal fund for a Safety Portfolio, providing low risk and profits that are well above average for its category.

The company does not have any foreign bond funds.

PH&N Bond 100.9

PH&N Short-Term Bond and Mortgage 99.7

Cash funds

There are two money market funds in the PH&N line-up, a Canadian dollar fund and a U.S. dollar entry. Both consistently generate above-average returns, in part because of their low MERs. We will divide this segment of the portfolio between them.

PH&N Canadian Money Market 97.8

PH&N $U.S. Money Market 100.4

PH&N Safety Portfolio summarized

Now let's take a look at the final composition of the PH&N Safety Portfolio.

PCT	PH&N SAFETY PORTFOLIO	WT. MVA	MVA
5.0%	Canadian Equity Plus	5.05	100.9
2.5%	U.S. Equity	2.27	90.6
2.5%	Euro-Pacific Equity	2.40	95.8
25.0%	Dividend Income	28.98	115.9
30.0%	Bond	30.27	100.9
20.0%	Short-Term Bond and Mortgage	19.94	99.7
7.5%	Canadian Money Market	7.34	97.8
7.5%	$U.S. Money Market	7.53	100.4
100.0%	Portfolio MVA	103.76	

Finally! We've been able to build a portfolio from within a single company that meets our goal of an average MVA higher than 100. This is further evidence of the very good performance of most of the PH&N funds over time.

The FundLine profile here looks like this:

The portfolio doesn't have quite as much diversification as we would like, but the heavy emphasis on safety, coupled with PH&N's small list of offerings, doesn't provide a great deal of leeway.

PHILLIPS, HAGER & NORTH GROWTH PORTFOLIO

The Growth Portfolio is not going to look a lot different from the Safety Portfolio, except in terms of asset mix. PH&N only has ten funds we can draw from (we don't include any balanced funds in these portfolios), so there's not a lot of selection.

Here's the extended asset mix we'll use.

	PH&N GROWTH
Canadian Equity	20.0%
U.S. Equity	20.0%
International Equity	20.0%
Special Equity	0.0%
Total Equity Assets	**60.0%**

. . .

Dividend Funds	15.0%
Domestic Bond	15.0%
Global Bond	0.0%
Total Income Assets	**30.0%**
Money Market	10.0%
Total Cash Assets	**10.0%**

Equity funds

Only one change from the Safety Portfolio here. Because we're giving each of these funds a 20 percent portfolio weighting, we'll use the 100 percent domestic Canadian Equity Fund in this case. The U.S. and Euro-Pacific funds round out this section.

PH&N Canadian Equity   100.5

PH&N U.S. Equity   90.6

PH&N Euro-Pacific Equity   95.8

Fixed-income funds

We'll divide the fixed income component equally between the Dividend Income Fund (although this is technically not a fixed-income fund at all, but a blue-chip stock fund) and the Bond Fund.

PH&N Dividend Income   115.9

PH&N Bond   100.9

Cash funds

This asset class gets a ten percent weighting in this portfolio, which we'll split between the two money market funds.

PH&N Canadian Money Market   97.8

PH&N $U.S. Money Market   100.4

PH&N Growth Portfolio summarized

Here is how our Growth Portfolio looks:

PCT	PH&N GROWTH PORTFOLIO	WT. MVA	MVA
20.0%	Canadian Equity	20.10	100.5
20.0%	U.S. Equity	18.12	90.6
20.0%	Euro-Pacific Equity	19.16	95.8
15.0%	Dividend Income	17.39	115.9
15.0%	Bond	15.14	100.9
5.0%	Canadian Money Market	4.89	97.8
5.0%	$U.S. Money Market	5.02	100.4
100.0%	Portfolio MVA	99.81	

In this case, the overall MVA came in a fraction below the 100 target level. This was due to the higher percentage of the portfolio allocated to the U.S. Equity Fund, and the lower percentage to the Dividend Income Fund with its extremely high MVA. However, this portfolio should produce excellent returns for our growth-oriented investor over the long term.

Here is how the FundLine looks:

Again, not quite as much diversification as we might like. But it's a small company. You can't have everything!

THE PITFALLS OF OVER-CONCENTRATION

By this point, you know how to build any type of mutual fund portfolio, using the FundLine and MVA. The appendix at the back of this book contains all the basic information you need.

There is one other point you should take away from this chapter. No matter how good a fund company is, you will end up with a less efficient portfolio by concentrating all your assets within a single firm. All fund groups have their weaknesses — either they don't offer certain types of funds, or those that are available in a particular category are mediocre or worse. As you saw in this chapter, we sometimes had to add funds to our portfolios that we were not happy with simply because there was no alternative.

We therefore caution against restricting yourself entirely to one company. No individual has access to the entire fund universe — you may have to eliminate certain funds because of minimum investing requirements, sales policies, provincial registration, etc. However, by broadening your range to the maximum extent possible, you greatly enhance your chances of building the most effective portfolio for your needs.

LOAD-FUND PORTFOLIOS

You've now seen several examples of how we use the FundLine and MVA scores to build high-performance, well-diversified portfolios. In this chapter, we'll apply the same process to the five largest load-fund companies in Canada. We don't go into quite the same level of detail in portfolio-building here, but we will explain why we are using each particular fund.

There is a two-fold purpose in doing this. First, some people hold most or all of their assets with a single company, such as Investors Group. If you're in that situation, you can use our model portfolios as a cross-check against your actual situation. You may find some changes are in order.

Second, we are frequently asked which mutual fund companies are best. This chapter will provide some objective answers to that question as it relates to the big load-fund firms. By examining the overall portfolio MVA and FundLine profile of each firm, you will be able to judge both the quality and diversity of their offerings within a specific context.

We will construct one sample portfolio for each selected company. For this chapter, we will use our most balanced model, a Growth/Income Portfolio. Basic asset distribution will be 50 percent equities, 40 percent fixed income, and 10 percent cash. We will vary the extended asset mix slightly so as to best accommodate the strengths of each company. However, we will only use funds that have been in existence long enough to have an MVA, so as not to skew the comparative results. All quoted rates of return are as of June 30/99.

INVESTORS GROUP

It is appropriate that we begin our load fund portfolio analysis with Investors Group. Not only is it the largest mutual fund company in Canada in terms of assets under management, but it is a firm that many people deal with exclusively because of its sales methods.

Most load mutual funds are sold through a variety of outlets: full-service brokers, discount brokers, financial planners, independent sales companies, etc. But the only way you can buy an Investors Group fund is from one of their own sales representatives. Over many years, these people have built a reputation for good service and helpful planning that has kept Investors Group at the top of the highly competitive mutual funds industry. They design portfolios for their clients that are attuned to each individual's objectives. Therefore, we want to stress that you should not panic if you have an Investors Group portfolio that is quite different from the model we've constructed here. It may be that your particular situation requires something other than the balanced approach we're using. If you think some changes in your own portfolio are warranted as a result of our findings, talk it over with your representative first.

Here is the extended asset mix we will use for Investors Group.

EXTENDED ASSET MIX

	INVESTORS GROUP
Canadian Equity	15.0%
U.S. Equity	15.0%
International Equity	15.0%
Special Equity	5.0%
Total Equity Assets	50.0%
Dividend Funds	15.0%
Domestic Bond	20.0%

. . .

Global Bond	5.0%
Total Income Assets	**40.0%**
Money Market	10.0%
Total Cash Assets	**10.0%**

Equity funds

The flagship Canadian stock fund offered by the company is Investors Canadian Equity, which has more than $3 billion in assets. We cannot understand why so much client money is concentrated here. The fund is a chronic underperformer, with an average annual compound rate of return of just 7.8 percent over the past five years. The safety record is poor in comparison with its peer group. All this adds up to an unimpressive MVA of 91.9.

The second-largest domestic stock fund in this group is Investors Retirement Mutual, with assets of more than $2.5 billion. This one has a slightly better risk rating, but it is a laggard in performance terms.

Our choice for the model portfolio is a fund that does not get a lot of attention from Investors Group clients, perhaps because of its mandate. It's the Investors Summa Fund, a socially responsible entry that avoids companies involved in such businesses as tobacco, alcohol, weapons manufacturing, etc. These limitations appear to have presented no problems for the manager, as this fund has far outperformed its larger stablemates, gaining an average of 17.3 percent annually over the past five years. To further enhance its appeal, this is a low volatility fund, which means risk is minimized. All these attributes show up in a very high MVA of 109.4. Ideally, we would like to split our domestic fund holdings by including a small-cap fund as well; however, Investors Canadian Small Cap II, which would be our fund of choice, has not been around long enough to make it possible to calculate an MVA. Therefore, the whole 15 percent Canadian equity allocation will go to Summa Fund.

We only have one logical choice for our 15 percent U.S. equity weighting — Investors U.S. Growth Fund. The companion North American Growth Fund doesn't come close in performance terms, and the small-cap U.S. Opportunities Fund is too new for an MVA score.

However, we aren't unhappy with Investors U.S. Growth, although it has shown signs of slowing down since the departure in 1998 of long-time manager Larry Sarbit. The fund still offers a fine performance record (average annual five-year rate of return of 24 percent) and has a very favourable risk profile.

The only pure international fund in the Investors' line-up is GS International Equity, managed by Rothschild/Global Strategy. However, it has not impressed us so far. Therefore, we'll use three region-specific funds to achieve this goal, giving each a five percent portfolio weighting. They are:

Investors European Growth Fund. This fund focuses on the developed countries of western Europe. Returns are average to slightly above for the European Equity category. The safety record is top-notch. MVA is 93.4.

Investors Pacific International Fund. The mandate is to invest across Asia, excluding Japan. This fund has been hot recently, gaining 57 percent in the past 12 months. Risk is on the high side. MVA is 97.3.

Investors Japanese Growth Fund. This one fills in the rest of the Asian puzzle. It's a below-average performer for the Japanese Equity category, but did manage to gain 30 percent in the year just completed. Medium risk for its type. MVA is 96.8.

Finally, in the equities section, we will include a five percent position in the company's best-performing fund in terms of MVA: Investors Real Property Fund. This fund invests in commercial real estate and generates profits through a combination of modest capital gains and steady tax-advantaged cash flow. It consistently produces above-average results in its category, but you need to keep that in perspective — we're talking a five-year average annual compound rate of return of 5.3 percent here. But the safety record is the best for any fund of its type and for people who want steady income at a reduced tax rate, this fund works very well. The MVA is an astounding 139.0.

Fixed-income funds

Our fixed-income allocation here is 40 percent. Of this, a 15 percent weighting goes to the Investors Dividend Fund. It's a huge fund, with over $5 billion in assets, that combines reasonable returns with a decent safety record. The MVA is a very respectable 108.5.

Our domestic bond holdings will be divided between two funds. Investors Corporate Bond, as the name suggests, specializes in debt issues of Canadian corporations. As a result, the risk is slightly higher than we find in the companion Investors Government Bond Fund which, somewhat surprisingly, also tends to have better returns. We'll assign each a ten percent weighting. Finally, in the fixed-income section, we'll add a small five percent position in the Investors Global Bond Fund for diversification.

Cash funds

The company only has one cash-type fund that qualifies for an MVA, Investors Canadian Money Market. It's a below-average performer, but it gets the nod by default.

Investors Group Portfolio summarized

Now let's take a look at our complete Investors Group Growth/Income Portfolio.

PCT	INVESTORS GROWTH/INCOME PORTFOLIO	WT. MVA	MVA
15.0%	Summa	16.41	109.4
15.0%	U.S. Growth	15.24	101.6
5.0%	European Growth	4.67	93.4
5.0%	Pacific International	4.87	97.3
5.0%	Japanese Growth	4.84	96.8
5.0%	Real Property	6.95	139.0
15.0%	Dividend	16.28	108.5
10.0%	Government Bond	9.60	96.0
10.0%	Corporate Bond	9.54	95.4
5.0%	Global Bond	4.00	79.9
10.0%	Canadian Money Market	9.18	91.8
100.0%	Portfolio MVA	101.57	

Here is how the FundLine profile works out:

Summa

U.S. Growth

European Growth

Pacific International

Japanese Growth

Real Property

Dividend

Government Bond

Corporate Bond

Global Bond

Canadian Money Market

Overall Portfolio

As you can see, Investors Group passes this test with flying colours. Not only were we able to create a portfolio with an average MVA of better than 100, but we also achieved almost perfect diversification, with only the Latin American box not filled. This shows that even with a group that has several below-average performers in its line-up, it is possible to create a well-balanced portfolio with above-average profit potential through careful planning.

MACKENZIE FINANCIAL CORPORATION

Mackenzie has taken over as the second-largest load fund company in Canada. It offers a broad range of investment options, divided into four fund groups: Industrial, Ivy, Universal, and Cundill. As well, the firm offers its own portfolios of funds under the STAR brand name.

Because there are so many STAR portfolios available, investors may prefer to choose one of those rather than creating their own personalized version. However, our analysis shows that, to date, most of the STAR entries have been average to below-average performers. If you're interested in an all-Mackenzie portfolio, we suggest you construct a model of your own, using our techniques. Then compare it to the STAR offerings. If you find one that comes close, go with it. However, we doubt that you will.

Here is the extended asset mix we will use in this case.

EXTENDED ASSET MIX

	MACKENZIE
Canadian Equity	15.0%
U.S. Equity	10.0%
International Equity	20.0%
Special Equity	5.0%
Total Equity Assets	**50.0%**
Dividend Funds	15.0%
Domestic Bond	20.0%
Global Bond	5.0%
Total Income Assets	**40.0%**
Money Market	10.0%
Total Cash Assets	**10.0%**

Equity funds

Mackenzie offers a wide range of Canadian equity funds, including Industrial Growth Fund, which at one time was the company's flagship and one of the largest funds in Canada. It has fallen on hard times in recent years, however, and is only a shadow of what it once was. For our 15 percent Canadian equity weighting, we will distribute our holdings equally among three quite different funds:

Ivy Canadian. This is a very conservative fund, run by Jerry Javasky. In the late '90s, he built up a large cash reserve to cushion his investors against possible stock market shocks, and the approach worked well in the big correction of late 1998. Returns are good (the fund has averaged 14 percent annually over the past five years). The safety record is excellent. MVA score is a fine 111.5.

Universal Canadian Growth. To offset the conservative Ivy style, we're adding a growth-oriented fund, run by well-respected managers Dina DeGeer and Dennis Starritt. Performance over the past three years has been slightly better than that of Ivy Canadian, and the safety record is also good. MVA is 109.7.

Ivy Enterprise. This is a small-cap fund, managed by Charles Roth. It's been having some problems recently, but the three-year returns are above average for its category and the risk rating is good for a fund of its type, despite a loss of 15.7 percent in the past year. MVA is 111.3.

Sharp-eyed readers will have observed that we have a lower U.S. equity content in this portfolio than we had in the Investors Group asset mix. That's because Mackenzie's pure U.S. equity funds are only so-so, or worse. However, the company offers several very interesting international and global funds, some of which contain U.S. content, so we'll make up the difference there.

For our 10 percent pure U.S. allocation, we'll use the Industrial American Fund. It invests in a diversified portfolio of U.S. stocks, with an emphasis on blue-chip issues, especially multinational corporations. The manager's style is value-oriented, an approach that was out of favour with investors until recently. That helps to explain why recent results have been weak in relation to the U.S. Equity category as a whole, thus pulling down the MVA to 82.9. We wish there were something better in the Mackenzie line-up, but there isn't. It's a weakness they need to address.

We can compensate for this to some degree, however, by adding the Ivy Foreign Equity Fund as part of our international component, with a five percent portfolio weighting. Despite the name, this fund focuses most heavily on U.S. stocks, with a smattering of other countries tossed in and a large cash position. Returns have been good — the fund averaged almost 15 percent a year over the past five years. Add an excellent safety record to the mix and you get a good MVA of 105.1.

Universal International Stock Fund might seem like a logical choice for this part of the portfolio, but it is too heavily concentrated in Europe and very weak in Asia outside of Japan. So we'll select some region-specific funds instead.

The Universal European Opportunities Fund gives us coverage of that continent, including some positions in the emerging markets of eastern Europe. Although it has slumped recently, it was one of the best performers in its category over the past three years, averaging almost 22 percent annually. Risk is about average, resulting in an MVA of 97.7. We'll give this fund a five percent portfolio weighting.

Universal Far East invests throughout Asia, except Japan. Historically, it's a below-average performer but it has looked much better recently with a one-year gain of 58 percent. Risk level is slightly better than average. MVA is 97.9. Portfolio weighting is five percent.

We'll complement the Far East Fund with Universal Japan to gain exposure to that turnaround situation. This fund has one of the best records in the Japanese Equity category, both in terms of performance and risk. One-year gain was 44.3%. MVA is 107.7. Here again, we'll use a five percent portfolio weighting.

We'll conclude the Mackenzie equity fund line-up with a five percent weighting in Universal Future, a specialty fund that focuses on high-tech stocks, although it includes other types of companies as well. It has been a good performer, averaging about 15 percent a year over the past five years, and the risk rating is surprisingly good for a fund of this type. MVA is 99.9.

Fixed-income funds

Mackenzie offers only one selection for our 15 percent dividend fund allocation, and it's not one we're happy with. It's the Industrial Dividend Growth Fund, and the word "Growth" in the name is a tip-off that this is not your classic dividend fund. A significant part of the portfolio is invested in securities that pay little or no dividends, so this is more correctly classified as a growth and income fund. It pays a 5c monthly distribution, but part of that represents a return of capital. We're somewhat surprised that a company with a fund line-up as broad as this does not have a single true dividend fund in its mix.

On the domestic bond side, our primary choice is Industrial Bond Fund. It's a strong performer, with an average annual compound rate of return of 10.7 percent over the past five years. Risk is about average and the MVA is a respectable 97.4. We'll give it a 15 percent portfolio weighting.

The other five percent of our domestic bond allocation will go into Ivy Mortgage, which offers an excellent safety record as its main attribute. Performance hasn't been particularly good in comparison to its peer group, but this fund adds a measure of stability to the overall portfolio.

We will also allocate five percent of the portfolio to a global bond fund and here we'll choose the Universal World Tactical Bond entry. It seeks to minimize risk by investing in the world's safest bond markets (e.g, the U.S., U.K., Germany) and also by holding large amounts of cash when interest rates are on the rise. Ironically, its safety profile to date is quite poor when compared to other foreign bond funds, but its performance is above average. The weak safety record pulls down the MVA to 79.9.

Cash funds

Our number one choice here, by far, would be the Industrial Cash Management Fund. Its low MER and above-average returns make it the best selection of its type in the company's line-up. However, it is only open to investors who buy Mackenzie funds on a front-end load basis. Since the overwhelming majority of people choose a back-end load option these days, that puts this fund out of their reach.

If you are eligible for this fund, by all means choose it. But since realism dictates our selections here, we'll go instead with the inferior Industrial Short-Term Fund for this portfolio.

Mackenzie Portfolio summarized

Here is where we net out with our Mackenzie Growth/Income Portfolio.

PCT	MACKENZIE GROWTH/INCOME PORTFOLIO	WT. MVA	MVA
5.0%	Ivy Canadian	5.58	111.5
5.0%	Universal Canadian Growth	5.49	109.7
5.0%	Ivy Enterprise	5.57	111.3
10.0%	Industrial American	8.29	82.9
5.0%	Ivy Foreign Equity	5.26	105.1
5.0%	Universal European Opportunities	4.89	97.7
5.0%	Universal Far East	4.90	97.9
5.0%	Universal Japan	5.39	107.7
5.0%	Universal Future	5.00	99.9
15.0%	Industrial Dividend Growth	15.33	102.2
15.0%	Industrial Bond	14.61	97.4
5.0%	Ivy Mortgage	4.84	96.8
5.0%	Universal World Tactical Bond	4.00	79.9
10.0%	Industrial Short-Term	8.69	86.9
100.0%	Portfolio MVA	97.80	

Here is the FundLine profile of this portfolio.

Ivy Canadian

Universal Canadian Growth

Ivy Enterprise

Industrial American

Ivy Foreign Equity

Universal European Opportunities

Universal Far East

Universal Japan

Universal Future

Industrial Dividend Growth

Industrial Bond

Ivy Mortgage

Universal World Tactical Bond

Industrial Short-Term

Overall Portfolio

The overall Mackenzie results don't look as good as those of Investors Group. The average MVA is significantly lower, and we have not achieved the same measure of diversification. Main weaknesses are the lack of a first-rate U.S. equity fund and the inability of most Mackenzie clients to gain access to the high-performance Industrial Cash Management Fund.

TRIMARK FUNDS

For a time, Trimark was a serious challenger to take over the position as the number one mutual fund company in Canada, a spot long held by Investors Group. But then its domestic equity funds went into a deep slump in the late '90s and people started pulling out money. As a result, Trimark has fallen back to fourth place in terms of total assets under management, and third among load companies. It's still big, with about $25 billion in its various funds. But not as big as before.

Unlike Investors Group and Mackenzie, Trimark's fund line-up is quite limited. As a result, we do not have the diversity of choice that's available from the other groups. Here is the extended asset mix we will use for them.

EXTENDED ASSET MIX

	TRIMARK
Canadian Equity	15.0%
U.S. Equity	0.0%
International Equity	35.0%
Special Equity	0.0%
Total Equity Assets	**50.0%**
Dividend Funds	0.0%
Domestic Bond	40.0%
Global Bond	0.0%
Total Income Assets	**40.0%**
Money Market	10.0%
Total Cash Assets	**10.0%**

Wow, this looks weird, you may be saying. Why no U.S. equities? Why no dividend fund? Because Trimark doesn't offer either, that's why. They also don't have a foreign bond fund and no specialty fund that's been around long enough to qualify for an MVA score. As you can see, building a well-diversified Trimark portfolio is a bit of a challenge. Let's see what we can do.

Equity funds

Trimark offers four diversified Canadian stock funds, plus two small-cap funds. This strikes us as overkill, especially given the gaps in their line-up, but that's what we're looking at. The small-cap funds haven't been in existence long enough to be considered for this model portfolio, nor has the new Trimark Enterprise Fund, managed by Kiki Delaney. So we have to make our domestic selections from among Trimark Canadian,

Trimark Select Canadian Growth, and Trimark RSP Equity. All have had recent managerial changes after a lengthy period of underperformance. At this point there is no indication of which will emerge as the premiere performer. Therefore, we will hedge our bets and take a five percent position in each.

We don't have much more latitude when it comes to the international funds. Our first choice will be the Trimark Fund, which had many years of high performance before hitting a rough patch recently. Although this is a global fund, we gain considerable exposure to the U.S. market here (53 percent of the portfolio in mid-1999). This fund has a new manager, Bill Kanko, who moved back to Trimark in the spring of 1999 after a stint with Mackenzie Financial. Investors hope he will rejuvenate the fund. We'll give it a 20 percent weighting in our mix. MVA is 89.7, which reflects the recent slippage in returns.

Our next selection is Trimark Indo-Pacific, which provides exposure to the Far East. As you might expect, given the recent strength in that part of the world, this has been Trimark's hottest fund lately with a one-year return of better than 50 percent. The downside is that the risk level here is worse than average. We'll give this one a ten percent weighting.

We would like to use the Trimark Europlus Fund in this portfolio, but it does not yet have an MVA score. So the final five percent equity position will go to Trimark — The Americas, which gives us some Latin American exposure as well as further adding to our U.S. stocks. This fund has been an underachiever, which explains the low MVA of 75.2, but it has looked better lately.

Fixed-income funds

With no dividend funds, no mortgage funds and no foreign bond funds from which to choose, this section of the portfolio will be composed entirely of Canadian bonds by default.

Our primary holding will be the Trimark Advantage Bond Fund. It includes some high-yield bonds in its mix to give it extra oomph, and has been an above-average performer over the past three years. MVA score is 99.2. We'll give it a 20 percent weighting.

We'll divide the rest of the bond weighting equally between these two funds:

Trimark Canadian Bond. About half of the portfolio is invested in Government of Canada issues. The rest is a mix of corporate bonds, provincial issues, a few preferred shares and T-bills. Performance has been above average for the Canadian Bond category and the safety record is good. MVA is 98.5.

Trimark Government Income. This fund focuses on shorter-term securities with a view to minimizing risk while providing regular monthly income. Returns tend to be slightly better than average for the Canadian Short-Term Bond category. MVA is 94.7.

Cash funds

Only one choice here — the Trimark Interest Fund, which offers above-average returns. MVA is 95.8.

Trimark Portfolio summarized

Here's how our Trimark Portfolio looks.

PCT	TRIMARK GROWTH/INCOME PORTFOLIO	WT. MVA	MVA
5.0%	Trimark Canadian	4.94	98.8
5.0%	Trimark Select Canadian Growth	4.86	97.2
5.0%	Trimark RSP Equity	4.63	92.5
20.0%	Trimark Fund	17.94	89.7
10.0%	Trimark Indo-Pacific	10.34	103.4
5.0%	Trimark – The Americas	3.76	75.2
20.0%	Trimark Advantage Bond	19.84	99.2
10.0%	Trimark Canadian Bond	9.85	98.5
10.0%	Trimark Government Income	9.47	94.7
10.0%	Trimark Interest	9.58	95.8
100.0%	Portfolio MVA	95.21	

Here is our Trimark FundLine profile.

Trimark Canadian

Trimark RSP Equity

Trimark Select Canadian Growth

Trimark Fund

Trimark Indo-Pacific

Trimark – The Americas

Trimark Advantage Bond

Trimark Canadian Bond

Trimark Government Income

Trimark Interest

Overall Portfolio

The overall MVA of this portfolio is the lowest we've seen thus far (although you haven't reached the end of the chapter yet; there's one that comes in lower). That's a reflection of the recent underperformance of most of Trimark's equity funds, and we would expect these results to improve going forward. This low portfolio MVA, which reflects the performance of the past three years, explains in a nutshell why Trimark has been suffering significant net redemptions.

Looking at the overall FundLine, there are some gaps in our coverage but we have not done badly considering the limited number of funds we have to work with.

FIDELITY INVESTMENTS

Fidelity has moved up to become the fourth-largest load company in Canada. They've traveled a long way in a decade — at the start of the '90s, they were only a minor force. The knock on Fidelity all along has been that they offer some fine U.S. and international funds but their domestic entries are weak. Let's see if that holds up as we construct our portfolio. Here's the extended asset mix we will use.

EXTENDED ASSET MIX

	FIDELITY
Canadian Equity	15.0%
U.S. Equity	15.0%
International Equity	20.0%
Special Equity	0.0%
Total Equity Assets	**50.0%**
Dividend Funds	0.0%
Domestic Bond	30.0%
Global Bond	10.0%
Total Income Assets	**40.0%**
Money Market	10.0%
Total Cash Assets	**10.0%**

Like Trimark, Fidelity has no dividend fund to offer. The company does have a number of interesting specialty funds, but none have been in existence long enough to qualify for an MVA score.

Equity funds

Fidelity's most attractive diversified Canadian equity fund is True North. It was originally created for Veronika Hirsch when she joined the company in 1996, only to leave shortly thereafter as a result of problems with securities regulators. The fund was taken over by Alan Radlo, who has done a fine job with it. Unfortunately, it hasn't been around quite long enough to receive an MVA score.

Our domestic equity choices therefore come down to the older Fidelity Capital Builder Fund and the small-cap Fidelity Canadian Growth Company Fund.

We're not happy about including Capital Builder in our mix. It is a chronic underperformer with a pitiful safety record. Over the past year, it lost 12.6 percent and the three-year average annual compound rate of return is just 1.9 percent. The MVA of 86.8 is actually somewhat generous, given this record. However, in terms of balance, we feel it is important to have some Canadian large-cap stocks. Therefore we will include it in the portfolio, but with only a five percent weighting.

The other ten percent of our domestic equity allocation goes to Canadian Growth Company. This is like ascending from hell to heaven. Managed by Alan Radlo, who also runs True North, this fund has generated a three-year average annual compound rate of return of 17.3 percent, one of the best results in the small-cap category. It has done this while managing to produce a safety rating that is one of the best for its type. Actually, there's a bit of cheating here. While the fund does have a small-cap bias, some of the holdings are anything but that — for example, a position in the huge Power Corporation of Canada. But let's not quibble. The MVA here is a terrific 123.6, which shows you how well Radlo has been doing.

Moving to the U.S. equity side, our primary holding will be Fidelity Growth America, to which we'll give a ten percent portfolio weighting. This fund has cooled off recently but still sports a very good five-year average annual compound rate of return of 22.2 percent. Safety rating is good and the MVA is 91.0.

We'll supplement this with a five percent weighting in Fidelity Small Cap America. This was one of the better U.S. small-cap funds available in this country but it has been on the skids lately, with a one-year loss of 12.3 percent. Predictably, the MVA slipped as well, all the way down to 70.9.

Our main international holding will be the very good Fidelity International Portfolio Fund. It's been a top performer for a long time, averaging 16 percent annually for the past five years, and has an above-average safety rating. MVA is an even 100.0. We'll put 10 percent of the portfolio here.

There are several other international funds that deserve to be included in our mix, but we can only give them relatively small allocations. They are:

Fidelity European Growth. This is one of the better European equity funds available, with an average annual gain of 17.8 percent over the past five years. Risk is higher than we would like, however, which pulls the MVA down to 93.0. Portfolio weighting: 2.5 percent.

Fidelity Far East. The top fund in the Asia ex-Japan category over the past five years, this fund produced an average annual return of 8.3 percent for investors at a time when many Asian funds were in negative territory. One-year return was 57.4 percent. MVA is 112.5. Portfolio weighting: five percent.

Fidelity Japanese Growth. The Japanese market got hot in 1999, and this fund did too, gaining more than 25 percent in the first half of the year. Good safety rating for its category. Portfolio weighting: 2.5 percent.

Fixed-income funds

On the domestic side, we have two choices, both quite good.

Fidelity Canadian Bond invests in a mix of government and corporate issues. Recent returns have improved to above average and the safety record is impressive. MVA is 97.4. We'll use this as our main domestic bond holding, with a 20 percent portfolio weighting.

The other ten percent we are allocating to Canadian bonds will go into the Fidelity Canadian Income Fund. This is a short-term bond fund, designed to minimize interest rate risk while at the same time providing somewhat better returns than you would normally get from a money market fund. MVA is 95.2.

We have a ten percent allocation for foreign bond funds, which we will divide equally between the Fidelity Emerging Markets Bond Fund and the Fidelity North American Income Fund.

The Emerging Markets Bond Fund went through a few tough years but was showing good signs of recovery in the first half of 1999. However, its high risk rating drags down the MVA to 76.5.

Fidelity North American Income invests in debt securities issued by Canada, the U.S., and Mexico. It took a big hit a few years ago when the Mexican peso was devalued, but has looked better recently. MVA is 98.8.

Cash funds

We have only one choice here, the Fidelity Canadian Short Term Asset Fund. It's a ho-hum performer, with a low MVA as money market funds go of 90.1.

Fidelity Portfolio summarized

Here is the bottom line on our Fidelity selections.

PCT	FIDELITY GROWTH/INCOME PORTFOLIO	WT. MVA	MVA
5.0%	Capital Builder	4.34	86.8
10.0%	Canadian Growth Company	12.36	123.6
10.0%	Growth America	9.10	91.0
5.0%	Small Cap America	3.55	70.9
10.0%	International Portfolio	10.00	100.0
2.5%	European Growth	2.33	93.0
5.0%	Far East	5.63	112.5
2.5%	Japanese Growth	2.76	110.2
20.0%	Canadian Bond	19.48	97.4
10.0%	Canadian Income	9.52	95.2
5.0%	Emerging Markets Bond	3.83	76.5
5.0%	North American Income	4.94	98.8
10.0%	Canadian Short Term Asset	9.01	90.1
100.0%	Portfolio MVA	96.83	

Here's the FundLine profile.

Capital Builder

Canadian Growth Company

Growth America

Small Cap America

International Portfolio

European Growth

Far East

Japanese Growth

Canadian Bond

Canadian Income

Emerging Markets Bond

North American Income

Canadian Short Term Asset

Overall Portfolio

Overall, Fidelity's portfolio MVA was disappointingly low. It should improve when True North becomes eligible for inclusion, but the surprisingly low MVAs from the two U.S. stock funds are a problem that the company needs to address.

We also were not able to attain the level of diversification we would normally like to see. Again, this should improve as Fidelity's various sector funds reach their third anniversary.

TEMPLETON FUNDS

For our final load fund portfolio, we'll look at the Templeton organization, the fifth-largest company in this category. Templeton is best known for its value-oriented global funds, led by the venerable Templeton Growth Fund, which has been churning out good profits for investors for decades. But is this just a one-fund company, or is there more to it? Let's see what our portfolio-building exercise produces. Here's the extended asset mix.

EXTENDED ASSET MIX

	TEMPLETON
Canadian Equity	15.0%
U.S. Equity	0.0%
International Equity	35.0%
Special Equity	0.0%
Total Equity Assets	**50.0%**
Dividend Funds	0.0%
Domestic Bond	30.0%
Global Bond	10.0%
Total Income Assets	**40.0%**
Money Market	10.0%
Total Cash Assets	**10.0%**

Like Trimark, the Templeton organization does not have a broad range of funds. Surprisingly, there is no pure U.S. stock fund in its line-up, although Templeton Growth does hold U.S. securities. There is no dividend fund, no mortgage fund and no specialty funds. So we are very limited in our scope.

Equity funds

Templeton offers only one domestic equity fund, Templeton Canadian Stock, so it gets a 15 percent portfolio weighting. It's not a bad fund, with slightly better-than-average-three year annual compound rate of return of 11.2 percent and a good safety record. MVA is 103.2.

In contrast, we have a number of global and international funds from which to choose. We couldn't have a Templeton portfolio without including a healthy slice of the Growth Fund, so we'll begin with that, giving it a ten percent portfolio weighting. Why not more? Because, good as its long-term history is, this fund has underperformed in recent years. Also, and this surprised us when we did the analysis, Templeton Growth has a very weak safety rating. That helps explain why the MVA comes in at a relatively low 90.8.

The companion Templeton International Stock Fund, which does not invest in North America, ranks much higher on the safety scale, although it's only average when compared to the entire category. Over the past three years, its results have also been somewhat better than those of Growth, averaging 14.7 percent annually. MVA is correspondingly higher, at 105.6. This fund will get a 15 percent weighting.

The rest of our international allocation will be divided between Templeton Emerging Markets and Templeton Global Smaller Companies, each of which gets a five percent portfolio weighting.

Templeton Emerging Markets Fund is run by Mark Mobius, one of the most colourful managers in the business. Emerging markets went through a rough time in the late '90s but this fund held up reasonably well and is the top performer in its category over the past five years. All funds of this type are high-risk, but this one is a little less so than normal. MVA is 74.8.

As the name implies, Templeton Global Smaller Companies Fund invests in small-cap stocks from around the world. Small caps have been a tough slog recently, but this one showed signs of picking up in the second quarter of '99. MVA is 80.7.

Fixed-income funds

We don't like putting 30 percent of a portfolio into one fund but we don't have a lot of choice here. Templeton Canadian Bond is the only domestic bond fund they offer, so it gets the whole weighting. To make matters worse, it's not a particularly good bond fund. Returns are consistently below average and risk is on the high side for a fund of this type. The low 88.1 MVA reflects all this. Here is a classic example of how investing all your assets with a single fund company can create serious problems.

If Templeton offered a good foreign bond fund, we would have been tempted to increase the weighting there, even though we are not keen on foreign bonds at this time. But, alas, the Templeton Global Bond Fund is even worse than its Canadian counterpart in both performance and safety terms. We give it a ten percent weighting with reluctance.

Cash funds

Yet again, there is just one cash-type fund available to us: Templeton Treasury Bill. It tends to be an average performer, nothing exciting. MVA is 92.6.

Templeton Portfolio summarized

Here is the final version of the Templeton Growth/Income Portfolio.

PCT	TEMPLETON GROWTH/INCOME PORTFOLIO	WT. MVA	MVA
15.0%	Canadian Stock	15.48	103.2
10.0%	Growth	9.08	90.8
15.0%	International Stock	15.84	105.6
5.0%	Emerging Markets	3.74	74.8
5.0%	Global Smaller Companies	4.04	80.7
30.0%	Canadian Bond	26.43	88.1
10.0%	Global Bond	7.18	71.8
10.0%	Treasury Bill	9.26	92.6
100.0%	Portfolio MVA	91.05	

The FundLine profile looks like this.

Canadian Stock

Growth

International Stock

Emerging Markets

Global Smaller Companies

Canadian Bond

Global Bond

Treasury Bill

Overall Portfolio

We actually achieved pretty good diversification here, given the limited number of funds from which to choose. But the portfolio MVA is appallingly low, dragged down mainly by the weak fixed-income and cash funds. The MVA would be higher in a more aggressive portfolio, in which a heavier weighting were given to equities. We wouldn't even advise trying to construct a safety portfolio using Templeton funds.

To answer the question we posed at the start of this section, no, Templeton is not a one-trick pony. There are other good equity funds in their line-up besides Growth. But the company is very weak on the fixed-income side. Investors would do far better to cherry-pick among the equity funds, rather than attempt to build a Templeton-only portfolio.

TO REITERATE

This is an appropriate time to reemphasize the point we made at the end of the last chapter: overconcentration of your assets in a single company can be dangerous to your financial health. Only one of Canada's five largest load fund companies, Investors Group, was able to produce a balanced growth/income portfolio with almost full diversification and an average MVA of more than 100. The rest failed the test to varying degrees, with Mackenzie the best of the other four.

Diversification is the key to success, not only in mutual fund selection but in the mix of companies you choose.

PACKAGE DEALS

The proliferation of mutual funds in recent years has created a great deal of confusion in the minds of investors. With all the choices now available, they find it difficult to mix and match the right combination of funds to create exactly the portfolio that best meets their needs.

The fund industry, always sensitive to what it perceives to be a new need on the part of investors, has responded predictably by creating packages of mutual funds, supposedly designed to suit every need. Don't know how to construct your own portfolio? Just buy one off the shelf!

Fund portfolios are the industry's latest craze. Over the past few years, dozens of fund packages have appeared on the scene to compete for your investment dollar. Some of these are designed in such a way that their performance can be tracked and meaningful comparisons made — for example, to the results generated by the average balanced fund. Others, especially the wrap accounts offered by the brokerage firms, are impossible to track, because the mix will be different for each individual client.

Some of the trackable portfolios are composed entirely of funds offered by a single company. These include the STAR portfolios (Mackenzie Financial), Investors portfolios (Investors Group), and MatchMaker portfolios (Bank of Montreal).

Others are built using funds from a number of companies. These include Keystone, which is operated by

Mackenzie, Artisan (Loring Ward), Choice Funds (CIBC), and Leaders (Scotiabank). One of our authors, Gordon Pape, is an advisor to CIBC Choice Funds.

Fund companies apparently believe that these packages represent huge potential sales. With the mutual fund universe now so large, even financial advisors are having problems finding the best choices. So the companies make it simple by offered selected packages of half a dozen or so funds, each package designed for a special purpose.

You may be tempted to go this route instead of building your own fund portfolio using the principles we've outlined elsewhere in this book. But before you make that decision, you should know more about what's available in the fund package market, and what you can expect in terms of performance, safety, and cost.

Here's the scoop on some of the main packages now on the market, competing for your investment dollar.

STAR

One of the pioneers in popularizing the concept is Gordon Garmaise, who, along with his wife, Ena, founded Garmaise Investment Technologies, a Toronto-based company that creates tailored portfolios and develops systems for helping people choose which one is best for their needs.

Garmaise, who holds a master of science degree in finance and economics from MIT, worked with Mackenzie Financial to launch the first portfolio system that really caught the public's attention. Named STAR, the program offers 17 portfolios in four categories, using only Mackenzie funds. They range in risk from conservative to highly aggressive.

Here are the STAR categories:

Registered: Eligible for registered plans; contain foreign content up to the 20 percent limit. Five portfolios.

Canadian: Eligible for registered plans; contain no foreign content funds, but do provide foreign exposure through derivatives. Five portfolios.

Investment: Blend of Canadian and foreign funds, not intended for registered plans. Four portfolios.

Foreign: Completely foreign content, no Canadian exposure. Three portfolios.

Several STAR portfolios have been around long enough to allow for some comparisons against regular balanced funds. The results vary, but only a couple make it into the second quartile. Most are high to middle third quartile, which is not bad but not sensational either. However, Garmaise cautions not to judge the portfolios on return alone. Risk also has to be taken into account and is a critical component in shaping the overall portfolio composition.

"You have to really control the downside in these portfolios," he says. "People tend to remember their losses much more than their gains. Limiting those losses when markets decline is one of the most important services we can render."

But, he admits, "We have underperformed somewhat, partly because some of our portfolios turned out to be not as well-diversified as we expected."

To put things back on course, the STAR portfolios went through a major overhaul in July 1998. Several funds were dropped from the mix; others were downgraded, and new funds were added.

"We learned a lot in the first three years," Garmaise says. "The program is even better now."

There is some evidence that this contention is correct. Several STAR portfolios performed much better during the year ending June 30/99, than they had previously. However, in most cases the three-year average annual compound rate of return was less than that of the average comparable balanced fund. Let's look at some numbers:

DOMESTIC BALANCED PORTFOLIOS

PORTFOLIO	AVERAGE ANNUAL COMPOUND RATE OF RETURN		
	1 year	2 years	3 years
Average Canadian balanced fund	0.6%	5.2%	9.8%
STAR Can. Balanced Growth & Income	-0.3%	4.8%	9.6%
STAR Can. Conservative Income & Growth	-1.2%	3.9%	N/A
STAR Can. Long-Term Growth	-1.9%	4.1%	N/A
STAR Can. Maximum Long-Term Growth	1.1%	5.7%	N/A

...

STAR Reg. Balanced Growth & Income	1.6%	4.4%	8.6%
STAR Reg. Conservative Income & Growth	0.5%	4.7%	7.6%
STAR Reg. Long-Term Growth	2.5%	4.3%	8.8%

Source: The Globe and Mail

Take a close look at these results. Of the seven STAR domestic portfolios, not a single one matched the average return of the Canadian Balanced category over the three-year period. In fact, you would have done much better by just putting your money into one of Mackenzie Financial's balanced funds and letting it go at that. Ivy Growth & Income generated an average annual compound rate of return of 12.7 percent over the same three-year period, while Industrial Pension did marginally better, at 12.8 percent. Even Industrial Balanced Fund turned in superior numbers, at 10.8 percent over the three years.

Looking at the one-year numbers, which reflect the portfolio rebalancing in mid-1998, three of the STAR entries outperformed the average, and did better than Ivy Growth & Income and Industrial Pension (but not Industrial Balanced). So Garmaise's contention that results will improve may turn out to be correct. However, to this point, the results show that investors would have been better off in a single balanced fund from Mackenzie rather than one of these packages.

Now let's look at the STAR international portfolios.

INTERNATIONAL BALANCED PORTFOLIOS

PORTFOLIO	AVERAGE ANNUAL COMPOUND RATE OF RETURN		
	1 year	2 years	3 years
Average global balanced fund	4.7%	8.5%	10.6%
STAR Foreign Balanced Growth & Income	5.4%	9.5%	9.7%
STAR Foreign Maximum Long-Term Growth	8.4%	7.8%	7.3%
STAR Inv. Balanced Growth & Income	1.9%	6.1%	9.2%
STAR Inv. Conservative Income & Growth	1.2%	7.3%	9.0%
STAR Inv. Long-Term Growth	-1.4%	4.9%	9.3%
STAR Inv. Maximum Long-Term Growth	3.1%	4.8%	6.7%

Source: The Globe and Mail

Here again we see a similar pattern. Not one of the STAR international portfolios did better than the average global balanced fund over three years. Again, two stand-alone Mackenzie funds outperformed the STAR portfolios over that time frame. Universal World Balanced RRSP Fund returned an average of 11.7 percent annually over the three years, while Universal World Asset Allocation Fund gained an average of 11.1 percent. Shorter-term, the STAR Foreign Maximum Long-Term Growth Portfolio outperformed both, and the averages, over one year, but it remains to be seen if it can retain that edge over the long haul.

Of course, we're looking at pure return numbers here, without the relative risk factor taken into account — a point that Garmaise places a great deal of emphasis on. And it is true that most of the STAR portfolios carry below-average risk for their categories. But in many cases you're sacrificing a significant amount of return for that lower risk. If you want to invest in a STAR portfolio and you're looking for the best combination of risk and return, only two portfolios meet the test, according to analysis done by Wilfred Vos of CIBC Securities. They fall into the Canadian Equity category: STAR Canadian Maximum Equity Growth and STAR Registered Maximum Equity Growth.

The STAR portfolios charge an extra ten basis points over the usual management fees for the component funds. That makes them cheap by portfolio standards.

Bottom line: The STAR portfolio concept has yet to prove itself. While the portfolios deliver on the promise of reduced risk for the most part, returns to date have been unimpressive, especially with the balanced portfolios. If it's a Mackenzie balanced product you want, you'd be better off buying one of their better-performing balanced funds.

KEYSTONE

Gordon Garmaise's latest project with Mackenzie is the Keystone portfolios. The principle is the same as with STAR but in this case several other companies also provide funds that can be used in the mix. They include

AGF, BPI, Beutel Goodman, Saxon, Sceptre, and Spectrum United.

"The advantage here is that we can add funds in areas where Mackenzie might not have a good alternative," Garmaise explains.

There are ten Keystone portfolios currently available. Five — the "Registered" series — are designed for RRSPs and other registered plans. The "Investment" series is intended for non-registered portfolios.

It's very early days for these portfolios, but here are some preliminary comparisons on the Canadian Balanced category. Results are to June 30/99.

DOMESTIC BALANCED PORTFOLIOS

PORTFOLIO	RATE OF RETURN
	1 year
Average Canadian balanced fund	0.6%
STAR Reg. Balanced Growth & Income	1.6%
Keystone Reg. Balanced Growth & Income	-0.5%
STAR Reg. Conservative Income & Growth	0.5%
Keystone Reg. Conservative Income & Growth	-0.4%
STAR Reg. Long-Term Growth	2.5%
Keystone Reg. Long-Term Growth	3.8%
STAR Reg. Maximum Long-Term Growth	3.0%
Keystone Reg. Maximum Long-Term Growth	3.5%

Source: The Globe and Mail

Mixed results here. The more conservative STAR portfolios outperformed their Keystone counterparts. But the more aggressive Keystone portfolios did better.

Like STAR, Keystone charges a premium of ten basis points (0.1 percent) over the regular management fees of the funds.

Bottom line: If you're a conservative investor, you'd be better off in a single low-risk balanced fund. More-aggressive investors may want to keep an eye on the Keystone portfolios that are tailored to deliver above-average returns.

ARTISAN FUNDS

Fifteen portfolios are offered in this line-up. They are run by Loring Ward Investment Counsel and distributed through a network of financial planning companies, including Equion Securities, Financial Concept Corporation, DPM Financial Planning Group, Summit Securities, and a number of others. These are third-party portfolios which include funds from AIM, Fidelity, Dynamic, C.I./BPI, and AGF. Each portfolio is designed to meet a specific investment need. The balanced entries range from "Most Conservative" to "Most Aggressive." As well, there are several targeted portfolios: Canadian Equity, U.S. Equity, International Equity, Global Fixed Income, and Canadian T-Bill.

The mix of funds you get will depend on your portfolio of choice. For example, if you purchase units in the Artisan International Equity Portfolio, you'll be buying a basket of outside funds that is made up as follows: 40 percent Fidelity International Portfolio Fund, 40 percent Hansberger Value Fund, 10 percent AGF International Value Fund, and 10 percent C.I. Emerging Markets Fund.

The weighting in each portfolio is determined by the investment counselling firm of Loring Ward, a Winnipeg-based company. The portfolios were launched in January 1998, so results to date don't tell us a lot about longer-term potential. However, the initial results are encouraging. Ten of the Artisan portfolios fall into the Canadian Balanced category. Over the year to June 30/99, every one of them outperformed the average return for that category. So did the Artisan Canadian Equity Portfolio. However, the U.S. Equity and International Equity entries did not meet the average returns of their respective categories.

The MER of the Artisan portfolios is relatively high, coming in at just under three percent in most cases (the T-Bill Portfolio is one percent). So in most cases you are paying a premium for the package versus simply buying the underlying funds.

For example, in the case of the International Equity Fund, the weighted MER of the individual funds works out to 2.58 percent. Buying them in the Artisan package produces an MER of 2.97 percent. So the added annual cost of doing it this way is 39 basis points (0.39 percent). That's the difference in the return you could expect from this package versus building your own portfolio using the same funds in the same proportions, which any financial planner could do for you.

Here are some one-year comparisons with the Keystone balanced portfolios, which use the same general approach. We've chosen the RRSP-eligible portfolios in both cases.

DOMESTIC BALANCED PORTFOLIOS

PORTFOLIO	RATE OF RETURN
	1 year
Average Canadian balanced fund	0.6%
Artisan RSP Moderate Portfolio	1.8%
Keystone Reg. Balanced Growth & Income	-0.5%
Artisan RSP Conservative Portfolio	0.5%
Keystone Reg. Conservative Income & Growth	-0.4%
Artisan RSP Aggressive Portfolio	2.1%
Keystone Reg. Long-Term Growth	3.8%
Artisan RSP Most Aggressive Portfolio	2.0%
Keystone Reg. Maximum Long-Term Growth	3.5%

Source: The Globe and Mail

Artisan's more conservative portfolios did better than those of Keystone. But the situation was reversed in the more growth-oriented portfolios. Three of the four Artisan portfolios beat the one-year average return for the Canadian Balanced category.

Bottom line: So far the Artisan funds are pretty good performers. But you'll pay a premium price to have your funds packaged for you in this way. Any financial advisor could emulate the portfolios, or you could do it yourself.

INVESTORS GROUP

There are seven "fund of funds" portfolios in the Investors Group line-up. All invest exclusively in other Investors Group funds, and all are designed to offer varying levels of risk. Some have been around for several years, so we have a pretty good idea of how they compare to funds in their peer group and to other Investors Group funds of the same type. Here are some examples, using figures to June 30/99.

CANADIAN EQUITY

FUND/PORTFOLIO	AVERAGE ANNUAL COMPOUND RATE OF RETURN			
	1 year	3 years	5 years	10 years
Investors Retirement Growth Port.	-6.6%	7.5%	9.0%	7.4%
Investors Retirement Mutual Fund	-9.9%	5.8%	8.2%	6.1%
Investors Canadian Equity Fund	-8.3%	6.0%	7.8%	8.3%
Average Canadian Equity Fund	-2.6%	11.0%	11.9%	9.2%

Source: The Globe and Mail

In this case, the Retirement Portfolio did better than either of the two stand-alone Investors Group Canadian stock funds for all periods out to five years. However, all significantly underperformed the average for all Canadian diversified equity funds.

GLOBAL EQUITY

FUND/PORTFOLIO	AVERAGE ANNUAL COMPOUND RATE OF RETURN			
	1 year	3 years	5 years	10 years
Investors Growth Portfolio	2.2%	14.8%	13.3%	12.0%
Investors World Growth Portfolio	11.2%	7.6%	8.3%	N/A
Investors Global Fund	4.8 %	14.2%	12.9%	12.2%
Average Global Equity Fund	10.9%	13.1%	11.8%	11.6%

Source: The Globe and Mail

In this case, the results are mixed. The Investors Group Growth Portfolio outperformed the average for the Global Equity category for all time periods longer than one year. But the World Growth Portfolio was a laggard. The Investors Global Fund was a much better choice than the World Growth Portfolio over all time periods and marginally outperformed the Growth Portfolio over a decade.

CANADIAN BALANCED

FUND/PORTFOLIO	AVERAGE ANNUAL COMPOUND RATE OF RETURN			
	1 year	3 years	5 years	10 years
Investors Income Plus Portfolio	-0.3%	8.7%	9.2%	8.0%
Investors Retirement Plus Portfolio	-0.9%	7.3%	8.3%	7.6%
Investors Mutual of Canada	-1.6%	10.5%	10.2%	9.0%
Average Canadian Balanced Fund	0.6%	9.8%	11.0%	9.0%

Source: The Globe and Mail

When we look at the Canadian Balanced category, it is quickly apparent that the two Investors Group portfolios were not the best place to be. Both produced worse results than the average Canadian balanced fund over all time periods. Except for the one-year results, Investors Mutual of Canada did significantly better than either of the portfolios.

The MERs of the portfolios are generally in line with those of regular Investors Group funds, so cost is not a major concern here.

Bottom line: Returns from the Investors Group portfolios aren't terrible, but they generally fail to match the averages for their respective categories. In most cases, you would do better by selecting a stand-alone fund from those offered by the company.

MATCHMAKER

This is an investment service offered by the Bank of Montreal, using their own First Canadian Funds. A total of 14 portfolios are offered, 12 of them "strategic" portfolios that are rebalanced periodically. As in the other programs, the idea is to optimize returns while keeping risk within tolerable levels. Each strategic portfolio contains a minimum of five funds. There are also two "savings" portfolios, each of which contains a GIC plus two funds. As with many of these portfolio plans, investors complete a questionnaire that is designed to direct them to the most suitable portfolio.

The MatchMaker portfolios have been around long enough to establish a three-year track record and some have done quite well. Here's a sampling from the Canadian Balanced category. The funds with "Registered" in the name are RRSP-eligible. Two versions of each non-registered portfolio are offered. Those designated "1" are more conservative than those designated "2." (This is one of the problems with all these portfolios. The names are often similar, and confusing.)

DOMESTIC BALANCED PORTFOLIOS

PORTFOLIO	AVERAGE ANNUAL COMPOUND RATE OF RETURN		
	1 year	2 years	3 years
Average Canadian balanced fund	0.6%	5.2%	9.8%
MatchMaker Registered Balanced 1	3.1%	6.3%	9.6%
MatchMaker Registered Growth 1	-0.1%	2.2%	8.3%
MatchMaker Strategic Balanced 1	2.6%	6.1%	9.0%
MatchMaker Strategic Balanced 2	2.9%	7.3%	11.0%
MatchMaker Strategic Growth 1	0.5%	3.3%	8.9%
MatchMaker Strategic Growth 2	1.1%	2.7%	8.9%
First Canadian Asset Allocation Fund	1.7%	5.7%	10.0%

Source: The Globe and Mail

Only one of these portfolios outperformed the category average over three years. The same was true when the MatchMaker portfolios were lined up against the First Canadian Asset Allocation Fund, which is in the same family.

Bottom line: Here again, there is no evidence that the packages can outperform the peer group average, or even do better than a stand-alone balanced fund over time.

SCOTIA LEADERS PROGRAM

This plan from Bank of Nova Scotia offers two portfolios of equity funds selected on the basis of achieving "Heavy Hitter" status in *Ranga Chand's World of Mutual Funds.* The program has been running since October 1996, and is the only one that uses equity funds exclusively. That means higher risk, but also potentially higher returns.

The results are not published in the monthly mutual fund surveys in the business press but can be calculated at the Scotiabank web site (the address to go to is www.scotiabank.ca/cgi-bin/Scotiabank/Leader/ leaderCalculator.cgi). One-year gain for the Global Equity Portfolio to June 30/99 was 4.6 percent. That compares to a return for the average Global Equity fund of 10.9 percent over the same period. The two-year average annual compound rate of return for the Leaders Program looks somewhat better, at 10.4 percent. But that is still below the 11.1 percent for the Global Equity category.

The Canadian Equity Portfolio showed a one-year gain of 0.45 percent to June 30, which was better than the average loss of 2.6 percent for the Canadian equity category. The two-year annual return for the Leaders Program was 2.8 percent, slightly below the average of 3.5 percent for the category.

Annual fees are 0.5 to one percent of the amount invested. Minimum is $10,000, but you don't benefit from the lowest fee schedule until you put in $100,000.

Bottom line: This package is quite expensive and the returns from both portfolios are below the average gains for the comparable mutual fund categories over two years.

CIBC CHOICE FUNDS

This program offers five balanced portfolios of selected third-party funds, ranging from Conservative to Very Aggressive. Each portfolio comes in a registered and a non-registered version. Funds may be chosen from any company that meets certain criteria (e.g., national distribution). Selection and monitoring is done by a panel that includes Gordon Pape (one of the co-authors of this book) and representatives from CIBC and T.A.L. Investment Counsel. There are no sales commissions charged, but an annual administration fee of 0.75 percent to 1.5 percent is assessed (larger accounts get the lowest rate). Minimum investment is $25,000.

This program is in its second year and underwent a major overhaul in mid-1999. As with most other packages, results so far are mixed. Over the 12 months to

June 30/99, two of the five portfolios marginally outperformed the average return in the Canadian Balanced category (which was only 0.6 percent) while the other three marginally underperformed it.

Bottom line: This is the most expensive of the packages reviewed here. However, the returns to date are only average to slightly below.

WRAPPING UP

Based on what we've seen so far, the mutual fund packages have not been particularly impressive, although none have been awful either. These plans are best suited for investors who prefer the convenience of one-stop fund shopping, buying a package that is tailored to fit their investment goals. Relative cost may become a factor going forward, but only once we have enough performance data to make useful comparisons between higher-cost programs and those with little or no incremental expense.

Keystone and Artisan appear to be the best bets at the present time. But that may change as more portfolio plans appear, and as performance numbers accumulate.

However, we believe that you can build your own mutual fund package more effectively using the FundLine principles contained elsewhere in this book.

FUND PACKAGES AT A GLANCE

PROGRAM	FUNDS	NATURE	SALES CHARGE	ANNUAL FEES
Artisan	Third party	Balanced	Yes	Varies
Choice	Third party	Balanced	No	0.75%-1.5%
Keystone	Third party	Balanced	Yes	0.10%
Investors	Investors	Balanced	Yes	No
Leaders	Third Party	Equity	No	0.5%-1%
MatchMaker	1st Canadian	Balanced	No	No
STAR	MacKenzie	Balanced	Yes	0.10%

INDEX PORTFOLIOS

When you are building investment portfolios, one of the most important considerations is identifying your selection style. The major style decision is whether to use an active, passive, or mixed approach to investing. Active investors search for and invest in undervalued securities or buy mutual funds that are managed by security selectors who follow an active approach. Passive investors believe that security prices fully reflect all available information and that the search for undervalued securities is fruitless. They follow an index strategy.

MARKET INDEXING ROOTS

Proponents of passive investing point out that an investment policy of randomly selecting common shares and buying and holding them has returned about 10 to 11 percent per year over the past 60 years. This gets right to the core of passive investing and market indexing.

Market indexing has its roots in the investment finance theory combination of Efficient Markets Theory and Portfolio Theory. If you believe in these two paradigms, you should concentrate your attention on your portfolio mix (safety/income/growth combinations) rather than individual stock selection. The first practical application of indexing was employed by the Wells Fargo

Bank in the United States in 1972, with the debut of the first index fund. Since then, indexing has grown enormously in popularity in the United States and the United Kingdom, although its growth has been quite slow in Canada, particularly at the retail investor level. The slow growth of indexing in Canada reflects a number of factors, including the general lack of understanding of passive investing by retail investors as well as the fear of missing out on high returns earned by "star" fund managers. The lack of promotion of index products by brokers and financial advisors (possibly because index products pay lower trailer fees and commissions than active products!) is another reason for the slow growth of indexing among retail investors.

PASSIVE INVESTING

Indexing takes a lot of emotion out of investing. In recent years, index products have far outshone active investments. In comparing the performance of indexes to actively managed mutual funds, the disparity is quite apparent.

For example, over the past five years Canadian market indexes have outperformed the average and median Canadian equity fund every year by an average of about three percent, well above the average management expense ratio (2.27 percent) of equity funds. Picking exceptions wasn't easy — only 25.6 percent of the 86 broadly diversified Canadian equity funds with five-year track records outperformed the TSE 300 Composite Index. In the Canadian large-cap category only six out of 48, or 12.5, percent beat the Toronto 35 Index. Meanwhile, index participation units such as TIPS 35 have almost perfectly matched their underlying index.

Over the past ten years the record for active investing is a little better. The average Canadian equity mutual fund has underperformed the TSE 300 Composite Index at a rate of about 0.70 percent per year — meaning that the average fund actually beat the index but the cost of doing so ate up the profits and more. Thirty-seven percent of the 59 funds in the sample beat the index. The large-cap funds didn't fare as well. Only 19 percent of the funds were able to overcome the 10.5 percent per annum compounded return of the Toronto 35 Index.

Keep in mind that, if anything, the mutual fund sample results are biased upwards, since the funds that merge or otherwise disappear do not appear in the sample. Typically such funds are very weak performers.

The record for Canada-domiciled U.S. funds is pretty dismal. Over the past five years the average U.S. fund has missed the S&P 500 benchmark by over six percent per annum. Admittedly, the S&P's 25.6 percent annual compounded rate of return is a tough target, but nevertheless only five out of 55 funds managed to beat it. Over the past ten years the differential narrows to three percent a year, with 20 percent of the funds beating the benchmark.

How do you carry out an indexing strategy? There are a number of useful vehicles. We have separated these into Canadian, U.S., and international indexing opportunities.

Canadian indexing

1. Index Participation Units

One of the most efficient investment products for passive investors is the so-called index participation unit or IPU. IPUs are exchange-traded securities that represent a basket of stocks, which in turn replicates a specific underlying market index. IPUs trade on exchanges just like stocks at a specific designated IPU-to-Index ratio.

Financial innovators tried for years to develop a tradable basket product that represents a market index. In the 1980s CIPs (Cash Index Participation Units), VIPS (Value of Index Participation Certificates), and Index Trust SuperUnits all debuted and subsequently disappeared in the U.S., due to either poor design or jurisdictional disputes among regulators, exchanges, and institutions. In Canada, the legal and securities structure was more accommodating to financial innovation; the Toronto Stock Exchange introduced its index participation unit version, called Toronto Index Participation Units, or TIPS, on March 9, 1990. The TIPS structure is so sound that it has served as prototype for subsequent IPUs, including SPDRs, based on the Standard & Poor's

500 Composite; and WEBS, based on individual Morgan Stanley Capital International indexes.

TIPS 35 and TIPS 100 are linked to the Toronto 35 and TSE 100 Indexes. Both have perfectly matched the decline in the corresponding indexes. Maybe the term "perfectly" bothers you, but that's the characteristic of a proper index product — since it has no cash drag, and little or no tracking error, it matches the index in bad times as well as good! Typically both TIPS IPUs are within three points (that is a negligible 3/100 of one percent) of the indexes they track.

TIPS 35 is pegged to the Toronto 35 Index, a large-cap index of 35 of Canada's largest public corporations including Alcan Aluminium, Noranda Mines, and Canadian Pacific Limited. TIPS 100 is pegged to the TSE 100 Index, which is composed of the 100 largest companies listed on the TSE 300 Composite Index.

TIPS 35 and TIPS 100 are listed on the Toronto Stock Exchange and trade in the same manner as stocks. Each is designed to represent one-tenth the value of the index it tracks. Dividends, based on the underlying index companies, are paid on a quarterly basis and are eligible for the dividend tax credit.

In June 1999, Barclays Global Investors Canada Limited filed a preliminary prospectus (dated June 21/99) to launch a new index participation unit based on the S&P/TSE 60 Index. The new IPU will be called iUnits S&P/TSE 60 or i60s. They began trading on the Toronto Stock Exchange in October under the trading symbol XIU. The new i60 may very well replace the TIPS 100 in the future in the FPX index calculations (see p.237). Like TIPS, the new i60s IPU are designed to trade at approximately one-tenth the value of the S&P/TSE 60 Index. If, for example, the S&P/TSE 60 Index is quoted at 444.38, the IPU will trade at about $44.44. Any "tracking error" (deviation of the IPU from one-tenth of the index) will reflect rounding effects due to index adjustments, accrued dividends, accrued management expenses, and impending takeovers. Like TIPS, the new IPU collects dividends on the underlying companies as paid, but will pay quarterly dividends to unitholders. The management expense ratio (MER) is a minimum of 15 basis points to a maximum of 17 basis points; thus there will be a small tracking error. TIPS, in contrast, have covered their expenses through security lending and the dividend float, operating with virtually no expenses, and have maintained a near-perfect tracking record as a result. Nevertheless, 17 basis points is a competitive MER. By contrast, index mutual fund management expense ratios are in the 80-to-110-point range.

The S&P/TSE 60 share index is a capitalization-weighted index comprising 60 of Canada's largest companies, including the big five Canadian banks. The S&P/TSE 60 Index is scheduled to replace the Toronto 35 and TSE 100 and TSE 200 index over the next year or so. (The TSE 300 Composite Index is expected to remain intact but divided into three major sub-indexes — the S&P/TSE 60, a mid-cap index, and a small-cap index.) All of the TSE indexes, including new and existing transitional ones, will be calculated and maintained by S&P. The new IPU will be RRSP-eligible.

Meanwhile, existing TIPS 35 and TIPS-100 will continue to trade. Ultimately they will either be merged with the new i60 or they will be delisted. Given the near-zero tracking error of the product, we see no problem with either option.

TIPS 35 and TIPS 100 make quarterly distributions, each consisting of up to three different components:

1. Dividend distribution, which is subject to the gross-up and dividend tax credit treatment.
2. Net realized capital gain distributions. These are gains that result from dispositions of shares from the TIPS trust at a price over cost. Gains will occur, for example, when there is a successful takeover of a TIPS-included company. Such an event will cause a disposition within the TIPS basket (deemed or real), which could trigger a capital gain. What actually happens is that the gain is immediately reinvested in the fund on behalf of the unitholder, and the number of TIPS units is consolidated (reduced) to leave the number of TIPS units outstanding unchanged. The net result is that the unitholder has a taxable capital gain (although no actual gain is received) for tax purposes. The

taxable capital gain is subject to the 75 percent inclusion rule. The taxable capital gain received is added to the unitholder's adjusted cost base, thus reducing the gain (or increasing the loss) which would otherwise be incurred when the units are eventually sold.

3. Accrued distribution amounts. These are payments (normally relatively small) which represent the payments made to the TIPS fund on the issue of new TIPS to account for the accrued distributions to date. These payments are treated as a return of capital. They are not taxable when received but reduce the adjusted cost base of your units by exactly the amount of the distribution.

2. Index Mutual Funds

Index mutual funds are an alternative to IPUs. Index mutual funds, like other equity mutual funds, invest in a portfolio of common shares. However, the objective of an index fund is to track, as closely as possible, an underlying market index. No time or effort is devoted to security selection — the objective is to keep the security acquisition and maintenance costs as low as possible. Canadian index funds have underperformed the TSE Total Return Index (which measures both capital appreciation as well as dividends) by about one percent per annum over the past five years, pretty well reflecting the management expense ratios. The combination of management expenses (0.8 percent) plus cash drag has caused the tracking error.

Canadian index mutual funds that track U.S. and global indexes are also available in Canada. Although generally IPUs dominate the index funds, one important advantage that index funds have is that the dividends can be easily reinvested.

RRSP-eligible versions (using T-bills and derivatives) are available for U.S. and global index funds.

There are eight index mutual funds focusing on the Canadian market.

The NN Canadian 35 Index Fund is the only one pegged to the Toronto 35 Index; it invests exclusively in TIPS 35 units. The remaining funds are all pegged to the

TSE 300 Composite Index. These funds are CIBC Canadian Index, First Canadian Equity Index, Green Line Canadian Index, GWL Equity Index A, Royal Canadian Index, Royal Canadian Premium Index, and Scotia Canadian Stock Index.

Here are two index funds with long track records:

TD Green Line Canadian Index Fund

This TSE 300-oriented index has a healthy 10-year record in tracking the TSE 300 Composite Index. But during the strong market, this fund, in part as a result of its low MER, beat the average of its group. This is one of the leaders among the Canadian index funds.

First Canadian Equity Index Fund

This fund is also focused on the TSE 300 Composite Index in the same proportion, with periodic adjustments when there are changes to the Index. In the year to June 30, 1999, when the average Canadian large cap fund lost 3.8 percent, this index fund lost 4.2 percent. But during up markets, this fund performed better than its peer group. The five-year average annual gain was 12.3 percent, just above average. These are not great numbers for an index fund. The MER is above average for Canadian index funds.

The Difference Between IPUs and Index Mutual Funds

TIPS and SPDRs represent units in a trust that holds a basket of securities designed to duplicate an index. The units are listed on an exchange and are traded the way common shares are. Mutual fund units, on the other hand, do not trade but are valued each day at their net asset value per unit (assets minus liabilities divided by number of units outstanding). You both buy and redeem mutual fund units from the mutual fund dealer (sometimes directly through your broker or sales representative).

The closest analogy to TIPS and SPDRs is closed-end investment funds, which hold portfolios of securities and are traded on the secondary market. However, closed-end funds typically trade at premiums or discounts to their net asset value. This won't happen with IPUs.

3. Index-Linked Term Deposits

Index-linked term deposits vary considerably. For example, CIBC introduced three-year and five-year GICs that come in four versions — each representing a mix of GIC, bond, and equity. The GIC payoff is tied to the GIC yield, the income component to the CIBC Wood Gundy bond index, and the equity yield to that of aggregate performance of a Toronto, a U.S., a Japanese, and a pan-European market index.

The underlying indexes linked to GICs range from the Toronto 35 Index to the Eurotop 100. Some of the payoffs at maturity are based on the closing level of the underlying index. Some base the payoff on the average monthly level of the underlying index. For some products the investor gets the increase in the index — in other cases, only a percentage of the increase. Some are capped, so they have a maximum potential profit.

A financial product aimed at retail investors should be advertised fairly; it should be transparent (you know what it is and where it fits into a portfolio); its return and risk features should be easy to describe; and it should be relatively simple to value.

Unfortunately, index-linked GICs can be difficult to describe and to value. For example, one GIC offered by a well-known trust company is linked to the markets of the G7 countries. This exotic product pays a floor rate of interest plus an increment that is pegged to an aggregate index of G7 markets, subject to a maximum of 35 percent over a three-year period. A 35 percent return over three years is actually 9.1 percent on an annual compounded basis. Not bad — but 9.1 percent hardly sounds as dramatic as 35 percent!

It's difficult to determine where an index-linked GIC fits into a portfolio. They look simple but the truth is that these products, which are retail versions of "heaven" bonds or structured notes in the derivatives markets, are very hard to value. An index-linked GIC is actually a term deposit plus a call option on the market. The basic equation for valuing call options is known as the Black Scholes option pricing model, and uses the heat exchange equation. This makes valuation difficult for anyone who is not trained in investment finance.

4. FPX Index Portfolios

Another opportunity for passive investing is with ready-made passive portfolios. Richard Croft and Eric Kirzner designed a set of indexes that are published daily in the *National Post*. These "FPX indexes" are passive and investable measures of representative diversified investment portfolios. These indexes are to be used as benchmarks to measure the performance of your own personal portfolio, or as fully investable portfolios if instead you choose to buy one of them.

Each of these diversified FPX indexes contains cash, fixed-income, and equity portions. The cash component, in the form of Government of Canada 91-day Treasury bills, is an insurance policy to provide nominal capital preservation and liquidity as well as protection against rising interest rates. The income component, in the form of "on-the-run" (or bellwether) government of Canada bonds of different maturities, is expected to provide nominal capital preservation and to generate periodic income cash flow for spending or reinvestment. The equity category, in the form of Index Participation Units such as TIPS and SPDRs, is primarily designed for both capital growth and dividend income, with an emphasis on growth.

The differences among the three indexes are primarily in the strategic asset allocation. The FPX growth portfolio is the most aggressive of the three and consists of 5 percent in 91-day T-bills; 25 percent in the medium-term Government bond; and 70 percent in TIPS 100, SPDRs, and WEBS.

The FPX balanced portfolio is a traditional 50/50 portfolio and has 10 percent allocated to a 91-day T-bill; 40 percent evenly split among the three Government of Canadas spanning the maturity structure; and 50 percent in equities, allocated among TIPS 100, SPDRs, and the five WEBS.

The conservative FPX income portfolio consists of 20 percent in a 91-day T-bill; 50 percent evenly split among the three Government of Canadas; and 30 percent in equities, allocated between TIPS 100 and SPDRs.

Each of the three indexes is based on an assumed portfolio size of $100,000. The indexes are denominated and expressed in Canadian dollars. Although each index is marked-to-market daily in Canadian dollars, the U.S. investments are held in U.S. dollars within the portfolio.

U.S. Index Products

1. IPUs

A variety of U.S. index participation units is available. The most popular are the Standard and Poor's Depositary Receipts, or SPDRs. SPDR units are traded in minimum increments of 1/64 of a dollar, or $0.016625. Like TIPS, SPDRs are quoted and traded in one-tenth the value of the S&P 500. For example, if the S&P 500 Index is at 1098.73, the core value of a SPDR will be U.S.$109.87. The market price will generally be about .3 percent to .5 percent higher.

The SPDR Trust expires in 2018. The dividends and other distributions of the 500 companies of the S&P 500 are collected and invested by the trust and then distributed on a quarterly basis to the unitholders. Dividends received from SPDRs are not eligible for the dividend tax credit. Furthermore, they are subject to tax withholding at source. The rate is 15 percent, so if you earn a dividend of $1,000 on your SPDR units, the U.S. government will withhold $150. You can recapture the tax as a foreign tax credit on your tax return.

The NASDAQ-100 shares, introduced in 1999, are based on the NASDAQ-100 Index of 100 mid- and large-cap companies traded on National Association of Securities Dealers stock exchange. The index has a heavy high-tech and Internet emphasis.

The Mid-Cap SPDRs, introduced May 4, 1995, are based on the S&P 400 MidCap Index, comprising mid-cap U.S. companies.

Select sector SPDRs, introduced on December 22, 1998, are specific sector indexes products that are subsets

of the S&P 500 Composite Index. There are nine different IPUs, based on the following: basic industries,
consumer services, consumer staples, cyclicals/transporta-
tion, energy, financial, industrial, technology, and utilities.

DIAMONDS, the first financial product based on the
Dow, were introduced January 20/98. The Dow Jones
Industrial Average is a large-cap index of 30 blue chip
companies traded on the New York Stock Exchange.

All of these U.S. index participation units are qualified
investments for RRSPs, Registered Retirement Income
Funds (RRIFs), and Deferred Profit Sharing Plans
(DPSPs) as RRSP-eligible foreign content.

2. U.S. Index Mutual funds

Two index mutual funds which invest in U.S. portfolios
are the TD Green Line U.S. Index Fund and CIBC U.S.
Equity Index RRSP Fund.

The TD Green Line U.S. Index Fund is pegged to the
S&P 500 Index. However, the tracking error has been
about 1.1 percent per annum over the past five years.
This is the original index fund launched by Green Line,
which now has eight such funds covering all the major
regions of the world.

Over the past two to ten years, this fund has been an
outperformer in its group, returning an average of 19.5
percent annually over the past decade. In fact, over the
past ten years, this was the best-performing fund in its
U.S. index class. TD Green Line also has an RRSP-eligible version (using T-bills and derivatives) and a Canadian
dollar version of the U.S. index fund.

The CIBC U.S. Equity Index RRSP Fund is, like the TD
fund, designed to track the S&P 500. The RRSP version
is relatively new, but so far, its strategy of replicating the
index with cash and S&P 500 futures has kept the tracking error low. This fund is designed strictly for RRSPs.
Holding it outside a tax-sheltered plan could cause
adverse tax consequences.

SPDRs are our choice for non-registered investing; the
Green Line or CIBC fund would be our choice for
RRSPs and RRIFs.

International indexing

1. International IPUs

Index Participation Units have made foreign investing a straightforward task. Their unique design allows them to track the underlying index very closely and you don't have to worry about hand-selecting different valuation methods and accounting standards in foreign countries.

Morgan Stanley World Equity Benchmark Shares (WEBS) were launched in May 1996. Like TIPS and SPDRs, each of these products represents a basket of securities that replicates the total return performance of a specific market index. The WEBS replicate specific Morgan Stanley Capital International (MSCI) indexes. BZW Barclays Global Fund Advisor advises the fund. There are 17 different series; each one is tied to a specific MSCI. (The MSCI World Composite index, launched in 1969, is the most widely used world performance index.) All MSCI are total return indexes with net dividends (after withholding taxes) deemed to be reinvested.

Morgan Stanley World Equity Benchmark WEBS are available for Australia, Austria, Belgium, Canada, France, Germany, Hong Kong, Italy, Japan, Malaysia, Mexico, the Netherlands, Singapore, Spain, Sweden, Switzerland, and the United Kingdom. Two of the more popular WEBS are Mexico and Japan.

WEBS Mexico is designed to track the MSCI Mexico (Free) Index, which consists of 39 stocks and represents about 73 percent of the capitalization of the Mexico market. The portfolio's largest holdings are in two classes of Telefonos de Mexico shares and Grupo Modelo C. Since their debut in 1996, the average tracking error has been about 2.8 percent per annum.

The tracking error is caused by the following factors:

1. *Cash drag.* WEBS hold a small portion of their portfolios in cash.
2. *Advisory fees.* At present, the advisory fee is running at a rate of about 1.39 percent per annum.
3. *Portfolio sampling.* Although WEBS are designed to replicate the specific underlying MSCI index, the approach used by the investment advisor Barclays Global Fund Advisors is to hold a basket of securities

that closely matches the index. The portfolio is allo-cated to a subset of the market, so results may vary positively or negatively from the index.

4. *Regulatory restraints.* Under the U.S. Single Issuer Rule, which is applicable to WEBS, no issuer in a port-folio can represent more than 25 percent of the portfo-lio. Accordingly, Telefonos de Mexico, which has two issues in the MSCI Mexico index of over 30 percent in aggregate, has to be underweighted in the WEBS portfolio to meet the rule. The portfolio is under-weighted in telecommunications.

5. *Revenue differential.* WEBS records dividends on the ex-dividend dates while the MSCI index estimates monthly dividends as 1/12 of the previous month's dividends.

WEBS Japan is pegged to MSCI Japan Index of 308 stocks, most of which are traded on the Tokyo Stock Exchange. They include such giants as Toyota Motor Corp., Honda Motor Corp., Matsushita Electric Industrial Company Limited, and Bank of Tokyo-Mitsubishi Limited. The index represents about 72 percent of the capitalization of the Japanese equity market.

WEBS

COUNTRY	TICKER	INDEX COMPANIES	NO. OF COMPANIES
Australia	EWA	MSCI	49
Austria	EWO	MSCI	24
Belgium	EWK	MSCI	20
Canada	EWC	MSCI	84
France	EWQ	MSCI	74
Germany	EWG	MSCI	69
Hong Kong	EWH	MSCI	38
Italy	EWI	MSCI	55
Japan	EWJ	MSCI	317
Malaysia	EWM	MSCI	76
Mexico	EWW	MSCI (free)	41
Netherlands	EWN	MSCI	22
Singapore	EWS	MSCI	32

. . .

Spain	EWP	MSCI	31
Sweden	EWD	MSCI	30
Switzerland	EWL	MSCI	43
United Kingdom	EWU	MSCI	144

2. International Index Funds

There are a few Canadian indexed global mutual funds.

The CIBC International Index Fund is pegged to the well-known Morgan Stanley Capital International Europe Australia and Far East Index (EAFE). EAFE is as representative an index of non-North America investing as you can find. The major components of the 1,075-company EAFE are the United Kingdom, Japan, Germany, France, and Switzerland.

The CIBC International Index Fund is a physical security-based portfolio. The fund manager's target is to track the EAFE index within 75 basis points. Curiously enough, the fund has positive tracking error so far in its relatively short life. This is most likely serendipity rather than skill — the fund used an approximation rather than a full replication strategy in its start-up period.

There is also a fully RRSP-eligible version of this fund, the *CIBC International Index RRSP Fund*. It also tries to track the EAFE index within 75 points. However, this fund uses a combination of Canadian T-bills and equity index futures to replicate the index. This use of cash and derivatives, means that the fund is fully eligible for an RRSP or RRIF. This version of the fund has potentially adverse tax consequences if held outside an RRSP.

Index Products and Defensive Protection

One knock against index securities is that since they are fully invested (except for index mutual funds that have small cash reserves), they don't provide protection against a bear market. In contrast, some fully managed equity mutual funds hold cash in tactical trading strategies, increasing the component as conditions warrant. The argument is that that in a bear market an insightful fund manager will increase the cash component, thus cushioning the blow and allowing the fund to outperform market indexes, or at least to lose less than the indexes.

There are two fallacies with this argument. First, the fund manager has to be right about assessing when a bear market has struck and to know when to increase the cash component. Yet studies show that fund managers haven't been too successful at this type of market timing. Second, by increasing the cash component, the fund manager is changing the asset allocation. Say an investor is holding a 20/30/50 portfolio, made up of a money market fund, an income fund, and an equity fund. If the fund manager increases the cash component of the equity fund by 10 percent, the investor is now holding a 25/30/45 asset allocation. Presumably, an investor who wanted to change the mix would have done so!

KEEPING MORE OF YOUR PROFITS

Canadian tax rates have eased a bit for lower-to-middle-income people, but they are still very high by international standards. So one of the most important criteria in selecting a mutual fund portfolio continues to be the amount of money you'll end up with in your pocket at the end of the day. Surprisingly, many investors give little or no consideration to the tax consequences of their actions until it's too late to do much about it.

You're liable for taxes on any profits you make from your mutual fund investments, whether as a capital gain, as a dividend cheque from the mutual fund company, or by having any distributions reinvested in additional fund units. But there are several ways to reduce the tax burden, if you know how.

The easiest way to cut taxes is to hold your mutual fund investments in some sort of tax shelter, such as a registered retirement savings plan (RRSP) or a registered retirement income fund (RRIF). Most Canadian mutual funds are eligible for such treatment, either without restriction or under the foreign content rules. (No more than 20 percent of the book value of your RRSP or RRIF can consist of foreign investments, but there are lots of ways around that, as we explain in the next chapter.)

If you can't tax-shelter your mutual fund investments, there are other ways to reduce Revenue Canada's bite by selecting your investments wisely. The corporate structure of the mutual fund you purchase will also have an effect on the taxes you pay, so you should be aware of what it is (most investors never bother to check).

There are two types of mutual fund structures:

Mutual fund trusts. This is the most common. A mutual fund trust will distribute all the income it takes in to unitholders in the form it received the money, so that the fund itself does not have to pay any taxes. This means any capital gains earned by the fund come to you as such, as do dividends, interest, rental income, etc. You'll receive a T3 supplementary form from the fund each year, showing the origin of all income distributed to you. For example, you may have received $1,000 from a fund last year, of which $500 represented your share of its total realized capital gains, $300 your share of dividends from taxable Canadian companies, and $200 your share of interest earned by the fund. Each of these individual amounts will be shown in a box on the T3 supplementary and each must be declared separately on your tax return at the appropriate line.

Mutual fund corporations. In this case, the fund itself is taxable on the income it receives from all sources. Once all taxes have been paid, the fund declares a dividend for distribution to shareholders. This means any income you receive from the fund (except for capital gains, which are treated separately) is in the form of a dividend from a taxable Canadian corporation, and is therefore eligible for the dividend tax credit. It doesn't matter whether the fund originally received the income in the form of interest, foreign dividends, or whatever — in your hands, it's all the same. The net result probably won't be any tax saving, since the fund has already paid appropriate taxes on the income before distributing the profits to shareholders. But it greatly simplifies the tax reporting of your income.

Now, here's a rundown on the types of profits your mutual funds may generate and the tax implications of each. As you'll see, in some cases the treatment will be different depending on whether the fund is structured as a trust or a corporation. Remember that fund units held inside a registered plan do not attract tax.

Capital gains. Whenever you sell units in a mutual fund for a higher price than you originally paid, you've made a capital gain. However, the amount subject to tax will be affected by several factors. These include:

Load charges – If you paid a commission to purchase the fund, this amount can be added to your purchase price for tax purposes, producing a higher "adjusted cost base."

Disposition costs – Any expenses associated with the sale of your units, such as a redemption fee, can be subtracted from the proceeds of the sale before calculating the tax owed.

Reinvested distributions – If you have directed that distributions from the fund be used to purchase additional units, these amounts can be added to the adjusted cost base.

Here's how some of these costs would affect your tax payable. Suppose, for example, you bought 100 shares in a no-load fund for $10 each (total $1,000) and later sold them for $15 each (total $1,500). You would have a capital gain of $500. However, if you paid a front-end load of five percent, you would add $50 to the amount of your original investment, producing an adjusted cost base of $1,050 and reducing the capital gain to $450. If you were charged a $25 fee for closing your account, you would subtract this from the gross proceeds of the sale, reducing the net amount to $1,475 and the capital gain to $425. Of this amount, 75 percent will be taxable.

Note that you must sell or otherwise dispose of your units (such as by contributing them to a self-directed RRSP or exchanging them for units in another fund) to trigger the tax liability. Unrealized capital gains are not taxed. The first 25 percent of any capital gain is free; the balance is added to your income and taxed accordingly.

One way to avoid a big tax bite when you eventually sell your fund units is by crystallizing capital gains when circumstances are right. Here's one way to do it, using as an example 500 units of XYZ Fund that were originally bought at $10 and are now worth $4 (funds can take that kind of beating occasionally). We'll assume the portfolio also holds 1,000 units of DEF Fund, each of which has a capital gain of $5. We'll say the current value of the DEF units is $65.

Purchase price of XYZ units	$5,000
Revenue from sale at current market	2,000
Loss	3,000
Amount eligible for capital loss (75 percent)	2,250
Revenue from sale of 600 shares of DEF Fund	39,000
Capital gain from sale of fund units	3,000
Taxable capital gain (75 percent)	2,250
Net capital gain for tax purposes	0
Tax payable	0

In this case, you crystallized the capital gain on 600 DEF Fund units, but the profit was offset by the loss on the sale of the units in XYZ Fund. You can now repurchase the 600 DEF units at the new cost base of $65, thereby reducing your future tax liability by $5 a share. The other 400 DEF shares retain their original cost base.

Capital gains distributions. Even if you don't sell your fund units, you may be credited with capital gains for tax purposes if the fund distributes some of the profits it makes from the sale of securities to unitholders. These will be indicated in Box 21 of the T3 supplementary slip. These capital gains are treated the same way for tax purposes as those explained above.

Capital gains distributions can sometimes leave mutual fund investors confused and angry. For example, we know of a case where an investor owned 1,000 units in Templeton Growth Fund in his regular brokerage account. Early in 1999, he received a T3 slip from the company, advising him he had to pay taxes on $1,330, his share of the money that Templeton Growth distributed to its unitholders at the end of their fiscal year in June 1998.

This investor couldn't believe it. Templeton Growth gained only a fractional 0.65 percent in 1999 — effectively, it broke even. He hadn't sold any of his units. So how could be possibly be on the hook for taxes on such a large amount of money?

Unfortunately, that's the way the system works. If Templeton Growth had gained 15 percent over the year, he probably wouldn't have thought twice about the tax. But in this situation, he actually ended up out of pocket for the year on this investment.

Here's how. He was a resident of British Columbia, in the highest tax bracket. Since the distribution consisted entirely of capital gains payments, he had to pay at a rate of 40.62 percent, the rate that applied to capital gains for the 1998 tax year. That added $540.25 to his tax bill. He was furious.

He would have been even angrier had he owned units of the Trimark Canadian Fund. During 1998, the total return on the fund was - 4.11 percent. However, investors received a distribution that totalled $2.3179 per unit. Of that, $0.1653 was received in the form of dividends, with the rest treated as capital gains.

For a top-bracket B.C. resident with 1,000 units, that would translate into a tax liability of $934.86. And this for a fund that *lost* money during the year!

This happens because most mutual funds are set up in the form of trusts. As such, they are required to distribute any money earned within the portfolio before the end of their fiscal year. Sources of income include interest, dividends, rental income, and realized capital gains — profits made when positions within the portfolio are sold. Any expenses incurred by the fund are deducted from the distributable amount first.

That's what happened in both the Templeton and Trimark cases — and many others as well. Although the unit value stayed flat or declined, transactions within the portfolio gave rise to the taxable distributions.

Dividends (Canadian). Any dividends from taxable Canadian corporations that are distributed to you must be declared for tax purposes. However, you're allowed to claim the dividend tax credit in connection with these payments, thus reducing the tax impact. If your fund is a trust, you'll find the actual amount of dividends credited to you in Box 23 of the T3 supplementary slip. The taxable amount of dividends eligible for the dividend tax credit appears in Box 32 and the amount of dividend tax credit you can claim will be shown in Box 39.

Dividends (foreign). If your mutual fund is a corporation, you don't have to concern yourself with this type of income. All the tax implications will be dealt with at the corporate level before distributions are made. If your fund is a trust, it's a different story. Any dividends from foreign sources will be shown separately on your T3 supplementary, as will any tax withheld at source. Taxes withheld by another country may be eligible for a foreign tax credit on your Canadian return. This won't be the case, however, if your mutual fund is being held in a RRIF or RRSP. Any foreign withholding tax paid in that situation is lost — you have no recourse under current tax regulations. However, recent amendments to the Canada–U.S. Tax Treaty have ended the requirement that tax be withheld on dividends paid to registered plans from U.S. companies, the main source of this problem in the past.

Note that dividends from foreign corporations received outside a registered plan are not eligible for the dividend tax credit.

Interest. Any interest income credited to you by a mutual fund trust will be shown in Box 26 of the T3 supplementary, headed "Other Income." This income will be subject to tax at your marginal rate (the rate you pay on the last dollar you earn) and is not eligible for any special tax treatment.

Rental income. If you own units in a real estate fund (either closed- or open-end), some of the income you receive may be from rents. This income is eligible for special treatment because capital cost allowance (CCA) may be used to shelter part or all of it from tax. The mutual fund company will normally make the necessary calculations on your behalf. However, you should be aware that any tax advantages gained in this way may be partially offset when you sell your units in the fund. Ask for full details from the mutual fund company before investing.

You'll pay tax at different rates depending on the type of distribution you receive from the mutual fund company. The applicable tax rates in all brackets for dividends, interest, and capital gains are below. They were prepared by Gena Katz, Principal in the National Tax Department of Ernst & Young, and are reproduced here with permission.

All rates assume the investment income is being earned on top of a base salary. They include federal and provincial income taxes, surtaxes, and provincial tax reductions. The basic personal tax credit is allowed for in the calculation.

Tax on capital gains, when applicable, is only paid on 75 percent of the total gain. The rates shown below take that into account and represent the effective rate for the full capital gain.

Dividend rates apply to the actual amount of dividends received from taxable Canadian corporations, not the grossed-up amount.

SPECIAL TIP: If you'd like a precise analysis of your tax situation and have access to the Internet, log on to the Ernst & Young web site (www.eycan.com) and go to the tax page. You'll find a special Personal Tax Calculator. Enter your estimated taxable income and your province of residence and it will determine your approximate tax liability and tell you your marginal tax rate for regular income, dividends, and capital gains. The section also offers an RRSP Tax Calculator and a weekly column, "EY Tax Mailbag." It's a free service.

1999 MARGINAL TAX RATES

BRITISH COLUMBIA

TAXABLE INCOME	INTEREST	DIVIDENDS	CAPITAL GAINS
$7,045 to $7,294	25.42%	6.85%	19.06%
7,295 to 19,794*	25.92%	7.49%	19.44%
19,795 to 29,590	25.42%	6.85%	19.06%
29,591 to 46,735	38.87%	23.67%	29.15%
46,736 to 55,866	40.04%	24.38%	30.03%
55,867 to 59,180	43.90%	26.73%	32.93%
59,181 to 62,391	48.97%	33.07%	36.72%
62,392 to 79,615	49.55%	33.46%	37.16%
79,616 and up	52.27%	35.30%	39.21%

ALBERTA

TAXABLE INCOME	INTEREST	DIVIDENDS	CAPITAL GAINS
$7,045 to $7,294	17.00%	4.58%	12.75%
7,295 to 10,141	17.34%	5.01%	13.01%
10,142 to 17,194*	29.53%	9.25%	22.15%
17,195 to 19,794*	25.47%	7.84%	19.10%
19,795 to 29,590	24.98%	7.23%	18.74%
29,591 to 45,279	37.94%	23.43%	28.46%
45,280 to 46,735	38.86%	23.98%	29.14%
46,736 to 59,180	40.03%	24.69%	30.02%
59,181 to 62,391	44.59%	30.40%	33.44%
62,392 and up	45.17%	30.79%	33.87%

SASKATCHEWAN

TAXABLE INCOME	INTEREST	DIVIDENDS	CAPITAL GAINS
$7,045 to $7,294	17.00%	4.58%	12.75%
7,295 to 7,536	17.34%	5.01%	13.01%
7,537 to 10,000	27.31%	9.91%	20.48%
10,001 to 14,000*	32.66%	16.29%	24.50%
14,001 to 19,794*	27.66%	9.91%	20.75%
19,795 to 20,216	27.16%	9.28%	20.37%
20,217 to 29,590	28.18%	9.75%	21.13%
29,591 to 40,280	41.93%	26.94%	31.45%
40,281 to 46,735	44.10%	28.46%	33.08%
46,736 to 59,180	45.27%	29.17%	33.95%
59,181 to 62,391	50.21%	35.34%	37.65%
62,392 and up	50.79%	35.73%	38.09%

MANITOBA

TAXABLE INCOME	INTEREST	DIVIDENDS	CAPITAL GAINS
$7,045 to $7,294	17.00%	4.58%	12.75%
7,295 to 8,242	17.34%	5.01%	13.01%
8,243 to 19,794*	29.75%	12.44%	22.31%
19,795 to 21,500*	29.25%	11.81%	21.93%
21,501 to 29,590	27.25%	9.31%	20.43%

. . .

TAXABLE INCOME	INTEREST	DIVIDENDS	CAPITAL GAINS
29,591 to 30,000	40.61%	26.01%	30.46%
30,001 to 46,735	42.61%	28.51%	31.96%
46,736 to 59,180	43.78%	29.23%	32.84%
59,181 to 62,391	48.37%	34.96%	36.28%
62,392 and up	48.95%	35.35%	36.71%

ONTARIO

TAXABLE INCOME	INTEREST	DIVIDENDS	CAPITAL GAINS
$7,045 to $7,294	17.00%	4.58%	12.75%
7,295 to 9,328	17.34%	5.01%	13.01%
9,329 to 11,735*	30.67%	8.96%	23.01%
11,736 to 19,794*	24.19%	6.99%	18.14%
19,795 to 29,590	23.72%	6.39%	17.79%
29,591 to 46,735	36.27%	22.33%	27.20%
46,736 to 51,199	37.44%	23.04%	28.08%
51,200 to 59,180	39.49%	24.29%	29.62%
59,181 to 60,155	44.05%	30.04%	33.04%
60,156 to 62,391	48.17%	32.53%	36.13%
62,392 and up	48.75%	32.92%	36.57%

QUEBEC

TAXABLE INCOME	INTEREST	DIVIDENDS	CAPITAL GAINS
$6,786 to $7,044	20.06%	12.73%	15.05%
7,045 to 7,294	34.26%	16.55%	25.70%
7,295 to 19,794*	34.54%	16.91%	25.91%
19,795 to 25,000	34.26%	16.55%	25.70%
25,001 to 29,590	37.27%	20.31%	27.95%
29,591 to 46,735	44.78%	29.71%	33.59%
46,736 to 50,000	45.95%	30.42%	34.46%
50,001 to 59,180	48.96%	34.18%	36.72%
59,181 to 62,391	51.60%	37.48%	38.70%
62,392 and up	52.18%	37.87%	39.14%

NOVA SCOTIA

TAXABLE INCOME	INTEREST	DIVIDENDS	CAPITAL GAINS
$7,045 to $7,294	17.00%	4.58%	12.75%
7,295 to 10,055	17.34%	5.01%	13.01%
10,056 to 15,000*	27.30%	7.89%	20.48%
15,001 to 19,794*	32.31%	14.14%	24.23%
19,795 to 21,000*	31.78%	13.47%	23.83%
21,001 to 29,590	26.78%	7.22%	20.08%
29,591 to 46,735	40.95%	24.94%	30.71%
46,736 to 59,180	42.12%	25.65%	31.59%
59,181 to 62,391	46.98%	31.73%	35.24%
62,392 to 79,258	47.56%	32.12%	35.67%
79,259 and up	49.23%	33.24%	36.92%

NEW BRUNSWICK

TAXABLE INCOME	INTEREST	DIVIDENDS	CAPITAL GAINS
$7,045 to $7,294	27.20%	7.33%	20.40%
7,295 to 19,794*	27.74%	8.01%	20.81%
19,795 to 29,590	27.20%	7.33%	20.40%
29,591 to 46,736	41.60%	25.33%	31.20%
46,737 to 59,180	42.77%	26.05%	32.08%
59,181 to 62,390	47.71%	32.21%	35.78%
62,391 to 96,874	48.29%	32.61%	36.21%
96,875 and up	49.68%	33.55%	37.26%

PRINCE EDWARD ISLAND

TAXABLE INCOME	INTEREST	DIVIDENDS	CAPITAL GAINS
$7,045 to $7,294	26.95%	7.26%	20.21%
7,295 to 19,794*	27.48%	7.94%	20.61%
19,795 to 29,590	26.95%	7.26%	20.21%
29,591 to 46,735	41.21%	25.10%	30.91%
46,736 to 48,873	42.38%	26.52%	31.79%
48,874 to 59,180	43.90%	27.45%	32.93%
59,181 to 62,391	48.97%	33.07%	36.72%
62,392 and up	49.55%	33.46%	37.16%

NEWFOUNDLAND

TAXABLE INCOME	INTEREST	DIVIDENDS	CAPITAL GAINS
$7,045 to $7,294	28.73%	7.75%	21.55%
7,295 to 19,794*	29.30%	8.46%	21.98%
19,795 to 29,590	28.73%	7.75%	21.55%
29,591 to 46,735	43.94%	26.76%	32.96%
46,736 to 58,721	45.11%	27.47%	33.83%
58,722 to 59,180	46.90%	28.56%	35.18%
59,181 to 62,391	52.32%	35.33%	39.24%
62,392 and up	52.90%	35.72%	39.67%

NORTHWEST TERRITORIES AND NUNAVUT

TAXABLE INCOME	INTEREST	DIVIDENDS	CAPITAL GAINS
$7,045 to $7,294	24.65%	6.65%	18.49%
7,295 to 19,794*	25.14%	7.26%	18.86%
19,795 to 29,590	24.65%	6.65%	18.49%
29,591 to 46,735	37.70%	22.96%	28.28%
46,736 to 59,180	38.87%	23.67%	29.15%
59,181 to 62,391	43.36%	29.28%	32.52%
62,392 and up	43.94%	29.67%	32.95%

YUKON TERRITORY

TAXABLE INCOME	INTEREST	DIVIDENDS	CAPITAL GAINS
$7,045 to $7,294	25.50%	6.88%	19.13%
7,295 to 19,794*	26.01%	7.51%	19.51%
19,795 to 29,590	25.50%	6.88%	19.13%
29,591 to 46,735	39.00%	23.75%	29.25%
46,736 to 59,180	40.17%	24.46%	30.13%
59,181 to 60,667	44.81%	30.26%	33.60%
60,668 to 62,391	45.53%	30.75%	34.15%
62,392 and up	46.11%	31.14%	34.58%

*Higher marginal income tax bracket results from the recapture of provincial tax reductions allowed at lower levels of income.

There are a few other important tax considerations to remember when buying mutual funds:

Make sure your registered and non-registered portfolios are structured so you pay the least possible tax. As a general rule, you should hold fixed income and money market mutual funds (those which are designed to generate interest) inside a registered plan, such as an RRSP or RRIF. That's because interest income is taxed at the highest rate, as you can see from the above tables. Keep equity, dividend, and real estate funds outside the registered plan, since profits earned by these types of funds are taxed more favourably. If your money is being professionally managed, check to see these basic tax guidelines are being observed. We have seen at least one case where an investment house replicated exactly the same portfolio in a client's registered and non-registered account. As a result, the customer was paying several thousand dollars a year in unnecessary taxes.

A Willowdale, Ontario, reader recently wrote to ask how maintaining tax-effective registered and non-registered portfolios could be done in an easy way.

"I try to save outside my RRSP (for a house, car, etc.) but you recommend income and mortgage funds for this purpose since they are better suited for short-term goals," he said. "Equities, on the other hand, are too volatile for short-term savings. But they are more tax-effective than interest-bearing investments outside an RRSP. How does an investor deal with these conflicts?"

In this kind of situation, we recommend investing in conservatively managed equity mutual funds outside the RRSP and keeping the savings component (e.g., the mortgage fund) inside a self-directed plan. Then, when you need the money, you can swap your equity units for the mortgage units inside the fund, sell the mortgage units, and use the cash for buying the house or whatever. However, you'll have to pay tax on any capital gains in the equity units at that point. See the next tip.

Remember that switching from one fund to another may trigger a tax liability. Revenue Canada takes the position that a switch is the same as a sale. If you've made a capital gain on the fund you're leaving, that profit will be subject to tax at the capital gains rate when you file your next return. Obviously, this won't apply if the switch takes place within an RRSP or RRIF. A few fund groups offer "umbrella" funds, which allow you to switch from one "section" of the fund to another without triggering a capital gain. AGF, C.I., Synergy, and AIM are among the companies that use this approach for some of their funds. However, the tax deferral is only temporary. When you eventually sell your units in the umbrella fund, taxes will have to be paid.

Buying funds at year-end may cause tax problems. Many funds make an annual profit distribution at year-end to unitholders of record on December 31, or earlier. If you buy into the fund a few days before, you'll receive the same payment as someone who has owned it all year. Sounds great? It's not. As financial advisor Stanley Tepner pointed out in *The Globe and Mail*, you end up paying tax on money you didn't earn. Here's how. Suppose you own 1,000 fund units which you just bought. They are valued at $10 each on December 31. The total value of your investment therefore equals $10,000. The fund manager declares a $1 distribution. You receive a cheque for $1,000. Because this is an open-end fund, the net asset value of the units is adjusted to $9, reflecting the distribution payment. You still have $10,000 in assets — only now you have to pay tax on $1,000 of that amount. You're out of pocket several hundred dollars, just because you bought in at the wrong time. The solution? Buy new units after the first of the year or choose funds that make distributions more frequently, thereby minimizing this effect.

Thomas Kingissepp of Maple Partners Financial Products offers this additional advice: "What is often overlooked is that the tax problem with buying mutual funds is a timing issue, not an additional tax. The distribution to the investor which gives rise to the tax is reinvested into additional units of the mutual fund. Thus, the investor's total cost base in the mutual fund has been increased and the investor will consequently have a smaller capital gain or a larger capital loss in the future when all of the units of the mutual fund are sold or transferred to an RRSP.

"Thus, the impact of the tax on the distribution increases the longer the investor holds the mutual fund and the longer the investor has to wait to obtain the tax benefit of the increased tax cost base. Conversely, a shorter holding period might mean that the impact of this tax is lessened. Thus, consider the magnitude of investment returns given up by waiting to buy until after the distribution, your expected holding period, purchases throughout the year as well as purchases after the first of the year, and funds that make more frequent distributions."

Finally, to close this chapter, here are some tax-wise mutual fund investing strategies for income and growth investors with money outside a registered plan.

For income investors

Select funds with distributions that attract minimal tax. Interest income gets no tax break, so you should avoid funds that pay mainly interest if you are investing outside a registered plan. Dividend distributions are the most desirable type, since they attract the lowest tax rate. Capital gains distributions will cost more in tax dollars, but are still better than interest payments.

Consider adding funds with tax-sheltered distributions. Real estate funds, both open-end (e.g., Investors Real Property Fund) and closed-end (e.g., Riocan REIT), shelter a portion of their distributions from rental income through the use of capital cost allowance (depreciation). So part of the money you receive is tax-deferred. In 1998, for example, Riocan unitholders received a total of $0.95 per share, of which 61.2% was not taxable. Here's how it worked out. We used the case of a top-bracket Ontario taxpayer. All figures are per unit. The $9 adjusted cost base is arbitrary. Numbers have been rounded to the nearest penny.

Riocan 1998 distribution per unit	$0.95
Amount not taxed	0.58
Taxable total	0.37
Amount eligible for capital gains treatment	0.06
Amount taxed at full rate	0.31
Total tax payable	0.18
After-tax income	0.77

...

Effective tax rate	18.9%
Previous adjusted cost base	9.00
New adjusted cost base ($9 - 0.58)	8.42

As you can see, the actual tax paid was only 18.7 percent of the total amount received. Compare that to a 1998 top bracket Ontario rate of 50.29 percent on interest income, 37.72 percent on capital gains, and 33.96 percent on dividends, and you can see the REIT is far more tax-efficient.

However, the untaxed portion of the distribution (about $0.58 a unit) has to be subtracted from the adjusted cost base — the amount you originally paid for the shares, less any previously untaxed distributions. This way, some of the money Revenue Canada loses now is recouped later when the units are sold, because the taxable capital gains will go up.

A similar situation applies with funds that specialize in income trusts, such as the Guardian Monthly High Income Fund. It paid out $0.72 a unit in 1998, of which $0.49 was not taxable.

For growth investors

Choose funds with a history of low distributions: If you don't need to generate steady income from your fund investments, select funds with a track record of good capital growth and small distributions.

Crystallize gains periodically. Manage your portfolio so that you control the timing of any tax liabilities, rather than being at the mercy of managers and markets. Look back at the example of the XYZ and DEF Funds we used to illustrate this point earlier in the chapter.

Don't buy into funds just before their fiscal year-end. Most funds make annual distributions in the last two weeks before their year-end. If you buy in just prior to a distribution, and the money is not in a registered plan, you'll be on the hook to pay taxes on what in your case will amount to a return of capital.

And don't assume all funds have a December 31 year-end. Most do, but some, like Templeton Growth, have other fiscal years (Templeton Growth's is June 30).

WRAPPING UP

Revenue Canada is going to take some of your investing profits, no matter what you do. But there are several ways to minimize the tax bite. These are the two keys:

1. Understand how different forms of investment income are taxed, and which offer the best advantages for investors.

2. Choose mutual funds or other types of securities that maximize after-tax returns in all non-registered portfolios.

WHO'S AFRAID OF THE FOREIGN CONTENT RULE?

Something very strange is happening in Ottawa. Despite pressures from every imaginable source, Finance Minister Paul Martin adamantly refuses to budge a centimetre on the 20 percent foreign content rule for registered plans. Never mind that it is costing Canadians millions of dollars a year in potential investment earnings. Ignore the fact that every study shows that greater international diversification reduces risk. Forget about the loopholes that are so gaping that they make the Grand Canyon look like a ditch. Mr. Martin will not be moved. Maybe at some point, he says. But not now.

The problem with this stance is that it is a sham. Knowledgeable investors can fill their RRSPs and RRIFs with foreign content if they wish to do so, and more such options are becoming available all the time. It's simply a matter of knowing how it's done and then selecting the investment products that best meet your specific needs.

Here are the choices currently available and our assessment of their effectiveness.

CANADIAN MUTUAL FUNDS THAT MAXIMIZE FOREIGN CONTENT

A Canadian fund may be fully RRSP-eligible and still have 20 percent of its portfolio in foreign securities. If you hold such a fund in your registered plan, the foreign content in its portfolio does *not* count towards your personal limit. If you want to increase the foreign content in a registered plan in this way, seek out Canadian funds that maximize their allowable international holdings. Using only this approach, you could effectively increase the foreign content in your RRSP to 36 percent. This would be achieved by investing 20 percent of your plan in international securities and the balance in Canadian mutual funds that maximize foreign content in their own portfolios.

Effectiveness rating: Excellent.

Pseudo-Canadian mutual funds (passive)

When the foreign content rule first began to emerge as a serious problem back in the early '90s, a few Canadian companies introduced a radical new concept. They would load up a mutual fund's portfolio with Treasury bills, to 80 percent of the assets, thus giving the fund full RRSP eligibility. They would then use the T-bills as security to invest in stock index futures on a foreign exchange. Initially, most of the funds focused on Standard and Poor's 500 futures in the U.S. but today you can invest in pseudo-Canadian index funds that have positions in all parts of the world. The range and variety of these funds is now extremely impressive. Index (passive) investing is still the basic approach used by this group, although some of these funds, such as C.I. American RSP Fund, include some active stock selection.

All these funds use derivatives to some degree. But don't let that scare you off. There is no leveraging involved here, which could result in an unacceptably high degree of risk in an RRSP. The fund's returns will normally reflect the performance of the underlying index or indexes.

So why are there such variations in the rate of return? Why did the CIBC U.S. Index RRSP Fund gain 23 percent over the year to April 30, 1999, while the Scotia CanAm Stock Index Fund added just 18.1 percent? Both are based on the Standard and Poor's 500 Index, after all. In this particular case, MER accounts for almost half a percentage point of the return differential — the CIBC fund has an MER of 0.9 percent, while the Scotia fund comes in at 1.34 percent. The higher the MER on an index fund, the greater the negative impact on the bottom line.

However, that's not enough to explain the difference in this case. Other factors may include the market timing for investing new cash, currency fluctuations (some funds are more active than others in terms of currency management), and the expiration date of the futures contracts they hold. (If the market has fallen between the time a contract was purchased and the time it expires, it has no value. Contracts on the S&P 500 mature in March, June, September, and December of each year.)

All this makes the management of these funds more complex than it may appear at first glance. So it isn't a case of all being cut from the same cloth. Some are indeed better than others. Here's a rundown on our top choices in various categories. The best way to hold them is in a self-directed RRSP.

> Note: These funds are strictly for registered plans. They aren't recommended for taxable accounts. Most companies have a non-RRSP version of the same fund available.

International Equity Funds

Top choice: Global Strategy Diversified World Equity Fund. This fund, run by Rupert Robinson of Rothschild International Asset Management in London, can invest in individual stocks as well as index futures, options, and forward currency contracts. Although the fund normally is exposed to a wide range of international currencies, Robinson may at times hedge some of the assets into Canadian or U.S. dollars to protect against the effects of anticipated currency declines.

At the start of 1999, about 47 percent of the fund's equity exposure was in U.S. markets, with slightly more than 50 percent of the assets in American currency. Europe accounted for about 36 percent of the equity exposure; Asia, including Japan, about 11.5 percent; the rest was scattered around. So this was very much a North America – Europe fund at that time. That explains its strong one-year performance (11.2 percent to the end of April 1999) and the very good three-year average annual compound rate of return of 15.2 percent.

Runner-up: Talvest Global RRSP Fund. Like the Global Strategy Fund, this one is very heavily weighted to the U.S. and Europe. Far East exposure is minimal, with only slightly more than five percent of assets in that part of the world.

Manager Guy Normandin takes an active approach to currency management, and lately has been hedging the portfolio in favour of Canadian dollars.

The three-year average annual compound rate of return of 17 percent to April 30/99 is actually better than the performance of the Global Strategy entry. However, the GS fund has looked better recently.

U.S. Equity Funds

Top choice: CIBC U.S. Index RRSP Fund. It may be just lucky timing that has allowed this fund, which is designed to track the S&P 500 Index, to outperform all its peers over the past two years, with an average annual compound rate of return of 32.1 percent to April 30/99. Plus, part of the gain is due to the fact the Canadian dollar has been so weak against its U.S. counterpart.

But you can't argue with success. This fund offers a winning combination of no load fees, a low MER, and exposure to a key U.S. index without eating into your foreign content. The returns are enhanced because the managers have a large part of the short-term portfolio in higher-yielding securities like GMAC discount notes.

Runner-up: Scotia CanAm Stock Index Fund. This fund also tracks the S&P 500 and is no-load; however, the MER is higher than that of the CIBC fund. The three-year average annual compound rate of return to April 30 was an excellent 24.7 percent. Wouldn't that look good in your RRSP? This portfolio does not use a currency hedging strategy, which is one of the reasons it did not do as well as the CIBC fund when the loonie was declining.

Best of the rest: Canada Trust AmeriGrowth Fund. This one is also based on the S&P 500. Returns are not quite as good as for the Scotia fund, but they aren't far off. It also benefits from being no-load.

C.I. American RSP Fund. Unlike the other recommended funds in the U.S. equity category, this one buys individual stocks as well as S&P 500 futures. Recent large positions included AT&T, American Express, Time Warner, and Chase Manhattan, among others. The fund's three-year average annual compound rate of return to April 30 was 20.3 percent — very good, but not up to the level of the pure S&P plays. A much higher MER (2.38 percent) is a major contributing factor to the lower returns.

European Equity Funds

Top choice: Global Strategy Diversified Europe Fund. This fund is run by the same person who manages the Global Strategy Diversified World Fund, Rupert Robinson of Rothschild Asset Management. It provides exposure to a broad cross-section of European nations through index futures on several key exchanges. The U.K. dominates the holdings, with Germany, France, and Switzerland coming up behind. There are some very small positions in eastern Europe as well.

Currency exposure is primarily to Europe but the manager can at times hedge back into Canadian or U.S. dollars.

Results have been good. The fund averaged 21.4 percent annually over the three-year period to April 30.

Runner-up: Canada Trust EuroGrowth Fund. Canada Trust offers several good funds that fall into the pseudo-Canadian class. This is another of them. The portfolio is heavily concentrated in the U.K., Germany- and France. Three, year average annual compound rate of return to April 30 was 19.5 percent. If you have an RRSP with Canada Trust, this and the AmeriGrowth fund should certainly be in it.

International Balanced Funds

Although most passively managed pseudo-Canadian funds focus on equities, there are some other types available for investors who want to reduce risk. The balanced fund category offers several good options.

Top choice: C.I. International Balanced RSP Fund. You'll find a little bit of everything here: individual stocks, index futures on major exchanges, some emerging markets exposure, bonds, short-term notes — it's all here but the kitchen sink. Recent emphasis is very much on developed Europe and the United States. Equities represented about 46 percent of the asset mix, bonds about 15 percent, and the rest was in cash and short-term notes. That's a huge cash position (38.5 percent) for a balanced fund, which means the downside risk is quite low.

The returns in the international balanced category fall well short of those for pure equity funds. However, this fund managed to gain 11.5 percent annually for the three years to April 30. That's a lot better than the average Canadian balanced fund.

Runner-up: Universal World Balanced RSP Fund. This fund has been coming on strong and ranks very close to the C.I. entry in our estimation. You won't go wrong with either. The three-year average annual gain here was 12.5 percent to April 30. Recent bond exposure was higher here (27 percent of the portfolio), while cash at 17 percent was much lower than in the C.I. entry.

Managers Michael Landry and Barbara Trebbi of Mackenzie Financial's U.S. operation were recently underweighting North America in this portfolio in favour of Europe. They also provided more exposure to Asia than the C.I. fund.

International Bond Funds

Top choice: AGF RSP Global Bond Fund. This fund had a bit of a rough time recently because of weak bond prices, but the one-year return to April 30 is still above average for the international bond fund category at seven percent.

Overall effectiveness rating for passive pseudo-Canadian funds: Good.

Pseudo-Canadian Mutual funds (active)

Until 1999, all pseudo-Canadian funds were passively managed for the most part. But now all that is changing. A number of companies have announced that they were launching clones of existing foreign content funds that are fully RRSP eligible. That means you can buy the same international fund in either an RRSP version or a non-RRSP version, something we have not seen before.

If this appears to be nose-thumbing on the part of the fund industry in Mr. Martin's direction, so be it. The fund companies seem to be operating under the assumption that the Finance Minister would rather have them circumvent the foreign content rule in this way than force him into a position where he has no choice but to change it.

The new funds operate in a manner that is somewhat similar to the mutual fund–linked notes that TD Securities have successfully marketed during the past two RRSP seasons.

Here's how they work. You, the investor, put cash into one of these funds — let's use the Trimark Select Growth RSP Fund to illustrate. That money is used to buy a portfolio of money market securities: T-bills, bankers' acceptances, corporate short-term notes, and the like. A third party (called a counterparty), likely a bank, then invests a comparable amount of money in units of the underlying foreign fund, which in this case is the Trimark Select Growth Fund. Through a forward contract arrangement between Trimark and the counterparty, the returns on the units held by the bank are "swapped" back to the unitholders in the RSP fund. The bank receives the equivalent of the return on the money market assets plus a fee for its trouble.

Complicated? You bet! Legal? Yes. Revenue Canada issued a ruling in August that declared these clones are on-side.

This innovation broadens the range of RRSP-eligible international funds significantly.

Here are some of the RRSP clones that had been announced at the time of writing.

Ivy RSP Foreign Equity Fund. This is a new addition to Mackenzie Financial's conservatively managed Ivy family. Responsibility for managing the underlying Ivy Foreign Equity Fund returned to veteran Jerry Javasky after the departure of Bill Kanko in early 1999. The underlying fund is heavily U.S.-oriented. The fund has a large cash cushion (20 percent) to protect investors in the event of a market drop. The underlying fund has been an above-average performer since its launch (Javasky managed it originally), and shows a 16.7 percent average annual compound rate of return for the five years to April 30. This makes the new clone an excellent candidate for an RRSP. Note that in the case of the two Mackenzie RRSP clones, you'll be charged a higher MER (40 to 50 basis points) than investors in the core fund will pay. So your returns here will be about half a percent a year below what investors in the underlying fund will receive.

Universal RSP Select Managers Fund. This is an RRSP clone of a Mackenzie fund that draws on stock picks from five of their top managers. The idea was copied from the highly successful AIM Global Theme Fund. Five managers of other funds select ten stocks each to make up the portfolio of this one. The managers are Brian Ashford-Russell of Henderson Investors, who specializes in global technology; Stephen Peak, also of Henderson (European stocks); Jim Broadfoot of Mackenzie's American operation (U.S. emerging growth stocks); Peter Cundill (global value); and Paul Baran (U.S. blue chip stocks).

The core fund got off to a very impressive start, with a gain of 42.1 percent for the six months to April. The managers are all top-drawer in their own areas of expertise and the inclusion of both growth and value styles of investing may contribute to reduced volatility. Our only concern is that the parent fund hasn't been around long enough to demonstrate its staying power, and it appears to be somewhat more aggressively managed than Ivy Foreign Equity. For those reasons, we would opt for the Ivy clone at this time.

Trimark Select Growth RSP Fund. Bill Kanko left Ivy Foreign Equity in April to take charge of Trimark Select Growth and the companion Trimark Fund. Both have good long-term records, but recent results have been sub-par. Kanko should breathe new life into these funds, however, so I expect an upturn in the numbers. One advantage in using this clone is that Trimark is going to try to structure the fund in such a way that the return will exactly mirror that of Select Growth. If they succeed, investors won't be penalized for buying the RRSP version.

AGF RSP American Growth Fund. The parent fund is one of the best of its type. Managed by Steve Rogers, it has produced some eye-popping numbers in recent years.

BPI RSP American Equity Value Fund. Another top U.S. entry, now part of the C.I. organization. The fund is managed out of Orlando by Paul Holland. Strong emphasis on high-tech stocks.

Fidelity RSP International Portfolio Fund. This is one of the best choices for RRSP investors who want global exposure. The parent fund has an excellent long-term record.

Effectiveness rating: Potentially excellent.

Index-linked GICs

When interest rates fell to their lowest levels since the early '60s, the bottom fell out of the lucrative GIC market. Financial institutions, in a scramble to revive investor interest and keep at least some of the money from flowing into mutual funds, resurrected a concept that had first been tried with limited success in the '80s — the index-linked GIC.

The idea is simple. Instead of receiving a specific rate of return on your invested money, your interest payment is calculated on the performance of an underlying stock index, such as the TSE 300. The formulas used for the calculation vary according to the issuer of the certificate, but the bottom line is that if the index scores a big gain during the term of your GIC, you'll do quite well. If the index goes down, you at least get your capital back.

The relevance of this to RRSP/RRIF investors is that many of these GICs are based on foreign indexes. The S&P 500 is the one most commonly used, but you can also buy index-linked GICs that are tied to a combination of overseas markets. Because these certificates are issued by Canadian financial institutions, they are fully RRSP-eligible. Even though the return is tied to the performance of a foreign stock exchange, you do not actually own any foreign content. So you can fill your registered plans with these things, if you wish.

Effectiveness rating: Average.

Index-linked notes

A variation of the index-linked GICs, these are notes issued by Canadian financial institutions and government agencies that base their return on a foreign market. They are RRSP/RRIF-eligible for the same reasons as the index-linked GICs. In some cases, these notes are publicly traded, which means they can be easily bought and sold on a stock exchange. They have never caught on with investors, however.

Effectiveness rating: Average.

Fund-linked notes

Still on the same theme, TD Securities has been very active over the past couple of years issuing and promoting special fund-linked notes, which were designed by TD and Midland Walwyn (now Merrill Lynch) and first offered for sale during the 1997 RRSP season. These notes offer a return linked to a specific international mutual fund. Think of them as a variation of index-linked GICs, and you won't be far off the mark in terms of how they work, except in this case a mutual fund, not a stock index, is the performance benchmark, and there is no guarantee against loss. The funds TD has used include Templeton Growth, Templeton International Stock, Fidelity European Growth, Fidelity Growth America, and Fidelity International Portfolio. Since the notes are 100 percent RRSP/RRIF-eligible, it means you can hold proxies for these funds in your registered plan without infringing on your foreign content. However, your return will not be as high as if you invested directly in the fund itself.

What you are actually buying is a ten-year bond issued by one of Canada's big banks. The return on that bond is directly related to the chosen mutual fund, but the bond qualifies as Canadian content; it doesn't matter how the rate of return is calculated.

But you pay a price for avoiding the foreign content rule. It starts with your initial purchase. For every $100 you invest, you'll pay $1 in sales commissions, so the net value of each note is actually $99. Once each year, the notes will receive interest which will reflect the distribution made by the underlying fund to its unitholders. However, an administration fee will be deducted. Typically, TD has charged about half a percent of the fund's average daily net asset value during the previous year. Consider this an extra management fee, on top of the fund's regular charges. The interest payments will be reinvested in additional notes.

At the end of ten years, the notes are redeemed for an amount equal to the net asset value of the underlying fund at that time, with some possible adjustments.

The notes are not listed on any stock exchange; however, you can cash out early by paying a redemption fee, similar to that of a back-end load mutual fund.

The average annual compound rate of return on these notes over time will probably work out to between 0.5 percent and 1.5 percent below that of the underlying fund. Although they are eligible for RRIFs, think twice about using them for such plans because the distributions are all automatically reinvested, meaning there is no cash flow.

If the new concept of actively managed pseudo-Canadian funds takes hold, as we expect it will, notes of this type may disappear because of their high cost and cumbersome nature. But you could still see them around during the 2000 RRSP season.

Effectiveness rating: Poor.

U.S.-dollar GICs and term deposits

If you buy foreign currency GICs and term deposits issued by a Canadian financial institution, they're considered to be domestic content in your RRSP. U.S.-dollar certificates are by far the most common. So if you're worried about the future direction of the loonie, you can hedge your bets by adding more U.S.-dollar strength to your retirement plan at virtually no risk.

Effectiveness rating: Excellent, if you don't mind the low return.

Foreign currency bonds

Canadian governments and corporations frequently issue bonds denominated in other currencies, such as Swiss francs, Euros, Japanese yen, and U.S. dollars. Why? Because many foreign investors don't like the currency risk associated with holding securities denominated in Canadian dollars, so we have accommodated them with bonds in their home currencies. All these bonds are 100 percent eligible for RRSPs and RRIFs. That's because the foreign content rules don't focus on the currency in which a security is denominated, but rather on the country of origin. Since all these bonds were issued by Canadian entities, they're RRSP-eligible. This means you can, if you wish, fill a self-directed RRSP with foreign currency holdings.

Bonds issued by organizations that have received a seal of approval from the Department of Finance, like the World Bank, can also be held without restriction in a registered plan. These bonds are usually denominated in major international currencies. Just be careful about adding a lot of foreign currency exposure at a time when the Canadian dollar is on the rise; you'll get whipsawed.

Effectiveness rating: Average.

Labour-sponsored venture capital funds

In the fall of 1998, the federal government did a U-turn in its policy on labour-sponsored funds and the foreign content rule. There has been a rule on the books for many years that anyone who owns shares in a qualifying small business in an RRSP can increase their foreign content about 20 percent on a three-for-one basis — three dollars worth of extra foreign content for each one dollar's worth of small business shares, as long as the total foreign content in the plan does not exceed 40 percent.

Labour-sponsored venture capital funds had lobbied for years to be classified as "small businesses" for purposes of this rule, knowing it would help to generate sales. Revenue Canada always said no. But in 1998, with the labour funds in serious trouble, the federal Department of Finance took another look at the whole situation and decided that a policy change was needed. Result: these funds now come under the small business rule and you can use any holdings in them to increase your foreign content. The change applies both to new purchases and to units you already have in your registered plan.

So if you buy $5,000 worth of a labour-sponsored venture capital fund for an RRSP, you can add another $15,000 worth of foreign content, as long as you stay under the 40 percent mark.

Effectiveness rating: Good.

WRAPPING UP

The 20 percent foreign content rule for registered plans is effectively a joke. It no longer needs to inhibit investors from creating geographically diversified portfolios with as much, or as little, domestic content as they wish. If you want to stick with mutual funds, you can now choose between a wide range of index offerings, or from a growing selection of RRSP-eligible clones of popular actively managed U.S. and international funds. You can also add a selection of U.S. or other foreign stocks to your portfolio by using the additional foreign content made available when you invest in labour-sponsored venture capital funds.

In fact, there are so many loopholes in this archaic rule that we have only given you a sampling here. If you go at it the right way, you could have 100 percent foreign content in your registered plans and no one could do anything about it.

INSURING YOUR FUTURE

Over the last three years, there's been a lot of talk about investment funds sponsored by insurance companies, or, as they are called in the industry, segregated funds. Most of the talk has been because mutual fund companies have begun marketing the concept as an add-on to their product offerings. (We provide complete reviews of all segregated fund products in *Gordon Pape's 2000 Buyer's Guide to Mutual Funds.*)

THE PROS AND CONS OF SEG FUNDS

Segregated funds are really insurance contracts that provide death benefits and principal guarantees. There is a risk premium attached to those guarantees, which is why segregated funds were traditionally not good investments. Before this new wave of segregated funds came to market, the insurance companies would not only issue the guarantees, they also managed the funds. Which was a recipe for poor performance.

Think about it: If you are the insurance company guaranteeing a worst-case scenario, it stands to reason you would manage the funds to avoid that scenario. So obviously the mandate of the fund was straightforward: first, avoid loss of principal at all costs; second, to produce positive returns. In that order.

So, historically, good segregated funds tended to weather downturns in the market reasonably well, but often fell short during periods when the financial markets were rising. And in the investment business, quite apart from the insurance business, the financial markets rise far more often than they fall. So you rarely read much about segregated funds in the financial press. They were seldom at the top of the performance parade, nor were they usually at the bottom.

There's been a major change in this segment over the last few years. It all started with a product line of new segregated funds from Manulife Financial, entitled Guaranteed Investment Funds (GIF). What made this original product so different was the underlying mandate of the fund manager. In this case, Manulife would buy units of a traditional mutual fund — like the Trimark Canadian Fund, or the AGF Growth and Income Fund — and then apply an insurance wrapper. In this way, Manulife managed the risks, and the fund manager concentrated on the returns.

The product was so successful that Manulife had to turn off the taps. They relaunched the product under a new label, GIF Encore, and it's the only line of Manulife segregated products investors can buy now.

Since the introduction of GIF, most of the major mutual fund companies have enlisted the assistance of an insurance company and have begun to market their own in-house family of segregated funds. Performance, then, is not the issue it once was. The issue today is the guarantee on your investment principal, and how much that guarantee costs.

Speaking of the guarantees

With so many mutual fund companies now aggressively marketing the guarantees surrounding segregated funds, we need to examine the guarantees more closely. Remember, mutual fund companies market segregated funds, they don't insure them. In the end, the guarantee is issued by an insurance company, and the value of the guarantee is directly related to the financial strength of the insurance company.

These are some of the features:

1. *Maturity guarantees.* All segregated funds come with some type of guarantee, which effectively limits or eliminates the potential loss of principal. The Office of the Superintendent of Financial Institutions dictates that segregated funds must have a minimum guarantee of 75 percent at maturity or death (we'll talk about the death guarantee in a moment). Most new companies, however, extend the guarantee to 100 percent of the original principal investment at both maturity and death. The maturity date is usually set ten years after the initial deposit. Of course, if the fund were to rise in value over the ten-year period, you would get the market value of the fund.

   For the record, we're not enthused about any segregated fund that has a 75 percent maturity guarantee. There is only a nine percent chance the underlying fund will be worth less than its original value ten years later — which means there is a possibility you may have to invoke the 100 percent maturity guarantee. But there is virtually no chance that the fund will be worth less than 75 percent of its original value — so there is no economic value to a 75 percent guarantee.

   We also have reservations about the cost of a 100 percent maturity guarantee. We'll explain in a moment. But first, let's understand what we mean by the guarantee. Say you invest $10,000 in a segregated equity fund with a 100 percent guarantee. Ten years later, your fund declines, leaving the total value of your investment at $9,000. Since the fund has a 100 percent guarantee, the insurance company would issue a "top up" payment, bringing the total value of your fund back up to $10,000. Presumably, because there is no risk of loss, the investor feels more secure about investing in the market.

   But remember, there is only a nine percent chance that your fund will be under water ten years from now. Here's where it gets interesting. We see some investors buying segregated bond funds. A bond fund holding a portfolio of Government of Canada bonds cannot lose money over a ten-year period. After all, the principal repayment is already guaranteed by the bond issuer, which as we said, in most cases is the federal government.

The same is true with a balanced fund. Half of the assets in most balanced funds are invested in government and high-grade corporate bonds; their principal is already guaranteed. If you buy a segregated fund, you are paying for a maturity guarantee that is already implicit in half the assets within the underlying fund. Where's the value in that? If you are looking at a segregated fund because of the maturity guarantee, then buy higher-risk funds. Buy all-equity funds and go for performance. After all, you are paying to have the risk eliminated.

Of course, a higher-risk fund will charge a higher MER to cover the cost of the insurance. But even with that, we think you have a better chance of getting real value for your investment dollar using a higher-risk, higher-performance segregated fund.

2. *Death benefit*. While we have concerns about a maturity guarantee that effectively promises the return of your principal ten years hence, we do think the death benefit has value, especially to older people who want to protect the value of their estate from any potential declines.

   While there is little chance your fund will be down ten years from the date of the initial deposit, we don't know when we will die. If your fund were to decline 20 percent six months after your initial deposit, your estate would be guaranteed, at a minimum, the initial deposit value. We think there is real value in the death benefit. (You know there is real value when investors have actually taken advantage of the guarantee and insurance companies have paid out death benefits.)

3. *Reset features*. Most segregated funds offer a reset feature, which goes hand in hand with the maturity guarantee and the death benefit. The reset features vary from fund company to fund company, and from insurance company to insurance company. Essentially, though, the reset feature allows you to reset the maturity and death benefit guarantee a specific number of times during the year.

This could be useful if the market were to rise after you made your initial deposit into the segregated fund. For example, suppose you invest $10,000, and six months later your fund is up 10 percent. Your investment is now worth $11,000, but your guarantee is only for $10,000. The reset privilege allows you to reset your maturity guarantee and death benefit to the new higher value. You have locked in your gains, and in the worst-case scenario at maturity, you will receive a minimum of $11,000.

Before getting too excited about this feature, remember that the maturity guarantee is still ten years hence. In other words, by resetting your guarantee to $11,000, you extend your maturity date. The new maturity date is now ten years from the date of the reset. You know our views on the maturity guarantee.

But from the perspective of the death benefit, the reset privilege has real value — and real costs to the insurance company. So much so, that Manulife had to rethink the reset privileges on their original line of Guaranteed Investment Funds (GIF). The new version of GIF — entitled GIF Encore — has drastically changed the reset options, making them automatic when tied to the death benefit. This is not a bad thing, but it does show how important it is to read all the fine print in your segregated fund contract before buying.

4. *Creditor protection*. Because segregated funds are insurance products, they enjoy a high degree of protection from creditors. This isn't absolute (the courts have denied protection in a few cases), but will be effective in many situations.

5. *Estate planning*. If the policy to which the fund is tied has a specific named beneficiary (not the estate), the assets in the fund will pass directly to that person on death, without probate delays or creditor claims.

There is one other significant tax advantage of segregated funds. The 20 percent foreign content limit does not apply to registered segregated funds, even if they are 100 percent foreign in nature. This is a neat loophole for holders of segregated funds (but a loophole that may be plugged by the federal government).

Because of the growing awareness of segregated funds, and the government's seemingly unlimited appetite for keeping Canadians locked into Canadian investments, the government plans to review the rules around segregated funds in January 2001.

At that time, segregated funds may be subjected to the same foreign content rules as their mutual fund counterparts. (Certain "grandfathering" rules may apply to some of the older funds.) If changes take effect, holders of segregated funds will have to calculate their foreign content as of the effective date and make sure that it is not over the 20 percent limit, or they will be nailed with penalties of one percent per month for amounts over the limit.

If you buy segregated funds, you'll pay a premium price in the form of higher management fees. You may feel that the cost is worth the added benefits, but be sure you look at all the options carefully before you act.

A SEGREGATED FUND PORTFOLIO
Aggressively buying the guarantee

The problem, as we see it, is not in the concept of the guarantee; it's in how investors use the guarantee in their portfolios. The fact that a guarantee exists differentiates a segregated fund portfolio from a traditional mutual fund portfolio — if not in terms of the real-world usefulness of the maturity guarantee, at least in terms of the role the guarantee plays on your psyche.

When we build traditional mutual fund portfolios using the FundLine and MVA process, we are interested in diversification. A well-diversified portfolio should not fluctuate as dramatically during the ebbs and flows of the business cycle. If we can reduce the week-to-week volatility, we believe you will be less likely to sell out in a panic. In other words, the greater your comfort level, the more likely you will hold your portfolio for the longer term. And long-term investors most generally get where they want to go.

With a segregated fund, you can argue that the guarantee serves the same purpose that portfolio diversification does for the traditional mutual fund portfolio. This suggests that a portfolio of segregated funds can carry higher risks than a portfolio of traditional funds because, presumably, there is no downside . . . longer-term.

We talked about this before, but it is so important, it bears repeating. Why would any investor buy a balanced segregated fund? A balanced fund has a portion of its assets invested in bonds and Treasury bills, almost all the time. We fail to see why any investor has to guarantee bonds or cash.

The bond component will eventually return the investor's principal. In the worst-case scenario, only half of a balanced fund is actually at risk (at least in terms of how the segregated fund investor defines risk). So you are paying full price to guarantee half the portfolio.

Now, you might think that the fund manager could use the guarantee to get more aggressive within the balanced fund. Not so! Remember, today's segregated fund is really just a traditional mutual fund with an insurance wrapper. The balanced fund manager has to manage the portfolio as if there were no guarantee. (After all, some of the unitholders will be in the segregated version; some will not.) They are all holding the same underlying fund. It's just that the segregated version has a higher MER than the non-segregated version. The higher MER is being used to fund the insurance contract.

Now, to be fair, insurance companies understand the varying levels of risk. That's why they levy different charges on different types of funds. It costs more to guarantee an aggressive equity fund than it does a balanced fund. But we think that, over the long term, the more-aggressive fund will overcome the extra costs with better performance numbers. Investors may be well served to buy more aggressive segregated funds. Ratchet up the potential performance, because you are paying for the downside guarantee.

THE CHAPMANS RETURN

In the section on "Putting the Pieces Together," we introduced the Chapman family. We will reintroduce them here in order to demonstrate how a segregated fund portfolio might affect their investment portfolio.

Let's review the Chapmans' investor profile. This time we will answer the questionnaire knowing that the portfolio has a principal guarantee.

Knowing the Chapmans' circumstances, the net worth, financial objectives, and time horizon parts of the questionnaire won't change. What might change is how the Chapmans answer the questions about risk. Remember, when they look at risk now, they have a principal guarantee, rather than year-over-year volatility issues. They also have, in some cases, reset privileges — they can reset their portfolio as its value increases. After all, the Chapmans have a 20-year time horizon, and any reset only stretches the principal guarantee out ten years.

In this run-through of the profile, we'll answer the questions around risk knowing that we have a guarantee to draw on.

Question 3
Liquidity

How important is it that you have cash available for emergencies or investment opportunities?

It is extremely important.	1
It is important.	2
It is slightly important.	4
It isn't important at all.	5
Liquidity Score:	4

There is no change in the way the Chapmans answer this question. Whether the funds are guaranteed will have no bearing on whether cash is needed over the short term for emergencies.

Question 4
Safety

After one year of investing, how much would the value of your long-term investment capital have to decline before you would sell it and take a loss?

I would sell if my investment declined by 5%.	1
I would sell if my investment declined by 15%.	2
I would sell if my investment declined by 25%.	3
I would sell if my investment declined by 50%.	4

. . .

I would not sell my investment.	5
Safety Score:	5

With this question, the Chapmans would never have to sell the fund in down years. The segregated fund principal guarantee would provide the necessary comfort.

Question 5

Current Income

How important is it that you receive an income stream from your investments over the period of your investment horizon?

It is extremely important.	1
It is important.	2
It is only slightly important.	3
It is not important at all.	4
Current Income Score:	4

There is no change in the way the Chapmans answer this question. Whether the funds are guaranteed will have no bearing on income requirements.

Question 6

Future Gains

How would you describe your reaction to financial news that may have a detrimental effect on your investments?

I would be very anxious and likely sell my investments.	1
I would be fearful and consider selling my investments.	2
I would be uncomfortable but would hold my investments.	3
I would remain calm and definitely hold my investments.	4
Future Gains Score:	4

There is significant change in the way the Chapmans would answer this question. Because of the guarantee, they feel more comfortable about their investments, regardless of the news of the day.

Question 7

Portfolio Variability:

How important is it that you never experience a loss in your portfolio during a given time period?

It is extremely important.	1
It is important.	2
It is only slightly important.	3
It is not important at all.	4
Portfolio Variability Score:	4

This question was answered more aggressively. In this case, the Chapmans place no importance at all on the possibility of a loss in their portfolio. With the guarantee, as long as the portfolio is held to maturity there is no risk of loss.

Question 8
Performance Review

Which performance numbers most concern you?

Monthly performance numbers.	1
Quarterly performance numbers.	3
Annual performance numbers.	5
Performance Review Score:	5

The Chapmans have no concerns about the shorter-term performance numbers.

Question 9
Speculation

Within the past five years, how often have you invested money into speculative investments?

I have never invested speculatively.	1
I have invested speculatively once.	2
I have invested speculatively twice.	3
I have invested speculatively three or more times.	4
Speculation Score:	2

The speculation score remains the same.

The time horizon score also remains the same, as the guarantee has no impact on the long-term objectives of the portfolio. With that in mind, here is the Chapmans' Personal Investor Profile based on the original scores from "Putting the Pieces Together," and the scores from the segregated fund questionnaire.

THE CHAPMANS' PERSONAL INVESTOR PROFILE

CATEGORY	INFORMATION FOUND WHERE?	ORIGINAL SCORES	SEGREGATED SCORES
A Net Worth	Question 1	7	7
B Financial Objectives	Question 2	10	10
C Risk Assessment Profile	Questions 3-8	14	20
D Time Horizon	Question 9	10	10
Total Score (A + B + C + D)		41	47

Based on the Chapmans' higher score, they fall into the Growth category, which leads to the following policy statement:

GROWTH								SCORE: 45 - 54
	Equities			Fixed Income			Cash	
Min	Policy	Max	Min	Policy	Max	Min	Policy	Max
40%	60%	80%	20%	30%	40%	5%	10%	15%

The extended asset mix for the Growth portfolio is as follows:

YEAR 2000 EXTENDED ASSET MIX

	NON-RRSP	RRSP
Canadian Equity	15.0%	30.0%
U.S. Equity	22.5%	7.5%
International Equity	22.5%	7.5%
Special Equity	10.0%	5.0%
Total Equity Assets	**70.0%**	**50.0%**
Dividend Funds	15.0%	35.0%
Domestic Bond	5.0%	10.0%
Global Bond	5.0%	0.0%
Total Income Assets	**25.0%**	**45.0%**
Money Market	5.0%	5.0%
Total Cash Assets	**5.0%**	**5.0%**

Note how we show the extended asset mix for both the RRSP and non-RRSP portfolios. We did this because foreign segregated funds don't take up foreign content room inside an RRSP. Since we can structure the asset mix without having to worry about foreign content — at least for the time being — we can use the more-aggressive non-RRSP asset mix when constructing this portfolio.

CLOSED-END FUNDS: UNEXPLORED TERRITORY

There are two types of investment company funds: open- and closed-ended. Closed-end funds (CEFs), unlike their open-end counterparts, are publicly traded rather than being bought or sold by mutual fund organizations. Closed-end funds are not well publicized in Canada and are generally misunderstood.

OPEN- VERSUS CLOSED-END FUNDS

Open-ended funds (often referred to as mutual funds) sell units to the public on a continuous basis and invest the proceeds in a portfolio of securities. The term open-ended refers to the continuous distribution of new units (subject only to a limit on the number of authorized units outstanding) and to the fact that the issuing fund will always redeem units at the current net asset value per unit (assets minus liabilities divided by the number of units outstanding). Units of open-ended funds are sold to the public at this net asset value per unit, plus, in some cases, a load or commission, and are sold back to the fund by the fundholder at the current net asset value at the time of redemption.

Closed-ended funds, on the other hand, do not sell shares continuously to the public. Like the open-ended fund, the CEF invests its assets in a portfolio of securities according to an investment plan or strategy. CEF units are traded on stock exchanges and over-the-counter markets; prices are determined by the usual auction process applicable to stock trading. Prices at any time may be well above or below net asset value, with the latter case (or discount to net asset value) more usual in recent years.

CEFs are often specialty funds. They concentrate on areas like precious metals (such as BGR Precious Metals Inc.), foreign securities (such as First Australian Prime Investments Fund or Canadian World Fund), and foreign currencies (First Mercantile Fund). Some, however, hold diversified portfolios of primarily Canadian securities (Canadian General Investments or United Corporations Ltd.).

In general, CEFs have lower management expense ratios than mutual funds since they do not have sales forces, they engage in limited marketing, and they have lower administration fees. CEFs are generally more transparent than mutual funds because there are no trailer fees.

Mutual funds and CEFs, although they may have similar investment objectives, are therefore subject to different evaluation techniques and performance measures. CEF valuation requires an evaluation of the discount as well as all other factors pertinent to open-ended funds.

The CEF is not a new idea. The first ones were introduced over 170 years ago in Belgium and they grew rapidly in popularity in other parts of Europe. Ironically, a financial crisis in 1890 involving the House of Baring and some South American loans interrupted the rapid closed-end fund growth. (Call it Baring Crisis Number One!) CEFs performed poorly in the Great Crash and investor interest waned. They have regained popularity in the past two decades and their growth has proliferated everywhere — except in Canada, where they are just catching on.

We like the CEF vehicle. It has some valuable and interesting aspects. The pricing method offers chances to buy at opportune times — when the discount is large. CEFs never suffer from the "new money/old money" syndrome associated with mutual funds. The "new money" syndrome refers to the fact that fund managers may have to invest the proceeds of new investor purchases at inopportune times (such as when there is a lack of good products or an overheated market). The "old money" syndrome refers to cases where the fund manager is forced to liquidate portfolio holdings (again, often at an inconvenient time, such as a depressed market) in order to meet redemptions from investors cashing out.

THE DISCOUNT DILEMMA

CEFs trade at discounts or premiums to net asset value — usually the former.

Since CEF units are traded rather than redeemed, they sell at a market-determined price, reflecting supply and demand. This price is rarely equal to its net asset value per unit. In Canada, the discount for the typical fund has averaged 10 to 20 percent in recent years, although the discount (or premium) varies with the fund and fund type.

The discount has become a technical measure of contrarian sentiment. The notion is that as small investors become increasingly pessimistic they bid down the shares relative to the net asset value, thus increasing the discount. Since in contrarian analysis the small investor is usually wrong at important turning points, an increasing discount is deemed bullish for the stock market.

Other reasons for the discount include imbedded tax liabilities on previously realized profits in the portfolio; accrued fees, salaries, and bonuses; the potential price impact of liquidating stocks within the portfolio; the maintenance costs of the portfolio; the degree of optimism and pessimism in the marketplace; the comparative advantage (skill) of the manager; and the opportunity to invest in restricted markets.

People sometimes buy CEFs for the wrong reasons. For example, some people are attracted by large discounts. Although buying at a discount may be useful, keep in mind that it could and often does just stay where it is. In our 20 years of following CEFs, we have never seen a sudden change in the level of a discount or premium.

THE CEF WORLD

There are about 35 CEFs traded in Canada, primarily in the form of fixed income and Canadian equity classes. Net asset values for many of the Canadian funds are published on Saturdays in *The Globe and Mail's* "Report on Business."

In the U.S. there are hundreds of CEFs, ranging from pure income funds to specialty country and regional funds. There are no restrictions preventing Canadians from trading these U.S. financial products. The funds listed in the U.S. are of course traded in U.S. dollars, so there is some foreign currency risk exposure as well. Net asset values, discounts and premiums, and one-year returns are quoted on Mondays in the *Wall Street Journal* under the heading "publicly traded funds" or "closed-end funds."

Types of CEFs

Income-Oriented CEFs

These CEFs hold "portfolios" of high-yield fixed income securities and earn cash flow on these investments. The net cash flow (cash flow minus management fees and administration costs) is passed on to the unitholders in the form of distributions.

Global and International Bond CEFs

Global fixed-income funds have virtually all of their assets in fixed-income securities, primarily bonds issued by foreign governments and foreign corporations. The primary objective is stable and regular income.

Global and International Balanced CEFs

The fund manager maintains a balanced portfolio of stocks and bonds, normally within a pre-specified range. The primary objective is stability of returns. Balanced funds are either formalized (the portfolio is fixed in some proportion, such as 40 percent bonds and 60 percent equities) or semi-discretionary (proportions can be changed when the advisor deems it wise).

Canadian Equity CEFs
The portfolio is invested in Canadian common shares subject to diversification and style constraints.

Global Equity Growth CEFs
The portfolio is invested in a global portfolio of common shares (including Canada) subject to diversification and style constraints.

International Equity Growth CEFs
The portfolio is invested in a portfolio of foreign common shares subject to diversification and style constraints.

Global Aggressive Equity Growth CEFs
These funds pursue a strategy of investing in a portfolio of very aggressive global common shares (including Canada) and look for unusually high growth.

Global and International Aggressive Equity Growth CEFs
These funds pursue a strategy of investing in a portfolio of very aggressive foreign common shares and look for unusually high growth.

Single-Country CEFs
Single-country CEFs invest all of their assets in specific countries. These funds have become popular in recent years, reflecting the increased investor interest in emerging and smaller equity markets, such as Chile, the Philippines, and South Korea. Single-country investment funds often represent the only investment vehicle available to a Canadian investor.

Regional CEFs
Regional CEFs invest all of their assets in specific regions. There are now funds specializing in regions as diverse as the Far East, Latin America, western Europe, eastern Europe, North America, the Pacific Rim, and Africa.

A review of Canadian income-oriented CEFs

Canadian income-oriented CEFs hold "portfolios" of high-yield fixed income securities and earn cash flow on these investments. The net cash flow (cash flow minus management fees and administration costs) is passed on to the unitholders in the form of distributions.

Following are capsules on some of the key Canadian closed-end income funds:

Citadel Diversified Investment Trust (CTD.UN)

CTD debuted September 16, 1997. The fund holds a portfolio of oil and gas royalty trusts (approximately 28 percent of portfolio), real estate investment trusts (26 percent), and income funds (46 percent). The remainder (10 percent) is in cash and short-term deposits.

The fund's primary objective is to generate high income for unitholders.

Distributions in 1998 were monthly, in irregular amounts, and totaled $0.646 per share. Approximately 80 percent of the value of these dividends represented a return of capital. Return of capital distributions are non-taxable although the distribution will reduce the adjusted cost base of the unitholder's units.

The fund recorded a 26.1 percent total return to July 1999, reflecting the healthy rebound of oil and gas royalty and income trusts. The fund trades at a discount to net asset value of about 4 percent, well below its 10.3 percent level at year-end 1998.

CTD has a mandatory repurchase program that requires that it repurchase shares when the discount to net asset value exceeds five percent. The program is subject to a maximum of 1.25 percent of the total number of units outstanding at the beginning of each calendar quarter.

Mailing Address:
National Bank Building
Suite 1710
150 York Street
Toronto, Ontario
M5H 3S5

Contact Name: Darren K. Duncan

Telephone: (403) 261-9674

Fax: (403) 261-8670

DDJ Canadian High Yield Fund (HYB.UN)

HYB is a closed-end investment trust with a fixed life to August 15/07. The fund debuted in August 1997 at a price of $25 in the form of an instalment receipt consisting of a $12.50 per unit payment made on closing and a second and final payment of $12.50 per unit due on August 31, 1998.

The fund's primary objectives are to provide an 8.5 percent to 9.0 percent annual investment return while maintaining the market value of the investment. The underlying strategy for achieving the objectives is to invest primarily in high-yield U.S. dollar-denominated fixed income securities issued by Canadian corporations.

HYB's total distributions received or receivable in calendar year 1998 were $2.20, including the January 15/99 payment (record date was December 31, 1998). HYB's total return was -5.04 percent for 1998.

The fund has recorded a 15.75 percent return to July 1999. The management expense ratio, at 1.20 percent, is at the upper end of closed-end bond funds, although well below the average bond mutual fund.

There are approximately 11.4 million HYB warrants outstanding. Each warrant allows the holder to buy one DDJ Canadian High Yield Fund at a $22.50 exercise price up to August 31/00.

Mailing Address:
151 Yonge Street, 7th Floor
Toronto, Ontario
M5C 2W7

Phone: (416) 681-6507

Fax: (416) 365-0501

First Asia Income Fund (FAI.UN)

FAI debuted in May 1997 at a price of $10, consisting of an initial payment of $6 per share and a second and final payment of $4 per share on May 14/98. The fund's primary objective is to provide high income to unitholders.

The portfolio consists primarily (about 85 percent) of debt securities of Australia, New Zealand, South Korea, the Philippines, and China and other Asian countries. It also has some exposure to U.S. debt securities. Distributions in 1998 were quarterly in irregular amounts. The fund has substantially lengthened the average maturity of the portfolio. As of July 1999 the average maturity was 11.1 years, as compared to 6.6 years earlier in the year.

As of July 1999, FAI was trading at a discount to net asset value of 24.46 percent, among the highest of the Canadian CEFs.

Mailing Address:
Suite 5300
Commerce Court West
Toronto, Ontario
M5L 1B9

Telephone: (416) 869-5500

Fax: (416) 947-0866

First Australia Prime Income Fund (FAP)

FAP's primary objective is to provide a monthly high income to unitholders. The fund's portfolio is devoted predominantly to the debt securities of Australia (about 85 percent), with the remainder of the portfolio allocated to New Zealand, South Korea, Thailand, China, and other issuers.

The fund has a strong long-term history (it debuted in 1986); however, performance has tailed off somewhat in recent years, reflecting primarily the weakness in the Australian dollar. In 1998, the fund reduced its distribution to 8 cents per month per share from the 9 cents per month distribution paid in 1997. The dividend was been maintained at this 8 cents per share level to July 1999.

FAP concluded a rights offering in early April 1999 under which shareholders received the right to subscribe for one FAP share plus one FAP share purchase warrant. The purpose of the rights offering was to finance the expansion of the company's portfolio investments in high-yield Asian debt securities. The offering was over-subscribed, with subscription requests totaling 122 percent of the securities offered.

Mailing Address:
> EquitiLink U.S.A
> 45 Broadway
> New York NY 10006

Phone: (800) 992-6341

Newcastle Market Neutral Trust (NMN.UN)

NMN is a closed-end investment fund that invests in a portfolio of hedge funds. The fund is managed by Newcastle Capital Management whose CEO, David Patterson, has considerable experience with both index investing and hedge investing. The fund debuted in August 1997 at net asset value per unit of $18.79 and an issue price of $20.

At present, there are 29 hedge funds in the portfolio positioned in eight different categories. Each of the hedge funds in which NMN invests is supposed to be market-neutral. True hedge funds have three important characteristics. First, a hedge fund will have a low, often zero, correlation with traditional investments such as stocks and bonds. Second, hedge funds are designed to isolate the portfolio manager's expertise. Third, the strategies employed within a hedge fund are often lever-aged ones, and liberal use is made of futures, forwards, options, and swaps involving commodities, currencies, financial instruments, and indexes.

Hedge funds are sometimes confused with specula-tive or performance funds, which are funds that seek exposure to specific risks such as foreign currency or industry sectors. However, speculative funds do not seek to eliminate the external risks associated with systematic market and economic changes. For example, a specula-tive fund manager would buy gold mining shares if he thought they had become undervalued, while a hedge fund manager with the same belief would not only buy undervalued gold mining shares but also sell short the market (for example, buy index put options) in order to isolate the shares from the market effect.

The highest concentration in NMN is in merger arbitrage, credit risk arbitrage, and convertible arbitrage. In merger arbitrage, the hedge fund manager buys the target firm in a merger or takeover and sells short the shares of the acquiring firm. In credit risk arbitrage, the focus is on high-yield, lower-quality bonds in which the purchase of the bonds is hedged with a short sale of equity securities of the same issuer. In convertible arbitrage, the fund manager normally buys convertible bonds or preferreds and sells short the underlying stock, thus isolating the undervalued convertible from the market effect.

The primary objective of Newcastle Market Neutral Trust is to pay $0.40 per unit per quarter (eight percent per annum based of the original issue price). However, the fund may only make distributions if the net asset value, after taking the distribution into effect, is greater than the initial NAVPU of $18.79. The fund failed to reach its $1.60 target distribution in 1998, paying only $0.69 per share. The omitted dividends are cumulative (that is, are accrued to the share). As at July 1999, the arrearage was $2.11 per share. The current NAVPU has risen to $18.45 and flirting with the $18.79 demarcation line. (The NAVPU has increased for eight straight months.)

At a special unitholders' meeting in February 1999, the fund managers sought approval to reduce the target payout to $0.30 per unit, and to reduce the minimum net asset value per unit required for the payment of distributions. Both motions were defeated by the unhappy unitholders.

Newcastle Management has waived its advisory fee since the dividends have been omitted and in fact under the original prospectus agreement will receive no fees until all of the back payments are made up and the fund is current on its distributions.

Mailing Address:
> Suite 330
> Scotia Plaza
> 40 King Street West
> Toronto, Ontario
> M5H 3Y2

Phone: (800) 422-1867

Polar Hedge Enhanced Income Trust (PHT. UN)

PHT is a closed-end investment trust with a fixed life to April 30/07. The fund debuted in May 1997 at a price of $15, paid in three $5 instalment receipts. The fund's primary objective is to provide a high portfolio return while maintaining the market value of the investment. The fund managers concentrate on convertible hedge positions (long convertibles/short underlying stocks). With convertible arbitrage, the fund manager normally buys convertible bonds or preferred and sells short the underlying stock thus isolating the undervalued convertible from the market effect.

Although the fund paid $0.907 in dividends, it suffered a dramatic drawdown in value in 1998. The original issue instalment receipt purchasers have lost much of their $15 investment. However, the fund had recorded a 14.8 percent gain as of July 1999 in addition to a 4.86 percent yield.

Mailing Address:
> 350 Bay Street
> 13th Floor
> Toronto, Ontario
> M5H 2S6

Contact Name: Paul Sabourin

Telephone: (416) 367-4364

Fax: (416) 367-0564

A review of Canadian closed-end equity funds

Canadian equity-oriented CEFs tend to focus on diversified portfolios of Canadian common shares. Following are capsules on some of the Canadian closed-end equity funds:

ARC Strategic Energy (AEF. UN)

AEF debuted in May 1998. The fund's portfolio is concentrated in energy securities and has an eclectic portfolio mix including exposure to junior, intermediate, and senior producers; turnaround situations; and early-stage companies.

Mailing Address:
Suite 4300
400 3rd Avenue S.W.
Calgary, Alberta
T2P 4H2

Telephone: (403) 292-0271

Fax: (403) 292-0693

Web: www.arcfinancial.com

BPI Global Opportunities II Fund

The BPI Global Opportunities II Fund was formerly the BPI Canadian Opportunities II Fund. The name was changed on November 5/98, to reflect a new set of investment objectives. The fund is now designed to be a globally diversified portfolio subject to a wide range of trading and investment targets including companies with dominance in their industries; companies at discounts to earnings and assets relative to global peers; short-term trading opportunities; and short selling of overvalued companies.

The fund should be evaluated strictly as of the November 5/98, new set of objectives. There is no discernible relationship between the pre-November and post-November objectives — this is an entirely new fund.

Mailing Address:
BCE Place
161 Bay Street
Suite 3900
Toronto, Ontario
M5J 2S1

Contact Name: Stephen J. Griggs

Telephone: (416) 216 2229

Fax: (416) 861 1715

Canadian General Investments (CGI)

Canadian General Investments is one of the oldest investment funds in Canada. It started as the Second

Canadian General Investment Trust in 1928. After shifting investment focus a number of times over the years, this closed-end investment fund adopted a strictly "buy Canadian" investment policy in March 1994. This policy change, implemented in conjunction with a listing on the London Stock Exchange, was a strategic move aimed at attracting foreign investors. The fund manager is MMA Investment Managers Limited. MMA employs both active selection for choosing securities and sector rotation for allocating funds to industries. The investment styles is bottom-up, an approach that is consistent with a constantly changing sector allocation.

The fund has a fully diversified portfolio representing all aspects the Canadian economy.

There are 3,688,730 warrants outstanding to buy CGI shares at $8.96 per share. These warrants are exercisable on June 30 in each year from 2000 to 2007.

The top ten holdings as of July 1999 were CT Financial Services Inc., BCE Inc., Imasco Limited, Suncor Energy Inc., Dia Met Minerals, Falconbridge Limited, Telesystem International Wireless Inc., Toronto Dominion Bank, Rio Alto Exploration Ltd., and Ritchie Bros. Auctioneers Incorporated. These ten companies comprised over 23 percent of the fund's overall portfolio.

Although CGI has been a top-performing equity fund for years, the relevant review period is really from the end of 1994, when CGI became a fully diversified Canadian equity fund. Until recently, CGI had substantially outperformed the TSE 300 Composite Index, the Toronto 35 Index, and virtually all Canadian mutual funds. However, its recent performance has dampened the record somewhat.

CGI's discount to net asset value as July 1999 had risen to 23.1 percent — well up from the 9.3 percent level at the start of the year. Over the past decade, the discount has been as low as 3 percent and as high as 40 percent. The fund managers have followed a policy of buying back and retiring shares when the discount is high. In fact, the manager has made issuer bids for shares in six of the last ten years. Accordingly, the number of shares outstanding has shrunk by about 40 percent over the past decade.

The company pays a dividend of $0.075 a quarter plus extras since the fund managers pursue a policy of paying out most of the income and realized capital gains as cash and share dividends. Total distributions including cash and stock were $3.30 per unit in 1997, $1.50 in 1998 and $0.225 per share thus far in 1999.

On October 5/98, CGI issued $60 million of class A preferred shares. The relatively low-cost preferred share issue was designed to enhance the return on equity and returns to shareholders through the leverage provided in lowering the firm's weighted average cost of capital.

Mailing address:
110 Yonge Street
Suite 1601
Toronto, Ontario
M5C 1T4

Telephone: (416) 366-2931

Fax: (416) 366-2729

Canadian World Fund (CWF)

Canadian World Fund Limited is a member of the same family as CGI. CWF was established in January 1994 as a closed-end fund with a global focus. The fund's substantial exposure to Latin America has hindered performance recently.

New Altamira Value Fund (NVL.UN)

NVL underwent a significant restructuring in 1998. The portfolio focus is now on value stocks in the form of small-cap, low P/E stocks, as well as fallen angels and turnaround situations. The number of names in the portfolio has been substantially reduced from around 150 to about 45.

The fund will terminate on December 31/01, and the net assets will be distributed to the unitholders unless an alternative to termination is approved. Alternatives include continuing the fund as a closed-end investment trust, converting the fund into an open-end mutual fund, and exchanging the units for units in one or more of the Altamira Funds.

Altamira's discount to net asset value has dropped from 21.7 percent at year-end 1998 to the mid-1999 level of 11.1%. The MER at about 1.12 percent is consistent with CEFs.

Mailing Address:
> The Exchange Tower
> 130 King Street West
> Suite 900
> Toronto, Ontario
> M5X 1K9

Telephone Number: (416) 507-7394

Fax: (416) 203-7488

Third Canadian General Investment Trust (THD)

THD's portfolio is comprised of 72.6 percent in CGI and 3.8 percent in CWF. The largest other significant holdings are City of London Investment Group PLC (2.3 percent) and Robert Fleming Holdings Ltd. (2 percent). The former is a privately-traded investment fund which invests in closed-end emerging markets funds. The latter is a U.K.-based investment banking and fund management group with the equivalent of C$160.7 billion under administration. The remainder of the portfolio is allocated to royalty and income trusts. Buying the Third Canadian General Investment Trust is identical to acquiring a portfolio consisting of about 73 percent CGI and 27 percent global investments, including the Canadian World Fund.

As at July 1999, THD was trading at a discount to net asset value of about 18 percent.

Mailing address:
> 110 Yonge Street
> Suite 1601
> Toronto, Ontario
> M5C 1T4

Telephone: (416) 366-2931

Fax: (416) 366-2729

United Corporations Limited (TSE: UNC)

UNC was one of Canada's first closed-end funds, having debuted in the 1930s. The portfolio until recently was solely managed by Cassels Blaikie Management. As of May 1999, Mulvihill Capital Management is advising the small-cap portion of the portfolio.

The portfolio composition is widely diversified. Just under 80 percent of the portfolio is allocated to Canadian equities. In fact, the proportionate industry weightings have a close resemblance to the TSE 300 Composite Index. Approximately 20 percent of the portfolio is allocated to foreign equities, primarily U.S. stocks and American Depositary Receipts (ADRs).

Mailing Address:

10th Floor
165 University Avenue
Toronto, Ontario
M5H 3B8

Telephone: (416) 947-2583

Fax: (416) 868-6199

Closed-end U.S.-dollar bond funds

Bond funds denominated in U.S. dollars are ideal investments for global currency diversification. If you generally have a need for some U.S.-dollar diversification, the closed-end U.S. global bond fund is one of the best routes. Closed-end bond funds, like bonds and other fixed-income securities, fluctuate in value with changing interest rates. An increase in interest rates, for example, depresses asset values, but improves the reinvestment rate.

One of our choices is the Templeton Global Income Fund (NYSE: GIM). The fund is advised by Neil Devlin of Franklin/Templeton. The fund's portfolio target is higher-grade foreign bonds of developed countries. At present, the portfolio has balanced global exposure although the heaviest allocations are to U.S. (about 21 percent), European (37 percent), Canadian (9 percent), and Latin America (22 percent).

The portfolio is long-weighted with an average term to maturity of over eight years. About 70 percent of the portfolio is in bonds rated Aa or higher. The monthly dividend of five cents a share represents an annual yield of about 8.0 percent, an attractive return on U.S. funds today.

First Commonwealth Fund (NYSE: FCO) is managed by Lawrence Freedman of EquitiLink International Management Ltd. and advised by EquitiLink Australia Ltd.

The fund invests in British Commonwealth countries, primarily high-grade Australian, Canadian, New Zealand, and U.K. bonds and other fixed-income securities.

The fund pays a dividend of seven cents a month plus the occasional extra based on capital gains. The long maturity of the portfolio (over eight years) means extreme interest rate sensitivity.

CEFs and Rights Offerings

CEFs make extensive use of rights offerings. First, some rights mechanics. In a typical rights offering, the company announces that shareholders of record as of a specific future date (the record date) will receive a specified number of rights per share (usually one right per share), which they can then use to buy additional shares on the basis of a specified number of rights (often three) for one new share at a specified price (the subscription price) up to a final date (the expiration date). If the rights are transferable they will trade on the same exchange as the common shares and be temporarily listed with a stock symbol. The shares will trade at a minimum value calculated as $[(P - S)/N]$ where P is the current price of the common share, S is the subscription price, and N is the number of rights required to buy a new share. In the early stage the rights will usually trade at a premium to this minimum value.

For example, the China Fund (NYSE: GC) issued rights to shareholders on the following terms: Each shareholder received one transferable right per share. Shareholders were then entitled to buy one common share by surrendering three rights plus $13 per share at any time up to May 13. So if you owned 300 shares you received 300 rights which entitled you to buy 100 shares at $13 per share. The shares were trading at about $19 per share at the time the rights began trading. The minimum value of a right was initially = $[(P - S)/N] = [(19 - 13)/3] = \$2$ each.

That is how rights offerings work. Now, what do you do if you receive rights in an offering? Here are our three "Rules for Rightsholders":

1. Always take action! Either sell your rights or exercise them! On the day that the shares begin trading without the rights (this is called the ex-rights date) the shares will drop by an amount approximately equal to a right (this is called the dilution effect). If you don't exercise or sell, you lose the amount of the dilution.

2. If you don't want to commit additional capital to your investment, sell the rights in the market. If so, sell the shares early in the period when the premium over intrinsic value is, everything else being equal, likely to be the highest.

3. The usual choice is to exercise them. Since the rights represent a call option, always wait until the final date before exercising — just in case the common stock falls below the subscription price during the period.

The Golden Rules of Selecting CEFs

1. Select CEFs whose managers build portfolios that really match the stated objectives. At least 60 percent of the portfolio should be exclusively allocated to the primary target, whether that is a specific country or a market segment.

2. Select CEFs whose performance generally remains within a specific risk category.

3. Hold some CEFs denominated in foreign currency.

4. Select management styles (active versus passive; value versus growth) that match your tastes.

5. Do not select CEFs based on the size of the discount or the level of management expense ratios. These are important but by no means critical factors.

MUTUAL FUND COUSINS: ROYALTY AND INCOME TRUSTS

Royalty and income trusts are classic flow-through investment vehicles. The trust, like a pooled fund, holds a "portfolio" of assets (such as natural resource, commodity, or real property; or financial assets such as stocks and bonds) and earns cash flow on these investments.

The net cash flow (cash flow minus management fees and administration costs) is passed on to the unitholders in the form of interest and dividends. The market value of the trust will reflect the long-term expected value of the cash flows. The market value should rise (fall) if interest rates drop (rise) and/or the price of the underlying asset (e.g., iron ore or common shares) rises (drops). Organized in a manner similar to closed-end investment funds, royalty and income trusts trade at market-determined prices rather than the net asset value per unit. Accordingly, they may trade at premiums or discounts to the net asset value per unit.

Royalty and income trusts, then, are simply pools of capital invested in specific portfolios of assets. If there are 1,000,000 units of the trust outstanding and you own 10,000 units, then you own one percent of the pool and are entitled to one percent of the distributions (which are based on the income of the fund after expenses and management fees).

ROYALTY TRUSTS

Harry Markowitz first published his work on diversification in 1952. Markowitz's model, which is now called Modern Portfolio Theory (MPT), and which would eventually win him a Nobel Prize, provided a fresh insight into how diversification works. This, in turn, would lead to an enhanced understanding of how stocks are priced and how they are priced relative to a market portfolio. Two generations of analysts, finance professors, students, and advisors have learned and applied the fundamental principle of diversification. The primary purpose of diversifying a stock portfolio is to eliminate the unique risk associated with the individual securities, leaving the overall systematic or market risk associated with the market itself. For example, if you were properly diversified, Bre-X's collapse in 1997 would have had a barely noticeable effect on your overall portfolio. Every asset allocation pie chart turned out by financial institutions today owes its origin to MPT.

Efficient diversification also means holding securities that normally react differently to market and economic events. One key diversification principle is purchasing power protection — holding assets that guard against unfavourable inflation rate movements. Although subject to sometimes severe short-term swings, real estate and commodities have over the long run been inflation hedges. A useful vehicle for holding a commodity- or real-estate-based investment is the Royalty Trust (RT).

There are different types of RTs—each geared to different investor income, investment and tax needs, and circumstances. The most popular are oil and gas, coal, and iron, although many innovative versions exist, including shipping terminals and hotels. Most of these trusts distribute income monthly or quarterly.

There are two key valuation and investment considerations. First is the cash-on-cash yield, which is the current one-year expected payout on the unit, divided by the current unit price. At the time of writing (July 1999) yields ranged from about 8 percent to as high as 25 percent. Needless to say, these are relatively high yields — much higher than those available on bonds and other conventional fixed-income securities. The problem is that this cash-on-cash yield is highly misleading on its own, because it ignores the life of the underlying assets or pool of assets. The cash-on-cash yield has to be measured against the actual yield on the portfolio. If cash-on-cash yields remain steady or rise when the market value of the assets in the portfolio are falling, the market values of the units will be falling and the fund will essentially be repaying capital to unit holders.

Accordingly, the cash-on-cash yield has to be measured against the expected life of the property or the Reserve Life Index, calculated by dividing the proven and probable reserves (normally only one-half of the probable reserves are used) by the annual rate of production. Obviously, the shorter the Reserve Life Index, the faster the reserves and portfolio assets will be depleted and the sooner the investment will cease to pay off.

Take the case of a representative oil and gas RT. The fund's annual distributions were recently $1.44 a unit, or 16.1 percent based on its $8.90 price. But with an estimated reserve life of only about eight years, this translates into an internal rate of return (IRR) of about 6.1 percent per annum if the reserves are not extended. The projected annual return is highly sensitive to this estimate. For example, if the life is extended to ten years the yield will be 9.89 percent per annum. Obviously, if management is successful in finding and/or developing new products and extending the estimated life of the property, values will rise.

A further problem is how the growth will be financed. If growth is continuously financed with the sale of new units, the existing unitholders suffer dilution unless the rate of return on the new projects at least equals the rate of return on the old — relative to the same cost of capital. So there is a "shell game" aspect to RTs that have short lives — since management must keep selling new units, invest in new projects or expand existing ones, or face rapid deterioration in unit values.

The royalty income and the amount of the distribution will also vary with the price of the underlying commodity of the fund (e.g., oil, gas, coal). The market value will rise (fall) if the price of the underlying asset (e.g., oil and gas) rises (drops).

So RT prices are a function of (i) cash-on-cash yield; (ii) estimated reserve life; (iii) changing interest rates; (iv) replacement development policies and skills of management; and (v) the price of the underlying commodity, including exchange rate implications.

Unitholders are allocated the depletion allowance, royalty tax credits, or capital cost allowance on the underlying properties. Accordingly, a portion of the distributions may be tax-deferred, depending on whether there is still a depletion or capital cost allowance pool. (Every trust is at a different stage.) Here's how the tax works. If an investor buys 1,000 units of Athabaska Oil Sands Trust at $24 per unit, receives $3,500 ($3.50 per share) in aggregate tax deferred distributions over time and $4,000 ($4 per share) in taxable dividends, and then sells the shares for $21.50 per share, the investor will have the following tax consequences (ignoring commissions):

	PER SHARE	TOTAL
Proceeds of disposition:	$21.50	$21,500
Adjusted cost base:		
Original Cost	$24.00	
Less: Tax-deferred dividends	$3.50	
Adjusted cost base	$20.50	$20,500
Capital gain	$1.00	$1,000

In these circumstances, the investor realized a capital gain of $1,000 or a taxable capital gain of $750, since only 75 percent of the gain is included in income. The $4,000 in taxable dividends will be included in income in the year received.

RTs are RRSP-eligible and are not considered foreign property as long as the non-Canadian property proportion of the portfolio doesn't exceed the 20 percent allowable limit.

RTs in general suffered through terrible years in 1998. The typical RT realized high cash-on-cash yields but at the expense of declining unit values. However, rising commodity prices led to a recovery in 1999.

REITs

A special case of the RT is the real estate investment trust, or REIT. REITs are organized as closed-end real estate investment funds, which means that their units are publicly traded. For illiquid assets such as real estate, the closed-end vehicle is the one that makes the most sense. Open-ended or "mutual" real estate funds are subject to new money and redemption problems that these closed-end forms avoid. (In fact, due to liquidity problems, real estate mutual funds all but disappeared in the 1991–92 real estate collapse.)

The typical Canadian REIT distributes about 85 to 95 percent of its income (rental income from properties), usually on a quarterly basis. Generally the taxable income earned by the trust flows through the REIT to be taxed in the hands of the Canadian holder. Furthermore, the REIT holder is entitled to a deduction for the pro rata share of capital cost allowance (depreciation on the properties). As a result, about 75 to 85 percent of the distributions are normally tax-deferred. However, the value of your tax-deferred receipts will reduce the adjusted cost base of your shares.

Here's how it works. If you buy 1,000 units of Riocan at $15.50 per unit, receive $3,000 ($3 per share) in aggregate tax-deferred distributions over time, and then sell the shares for $17.50 per share, you will have a capital gain of $5,000 = [1000 × ($17.50 - $15.50 + $3.00] before adjustments for commissions. The gain will be subject to capital gain treatment; that is, 75 percent of the gain, or $3,750, is included in income and taxed at your normal rates. REITs are RRSP-eligible and are not considered foreign property as long as the real estate portfolio doesn't contain non-Canadian property in excess of the 20 percent allowable limit.

REITs generally match the performance of real estate prices. You'll find a generally high correlation between the C.M. Oliver Canadian REIT index and real estate prices.

The typical Canadian REIT yields about seven to eight percent at present, well above the rates on preferred shares and other fixed-income securities. REITS seem too good to be true. But remember, as the "no free lunch" theorem of investment finance tells us, question anything that seems is too good to be true. And there are two catches with REITs.

Since you are a unitholder rather than a shareholder, you are potentially jointly and severally liable with all other unitholders (plus the trust itself) in the case of insolvency. Instead of limited liability, you are relying on the REIT management to have property, casualty, and liability insurance, prudent lending policies, and other safeguards in place. Nevertheless, there is the possibility, albeit a low one, of a problem — say, a catastrophic fire or a building collapse, something that isn't covered by insurance.

The second problem is less transparent. Real estate properties depreciate in value without significant maintenance payments and renewal of facilities. Since most or all of the REIT's income is being distributed and the capital cost allowance is being allocated to you, you are in a sense getting your own capital back. The book value of the real estate properties will be steadily depleting. Of course, if the properties are appreciating in value, this could offset the depletion factor. The point is that the long-term income stream is quite variable, certainly more variable than some advisors would have you believe.

The way we see it, REITs have their place in a long-term investment portfolio. For timers or tactical asset allocators, REITs are ideal for trying to pick real estate market bottoms.

INCOME TRUSTS

Income Trusts (ITs) hold "portfolios" of high-yield fixed-income securities and earn cash flow on these investments. The net cash flow (cash flow minus management fees and administration costs) is passed on to the unitholders in the form of distributions. Most of these trusts distribute income monthly or quarterly.

The cash-on-cash yield has to be measured against the actual performance of the portfolio. If cash-on-cash yields remain steady or rise when the market value of the assets in the portfolio is falling, the market values of the units will decline and the fund will essentially be repaying capital to unitholders. For a poorly designed or functioning fund investors could be looking at the worst of all tax worlds — one in which they have high taxable income due to high interest income coupled with declining prices, for which there is little or no offsetting tax benefit. For example, take the case of Triax Diversified Income Trust, whose primary objective is to provide a high portfolio return while maintaining market value of the investment. If you make the mistake of focusing strictly on the cash-on-cash yield you'll see that the fund's $1.45 in distributions over the past 12 months translates into a yield of over 13 percent based on the recent unit price. The problem is that over that same 12-month period Triax actually lost value for unitholders on a total return basis. Not that it is a bad investment. To the contrary, it has a solid investment strategy and a good plan. It's just that the current yield is misleading.

Some of the newer ITs offer unitholders a continuous right to redeem units. For example, one fund allows unitholders a privilege as follows: "Units tendered within five business days of the last day of the month are redeemed as at that final date with payment on or before the eighth business date following the redemption date. Units tendered after that date are redeemed on the last business day of the next month. The redemption price is the NAVPU less the lesser of (i) four percent of the NAVPU and (ii) $1.00 per unit. In February each year the redemption price is the NAVPU without adjustment." The effect of this feature should be to substantially limit the discount to net asset value that often plagues CEFs.

Many of the income trusts have ambitious objectives (an eight to nine percent annual return target is the typical objective of many of these trusts). As with their investment cousins, royalty trusts, some income trusts have been maintaining high distributions at the expense

income trust units. The fund's focus is on gas and oil royalty trusts.

The fund has maintained a monthly distribution thus far, although its original target of $0.09 per month has turned out to be overly optimistic. The distribution was cut to $0.08 per month in May 1998; to $0.07 per month in September 1998; and then to $0.06 per month in May 1999. Approximately 87 percent of the $0.96 per unit in distributions in 1998 was a return of capital. EIT suffered a fate similar to most royalty trusts in 1998: distributions financed by declining share prices in a manner that is consistent with the repayment of capital.

Enervest staged a nice recovery in 1999 and recorded a healthy 42.9 percent gain as of July 1999.

Under the fund's dividend reinvestment plan, distributions plus up to an additional $1,000 can be reinvested as per the cash distribution date. Given that much of the distributions are tax-deferred we do not recommend this fund for RRSPs or other tax shelters.

Mailing Address:
Suite 2950
700 – 9th Avenue S. W.
Calgary, Alberta
T2P 3V7

Contact Name: Ms. Andrea Watkins

Telephone: (403) 571-5550

Fax: (403) 571-5554

First Premium Income Trust (FPI. UN)

The fund debuted in June 1996 at a price of $25. The fund's objective is to make quarterly distributions of at least $0.50 per unit, which translates into a cash-on-cash yield of 7.7 percent, based on the market price as of July 1999. FPI holds a diversified portfolio of Canadian common shares spanning the major industry sectors. The largest allocations are to utilities (24 percent) and financial services (26 percent). The ten largest holdings are BCE Inc., Royal Bank of Canada, Bank of Nova Scotia, Imasco Limited, Canadian Imperial Bank of Commerce, Donohue Inc. Class A,

Imperial Oil Ltd., Alcan Aluminum, Toronto-Dominion Bank, and Noranda Inc.

The overall investment performance remains on target. The fund's annual compounded rate of return based on its original issue price of $25 is over 12 percent per annum. Option premiums remain relatively high, given the volatility in the market. The fund, with its solid base, should continue to generate healthy returns for investors. FPI has met both of its scheduled $0.50 per unit distributions as of July 1999. PFI has called for a special meeting of shareholders to approve its plan to add writing cash covered put options to complement its covered call option writing strategy. The plan is likely to be approved, and will add additional flexibility to the trading arsenal.

First Premium Oil and Gas Income Trust (FPG.UN)

The primary objective of the First Premium Oil and Gas Trust is to provide a quarterly dividend of at least $0.1875 per unit. The fund met its distribution targets in 1998 but was unable to make its first quarterly dividend in 1999, due to some substantial portfolio losses. Management does not expect to make any distributions in 1999. The fund lost 11.8 percent in 1998, but had staged a healthy 22.2 percent rebound to July 1999.

The base portfolio is Canadian and U.S. oil and gas stocks consisting primarily of companies included on the TSE 300 Oil and Gas Sub-Index. The fund is also allowed to invest up to 20 percent of its portfolio in companies included in the Standard & Poor's 500 Energy Sub-Index. As with the other First Premium funds, covered writing strategies are employed. FPG intends to add cash covered put options to its portfolio strategies.

First Premium U.S. Income Trust (FPU.UN)

FPU debuted in February 1997 with identical objectives to that of First Premium Income Trust: provides quarterly distributions of a least eight percent per annum, based on the original purchase price. FPU holds a diversified portfolio of stocks selected from the top 50 of the Standard & Poor's 100 Index. The largest allocations as of July 1999 were in technology (32 percent), consumer cyclicals (13 percent), communications (12 percent), financial services

(11 percent), and health care (9.6 percent). The ten largest holdings were Cisco Systems Inc., Microsoft Corporation, BankAmerica Corporation, AT&T Corporation, Bristol-Myers Squibb Company, Intel Corporation, Northern Telecom Limited, Pharmacia & Upjohn, MCI WorldCom Inc., and Wal-Mart Stores, Inc.

Since its debut in February 1997, the First Premium U.S. Income Trust has made each of its targeted $0.50 a share quarterly distributions as well as four special distributions. Distributions in 1998 totaled $3.25, comprising $2 per unit in regular distributions and $1.25 in special distributions. As of July 1999, the fund had met its scheduled $0.50 per unit distributions plus a $0.50 special distribution in June 1999. FPU intends to add cash covered put options to its portfolio strategies.

First Premium Income Trust (FPI.UN)
First Premium Oil and Gas Income Trust (FPG.UN)
First Premium U.S. Income Trust (FPU.UN)

Mailing Address:
Standard Life Centre
121 King Street West
Suite 2600
Toronto, Ontario
M5H 3T9

Telephone: (416) 681-3966

Income Financial Trust (INC.UN)

Income Financial debuted in February 1999. The fund's primary objective is to provide a monthly cash distribution of $0.17708 per unit or $2.12496 per annum, which translates into an 8.5 percent nominal annual yield based on the initial issue price. The effective annual equivalent to this nominal yield is 8.83 percent. The targeted return is equivalent to a 10.40 percent pretax interest equivalent return on a nominal basis and 10.81 percent on an effective basis.

The fund has a termination date of January 1/09, at which time unitholders may redeem their units at a redemption price equal to the net asset value per unit.

Quadravest Inc., the same company that manages Split Yield Corporation Capital Shares, manages the fund.

The portfolio is concentrated primarily (at least 75 percent by the by-laws) in financial services companies listed on the Toronto Stock Exchange Financial Services Index, the Standard & Poor's Financials Index, and the Standard & Poor's MidCap Financials Index. In a strategy similar to that employed with Split Yield, the manager will also write call options against all or part of the portfolio from time to time to enhance returns.

An interesting feature of INC is that unitholders have a continuous right to redeem units. Units tendered within five business days of the last day of the month are redeemed as at that final date with payment on or before the eighth business date following the redemption date. Units tendered after that date are redeemed on the last business day of the next month. The redemption price is the NAVPU minus the lesser of (i) four percent of the NAVPU and (ii) $1 per unit. In February each year the redemption price is the NAVPU without adjustment. The effect of this feature should be to substantially limit the discount to net asset value that often plagues CEFs.

Since the initial distribution (record date March 31/99) all monthly distributions have been met thus far in 1999.

Mailing Address:
Royal Trust Tower
77 King Street West
Suite 2505
P.O. Box 341
Toronto, Ontario
M5K 1K7

Telephone: (416) 304-4444

Fax: (416) 304-4441

Labrador Iron Ore Royalty Income Fund (TSE: LIF. UN)
LIF holds an overriding seven percent royalty (on the sales) and an 11.98 percent equity interest in, and of, the Iron Ore Company of Canada, a huge iron ore producer operating for some 34 years in the Labrador City area.

The trust has recently been paying $0.20 per share in interest and $0.05 per share in dividends quarterly. The yield has been solid but it has been at the expense of declining unit values — to all intents and purposes investors until recently have been receiving their capital back. Sales revenue is closely tied to iron ore pellet prices, which have ranged between $34 and $36 a tonne in recent years. However, negotiations in May 1999 between the Iron Ore Company of Canada and its customers resulted in a decrease of 11 to 14 percent in concentrate and pellet prices for 1999.

Ownership of Labrador is a long-term proposition, if you want it to be. Your investment will not run out — there are about 40 years' worth of production in the proven and probable reserves, based on current production levels.

Mailing Address:
> 26th Floor
> Scotia Plaza
> 40 King Street West
> Toronto, Ontario
> M5W 2X6

Contact: Roseanne Moloney

Telephone: (416) 863-7133

Fax: (416) 863-7425

MCM Split Share Corp. Class A (MUH.A)

MUH debuted in February 1998 at an issue price of $15. The fund's objective is to pay a quarterly dividend (the target is $0.30 per quarter) to unitholders while preserving or enhancing capital and to return the original issue price to investors at the fund's termination date of February 1/08. The fund's strategy is to hold a portfolio of Canadian common shares listed on the TSE 300 Composite Index, a portion (up to 20 percent) in U.S. common shares listed on the Standard & Poor's 100 Index, and to write call options against all or part of the portfolio to enhance returns.

Thus far, the fund has maintained its $0.30 per quarter distribution on the class A shares since inception.

The largest allocations as of July 1999 were to industrial products (25 percent), utilities (18 percent), and financial services (15 percent). The ten largest holdings are BCE Inc., Northern Telecom, Canadian National Railway Company, Canadian Pacific, Petro-Canada,

Toronto-Dominion Bank, Bank of Nova Scotia, Bombardier, Alcan Aluminum, and AT&T Corp.

Mailing Address:
> Standard Life Centre
> 121 King Street West
> Suite 2600
> Toronto, Ontario
> M5H 3T9

Contact Person: David Middleton

Telephone: (416) 681-3900

Fax: (416) 681-3901

Sixty Plus Income Trust (SIX.UN)

Sixty Plus Income Trust debuted in February 1998 at an issue price of $25 per unit. The fund's objectives are to provide unitholders with a stable stream of quarterly distributions of at least $0.50 per unit and to return the original issue price of the units on the termination date of January 1/09.

The fund's portfolio is invested primarily in common shares selected from the new S&P/TSE 60 Index (hence the 60 Plus name), which debuted in January 1999. Up to 20 percent of the fund's portfolio (at cost) can be invested in the common shares of the top 60 corporations (by market capitalization) from the S&P 100 Index or ADRs of the top 60 companies by market capitalization whose ADRs are listed on the NYSE or NASDAQ.

As with the other Mulvihill Capital Management issues (see the First Premium series and MCM Split Shares) the fund manager may from time to time write call options against part or the entire investment portfolio.

As with Income Financial Trust, Sixty Plus Income Trust unitholders will have a continuous right to redeem units. Units tendered within five business days of the last day of the month are redeemed as at that final date with payment on or before the fifteenth date following the redemption date. Units tendered after that date are redeemed on the last business day of the next month. The redemption price is the NAVPU minus the lesser of (i) 4 percent of the NAVPU and (ii) $1 per unit. In

December each year the redemption price is the NAVPU without adjustment.

Sixty Plus paid its first cash distribution of $0.80 per unit to unitholders of record June 30/99. This is a pro-rated amount representing the distributions for the first two quarters of 1999 ($0.30 for first quarter and $0.50 for second quarter).

Mailing Address:
    Standard Life Centre
    121 King Street West
    Suite 2600
    Toronto, Ontario
    M5H 3T9

Telephone: (416) 681-3925

Split Yield Corporation Capital Shares (YLD)

YLD was listed on the TSE on April 16, 1998. The fund's objective is to pay a high quarterly dividend ($0.45 per quarter is the target) to unitholders while preserving or enhancing capital. The fund's strategy is to hold a port-folio of Canadian common shares listed on the Toronto 100 Index, of U.S. common shares listed on the Standard & Poor's 100 Index, and to write call options against all or part of the portfolio to enhance returns.

YLD's objectives are similar to MUH's, although it targets for a larger quarterly dividend. The $0.45 per quarter goal represents a very aggressive 12 percent target return based on the initial issue price of $15. This fund has a well-designed investment strategy and management expertise in covered writing.

Shareholders of record as at January 29/99 (ex-divi-dend date was January 27/99) received a $0.45 per share quarterly dividend plus a $0.45 per share special divi-dend. An additional distribution of $0.45 per share was made in April 1999. The fund has recorded a total return in the year to date of 12.6 percent. The fund's aggressive strategy is paying off, as it has thus far managed to main-tain both its share value and its 12 percent yield based on issue price dividend yield.

Mailing Address:
Royal Trust Tower
77 King Street West
Suite 2505
Toronto, Ontario
M5K 1K7

Telephone: (416) 304-4444; (877) 478-2372

Fax: (416) 304-4441

WEB: www.splityield. com

Triax Diversified High Yield Trust (TRH. UN)

TRH has a very clear investment objective: paying investors a monthly income equal to or greater than the yield on ten-year government of Canada bonds plus two percent. The fund holds a portfolio of primarily high-yield corporate bonds. The largest holdings as of July 1999 included mid-term and longer-term bonds of Air Canada, Celestica Inc., Clearnet Communications, Metronet Communications, Microcell Telecommunications, Norampac, Rogers Cable Systems, Sun Media, and Western Star Truck Holdings.

Including the $0.15 per unit distribution made on January 15/99 (record date December 31/98), the fund paid $1.20 per unit in 1998. However, the fund lost 9.5 percent on a total return basis in 1998. As of July 1999, Triax had distributed $0.60 per share while maintaining a stable unit price.

Mailing Address:
BCE Place
161 Bay Street
Suite 4700
Toronto, Ontario
M5J 2S1

Telephone: (416) 362-2929; (800) 407-0287

Fax: (416) 362-2199

WINNING THE INVESTMENT RACE

Every successful investor eventually comes to understand one fundamental truth about the process – this is a marathon, not a sprint.

How well, or badly, your securities perform over one, two, or three years is not important in the grand scheme of things. What matters is how well they do over 10, 20, and 30 years. Sometimes it's difficult to keep that in perspective, especially when a particular mutual fund is tanking. For example, investors bailed out of the AIC Advantage Fund in droves in 1999 when performance dropped sharply after shares in banks and mutual fund companies took a hit. They ignored the fact that over the previous decade the fund had returned better than 17 percent a year, an outstanding performance by any standard. When AIC Advantage bounces back, as it inevitably will, many people will regret their hasty decision.

Every investor has to be prepared to accept both good and bad times. What's important is to maximize returns when conditions are good and minimize the losses when the bad times come. A well-designed portfolio with carefully selected securities that meet your specific needs is the best way to achieve that.

What kind of returns should you expect? Over the long haul, an aggressive growth portfolio that averages better than 10 percent annually is doing extremely well. If you're able to generate an average annual return in the 12 percent range over a decade, consider yourself a super-investor. Even the best of the pros would have difficulty matching that.

The less risk you're willing to accept in your portfolio, the lower your probable return. Those who opt for our Safety Portfolio should expect to do no better than about five percent annually under the kind of interest rate conditions that prevailed through most of the 1990s. When interest rates are high, a Safety Portfolio will perform much better. However, that kind of economic environment does not show up on any of our radar scopes at this time.

So it's important that you maintain a realistic perspective in terms of your performance expectations. If you give safety a high priority, don't then turn around and expect your portfolio to generate annual returns of eight to ten percent. That may seem like an obvious statement. However, we receive dozens of questions every year from people asking exactly that: "Where can I invest my money to get ten percent a year with no risk?" The answer: nowhere.

Nor do you need ten percent returns to build a sizeable nest egg. An investment of $3,000 a year that earns six percent annually over 30 years will grow to more than $235,000 at the end of that time. Of course, we don't recommend that anyone with that long a time horizon invest in such a conservative manner. But if that's your decision, you can still achieve some respectable results.

What it all comes down to in the end is self-discipline. You must make the effort to select those securities that best suit your goals, either on your own or with the help of a financial advisor. Then you must use those securities and the tools we've given you in this book to construct an appropriate portfolio. Finally, you need to monitor that portfolio constantly to ensure that it's performing as you intended. If it's not, find out why and make needed changes.

Don't be impatient. At the outset, the results may seem to be slow in coming. But it's like a snowball rolling downhill. As it gathers momentum, it grows larger and larger, until by the time it reaches the bottom it is ten times or more its original size.

That's what will happen to your investments if you choose them with care and look after them properly.

We've done all we can to help. Now it's your turn.

Fund Name	Fund Type	Sub-Type	MVA	Canadian Equity	U.S. Equity	Europe	Japan	Far East	Latin America	Special Equity	Dividend	Fixed Income	Global Fixed Income	Money Market	Short Term	Mid Term	Long Term	Foreign Currency	Sector Specific	Small-cap	Mid-cap	Large-cap	Top Down	Bottom Up	Value Method	Sector Rotation	Momentum	Indexation
@rgentum Canadian Small Company Pfl	CdnEq	SCDivr		◆																◆				◆			◆	
@rgentum Discovery Portfolio	CdnEq	SCDivr		◆																◆				◆			◆	
@rgentum Income Portfolio	Balan	CdnSAA		◆	◆							◆				◆								◆			◆	
@rgentum International Master Portfolio	FgnEq	Global			◆	◆												◆			◆	◆	◆				◆	
@rgentum Market Neutral Portfolio	USEq	Divers			◆													◆					◆				◆	
@rgentum Quebec Balanced Portfolio	Balan	CdnSAA		◆								◆				◆					◆	◆		◆			◆	
@rgentum Short Term Asset Portfolio	FixInc	CdnMkt											◆	◆	◆													◆
@rgentum U.S. Master Portfolio	USEq	Divers			◆													◆			◆	◆		◆			◆	
20/20 Aggressive Global Stock	FgnEq	Global			◆	◆												◆			◆	◆		◆			◆	
20/20 Aggressive Growth	USEq	Divers	81.3		◆															◆	◆	◆		◆			◆	
20/20 Canadian Resources	CdnEq	Resorc	93.1							◆									◆					◆			◆	
20/20 Emerging Markets Value	FgnEq	Emerg	66.9				◆	◆	◆									◆						◆	◆		◆	
20/20 India	FgnEq	India	107.2				◆	◆										◆			◆			◆	◆		◆	
20/20 Latin America	FgnEq	Latin	71.4						◆									◆						◆	◆		◆	
20/20 Managed Futures Value **	Spclty	Other	81.7							◆								◆	◆				◆					◆

Fund	Category	Type	Score
20/20 RSP Aggressive Equity *	CdnEq	Growth	84.0
20/20 RSP Aggressive Smaller Companies	CdnEq	Growth	
ABC American-Value	FgnEq	NrthAm	
ABC Fully-Managed	Balan	CdnSAA	96.7
ABC Fundamental-Value	CdnEq	Value	97.0
Acadia Atlantic	Balan	CdnSAA	
Acadia Balanced	Balan	CdnSAA	79.5
Acadia Bond	FixInc	CdnBnd	91.6
Acadia Canadian Equity	CdnEq	Divers	
Acadia Diversified	Balan	CdnSAA	
Acadia International Equity	FgnEq	IntlEq	
Acadia Money Market	FixInc	CdnMkt	84.8
Acadia Mortgage	FixInc	Mortge	86.2
Acker Finley QSA Canadian Equity	CdnEq	LCDivr	
Acuity Bond	FixInc	CdnBnd	
Acuity Canadian Balanced	Balan	CdnSAA	
Acuity Canadian Equity	CdnEq	Divers	
Acuity High Income	Balan	CdnSAA	95.5
Acuity Money Market	FixInc	CdnMkt	
AGF American Tactical Allocation	Balan	GblTAA	117.6
AGF Canadian Bond	FixInc	CdnBnd	95.6

Fund	Category	Value
AGF Canadian Growth & Income	Balan	85.3
AGF Canadian Growth Equity	CdnEq	91.2
AGF Canadian High Income	CdnEq	110.2
AGF Canadian Money Market	FixInc	87.4
AGF Canadian Stock	CdnEq	97.8
AGF Canadian Tactical Asset Allocation	Balan	97.9
AGF Dividend	CdnEq	104.3
AGF European Asset Allocation	Balan	103.2
AGF Global Government Bond	FixInc	88.6
AGF Global Real Estate Equity	SpcIty	
AGF International Group-American Growth	USEq	95.0
AGF International Group-Asian Growth	FgnEq	94.8
AGF International Group-Canada Class	CdnEq	
AGF International Group-China Focus	FgnEq	84.8
AGF International Group-European Growth	FgnEq	87.1
AGF International Group-Germany Class	FgnEq	104.8
AGF International Group-Intl Stock	FgnEq	
AGF International Group-Japan Class	FgnEq	114.2
AGF International Group-Short Term Inc	FixInc	66.0
AGF International Group-Special U.S.	USEq	64.1
AGF International Group-World Equity	FgnEq	89.2

Fund	Category	Sub-category	MVA Score
AGF International Value	FgnEq	Global	99.5
AGF RSP Global Bond	FixInc	GlbBnd	86.5
AGF RSP International Equity Allocation	FgnEq	Global	87.9
AGF U.S. $ Money Market Account	FixInc	USMkt	95.8
AGF U.S. Income	FixInc	GlbBnd	82.7
AGF U.S. Short Term High Yield	FixInc	GlbBnd	61.3
AGF World Balanced	Balan	GblTAA	96.4
AIC Advantage	CdnEq	FinSer	99.0
AIC Advantage Fund II	CdnEq	FinSer	
AIC Advantage Seg II 100% (Transam)	CdnEq	Divers	
AIC American Advantage	USEq	Divers	
AIC American Advantage Seg 100% (Transam)	USEq	Divers	
AIC American Income Eq Seg 100% (Transam)	Balan	GblSAA	
AIC American Income Equity	Balan	GblSAA	
AIC Diversified Canada	CdnEq	Growth	118.3
AIC Diversified Canada Seg 100% (Transam)	CdnEq	Growth	
AIC Income Equity	Balan	CdnSAA	
AIC Income Equity Seg 100% (Transam)	Balan	CdnSAA	
AIC Money Market	FixInc	CdnMkt	92.9
AIC Money Market Seg 100% (Transam)	FixInc	CdnMkt	
AIC Value	FgnEq	NrthAm	96.6

Fund	Type	Category	Value
AIC Value Seg 100% (Transam)	FgnEq	NrthAm	
AIC World Advantage	FgnEq	IntlEq	
AIC World Advantage Seg 100% (Transam)	FgnEq	IntlEq	
AIC World Equity	FgnEq	IntlEq	105.7
AIC World Equity Seg 100% (Transam)	FgnEq	IntlEq	
AIM American Aggressive Growth	USEq	Divers	
AIM American Premier	USEq	LgCap	101.0
AIM Canadian Balanced	Balan	CdnTAA	96.4
AIM Canadian Bond	FixInc	GlbBnd	98.0
AIM Canadian Premier	CdnEq	LCDivr	98.5
AIM Cash Performance	FixInc	CdnMkt	92.4
AIM European Growth	FgnEq	Europe	99.0
AIM Global Health Sciences	Spclty	GlobST	88.8
AIM Global Technology	Spclty	GlobST	
AIM GT America Growth	USEq	Divers	70.0
AIM GT Canada Growth	CdnEq	Growth	98.0
AIM GT Canada Income	Balan	CdnSAA	
AIM GT Canada Money Market	FixInc	CdnMkt	
AIM GT Canada Value	CdnEq	LCValu	
AIM GT Global Bond	FixInc	GlbBnd	92.4
AIM GT Global Growth & Income	Balan	GblSAA	111.4

Fund	Category	Type	MVA
AIM GT Global Health Care	Spclty	GlobST	
AIM GT Global Infrastructure	Spclty	GlobST	87.4
AIM GT Global Natural Resources	CdnEq	Resorc	97.1
AIM GT Global Telecom	Spclty	GlobST	83.3
AIM GT Global Theme Class	FgnEq	Global	
AIM GT Latin America Growth	FgnEq	Latin	76.4
AIM GT Pacific Growth	FgnEq	PacRim	103.0
AIM GT Short-Term Income Series A	FixInc	ST Bnd	83.2
AIM GT Short-Term Income Series B	FixInc	ST Bnd	78.1
AIM International Value	FgnEq	Global	88.2
All-Canadian CapitalFund	CdnEq	Divers	79.0
All-Canadian Compound	CdnEq	Divers	79.2
All-Canadian ConsumerFund	CdnEq	Consum	99.4
All-Canadian Resources Corporation	CdnEq	Resorc	80.9
Alpha Money Market	FixInc	CdnMkt	
Alpha Quantitative Equity	CdnEq	Divers	
Alpha Quantitative Value	CdnEq	Value	
Alpha U.S. Small Cap Value	USEq	SmCap	
Altafund Investment Corporation	CdnEq	Divers	81.0
Altamira Asia Pacific	FgnEq	PacRim	93.5
Altamira Balanced	Balan	CdnTAA	91.7

Fund	Type	Category	Value
Altamira Bond	FixInc	CdnBnd	104.0
Altamira Capital Growth	CdnEq	LCGrwt	97.5
Altamira Dividend	CdnEq	Dividnd	101.6
Altamira e-business	Spclty	GlobST	
Altamira Equity	CdnEq	Divers	90.2
Altamira European Equity	FgnEq	Europe	92.6
Altamira Global Bond	FixInc	GlbBnd	78.3
Altamira Global Discovery	FgnEq	Emerg	63.9
Altamira Global Diversified	FgnEq	Global	90.3
Altamira Global Small Company	FgnEq	Global	
Altamira Growth & Income	Balan	CdnTAA	76.5
Altamira High Yield Bond	FixInc	GlbBnd	94.8
Altamira Income	FixInc	CdnBnd	95.4
Altamira Japanese Opportunity	FgnEq	Japan	105.0
Altamira North American Recovery	CdnEq	Divers	96.8
Altamira Precious & Strategy Metal	CdnEq	PrMetl	86.3
Altamira Precision Canadian Index	CdnEq	LCDivr	
Altamira Precision Intl RSP Index	FgnEq	IntlEq	
Altamira Precision U.S. RSP Index	USEq	Divers	
Altamira Resource	CdnEq	Resorc	81.3
Altamira Science & Technology	Spclty	GlobST	94.2

Fund	Category	MVA Score
Altamira Select American	USEq / SmCap	68.6
Altamira Short Term Canadian Income	FixInc / CdnMkt	
Altamira Short Term Global Income	SpcIty / Crrncy	68.6
Altamira Short Term Government Bond	FixInc / ST Bnd	93.4
Altamira Special Growth	CdnEq / SCGrwt	105.1
Altamira T-Bill	FixInc / CdnMkt	
Altamira US Larger Company	USEq / LgCap	88.5
APEX Asian Pacific	FgnEq / PacRim	95.7
APEX Balanced (AGF)	Balan / CdnTAA	89.6
APEX Balanced (Dynamic)	Balan / CdnSAA	
APEX Canadian Growth (AGF)	CdnEq / LCDivr	89.6
APEX Canadian Stock	CdnEq / Divers	
APEX Cdn Value (Dynamic)	CdnEq / Value	
APEX Fixed Income	FixInc / CdnBnd	92.4
APEX Global Equity	FgnEq / Global	
APEX Growth & Income	Balan / CdnSAA	
APEX Money Market	FixInc / CdnMkt	86.5
APEX Mortgage	FixInc / B & M	84.4
APEX U.S. Equity	USEq / Divers	
Artisan Aggressive Portfolio	Balan / CdnSAA	
Artisan Canadian Equity	CdnEq / Divers	

Fund			
Artisan Canadian Fixed Income	FixInc	CdnBnd	
Artisan Conservative Portfolio	Balan	CdnSAA	
Artisan Global Fixed Income	FixInc	GlbBnd	
Artisan International Equity	FgnEq	Global	
Artisan Moderate Portfolio	Balan	CdnSAA	
Artisan Most Aggressive Portfolio	Balan	CdnSAA	
Artisan Most Conservative Portfolio	Balan	CdnSAA	
Artisan RSP Aggressive Portfolio	Balan	CdnSAA	
Artisan RSP Conservative Portfolio	Balan	CdnSAA	
Artisan RSP Moderate Portfolio	Balan	CdnSAA	
Artisan RSP Most Aggressive Portfolio	Balan	CdnSAA	
Artisan RSP Most Conservative Portfolio	Balan	CdnSAA	
Artisan U.S. Equity	USEq	Divers	
Associate Investors	CdnEq	Value	114.6
Astra 110	Balan	CdnSAA	
Astra 110 - Series II	Balan	CdnSAA	
Astra 125	Balan	CdnSAA	
Astra American Equity	USEq	Divers	
Astra Balanced	Balan	CdnSAA	
Astra Bond	FixInc	CdnBnd	
Astra Bond - Series II	FixInc	CdnBnd	

Fund	Category	Subcategory	Score
Astra Canadian Equity	CdnEq	Divers	
Astra Canadian Equity - Series II	CdnEq	Divers	
Astra Canadian Index	CdnEq	Divers	
Astra Demographic Tendency	CdnEq	Divers	
Astra Dividend	CdnEq	Divdnd	
Astra Dynamic	Balan	CdnSAA	
Astra International Equity	FgnEq	IntlEq	
Astra Money Market	FixInc	CdnMkt	
Astra Secure	CdnEq	Divers	
Astra US RSP index	USEq	Divers	
Atlas American Advantage Value	USEq	LgCap	86.4
Atlas American Large Cap Growth	USEq	LgCap	94.1
Atlas American Money Market	FixInc	USMkt	95.2
Atlas American RSP Index	USEq	Divers	
Atlas Canadian Balanced	Balan	CdnSAA	113.7
Atlas Canadian Bond	FixInc	CdnBnd	92.8
Atlas Canadian Emerging Growth	CdnEq	SCGrwt	85.9
Atlas Canadian High Yield Bond	FixInc	CdnBnd	91.4
Atlas Canadian Income and Growth	Balan	CdnSAA	
Atlas Canadian Income Trust	CdnEq	Divdnd	
Atlas Canadian Large Cap Growth	CdnEq	LCDivr	102.9

Fund	Type	Style	Value
Atlas Canadian Large Cap Value	CdnEq	LCDivr	97.1
Atlas Canadian Money Market	FixInc	CdnMkt	92.8
Atlas Canadian Small Cap Growth	CdnEq	SCDivr	
Atlas Canadian Small Cap Value	CdnEq	SCDivr	105.7
Atlas Canadian T-Bill	FixInc	CdnMkt	88.2
Atlas European Value	FgnEq	Europe	93.5
Atlas Global Value	FgnEq	Global	93.4
Atlas International Emerging Markets Gth	FgnEq	Emerg	
Atlas International Large Cap Growth	FgnEq	IntlEq	
Atlas International RSP Index	FgnEq	IntlEq	
Atlas Latin American Value	FgnEq	Latin	81.1
Atlas Pacific Basin Value	FgnEq	PacRim	102.9
Atlas World Bond	FixInc	GlbBnd	79.0
Azura Balanced Pooled	Balan	GblSAA	92.7
Azura Balanced RSP Pooled	Balan	CdnSAA	
Azura Conservative Pooled	Balan	CdnSAA	105.2
Azura Growth Pooled	FgnEq	Global	82.3
Azura Growth RSP Pooled	CdnEq	Divers	
Azura RSP Aggressive Growth Pooled	CdnEq	SCDivr	
B.E.S.T. Discoveries	Labour	LSVC	
Beutel Goodman American Equity	USEq	LgCap	75.9

Fund	Category	Category	MVA Score
Beutel Goodman Balanced	Balan	CdnSAA	98.8
Beutel Goodman Canadian Equity	CdnEq	Divers	98.9
Beutel Goodman Income	FixInc	CdnBnd	99.3
Beutel Goodman International Equity	FgnEq	IntlEq	90.0
Beutel Goodman Money Market	FixInc	CdnMkt	98.0
Beutel Goodman Private Balanced	Balan	CdnSAA	106.4
Beutel Goodman Private Bond	FixInc	CdnBnd	94.1
Beutel Goodman Private Foreign Equity	USEq	Divers	87.1
Beutel Goodman Small Cap	CdnEq	SCDivr	116.8
Bissett American Equity	USEq	LgCap	88.6
Bissett Bond	FixInc	CdnBnd	97.1
Bissett Canadian Equity	CdnEq	LCDivr	106.2
Bissett Dividend Income	CdnEq	Divdnd	109.9
Bissett Income Trust	CdnEq	Divdnd	
Bissett International Equity	FgnEq	IntlEq	99.5
Bissett Microcap	CdnEq	SCDivr	
Bissett Money Market	FixInc	CdnMkt	99.8
Bissett Multinational Growth	FgnEq	NrthAm	100.2
Bissett Retirement	Balan	CdnSAA	106.0
Bissett Small Capital	CdnEq	SCDivr	106.7
BNP (Canada) Bond	FixInc	CdnBnd	87.6

Fund	Type	Category	Value
BNP (Canada) Canadian Money Markets	FixInc	CdnMkt	85.5
BNP (Canada) Equity	CdnEq	LCDivr	101.2
BPI American Equity Value	USEq	LgCap	99.3
BPI American Equity Value Segregated	USEq	LgCap	
BPI American Small Companies	USEq	SmCap	62.5
BPI Asia Pacific	FgnEq	PacRim	
BPI Canadian Bond	FixInc	CdnBnd	90.7
BPI Canadian Bond Segregated	FixInc	CdnBnd	
BPI Canadian Equity Value	CdnEq	LCDivr	92.0
BPI Canadian Equity Value Segregated	CdnEq	LCDivr	
BPI Canadian Mid-Cap	CdnEq	Divers	
BPI Canadian Mid-Cap Segregated	CdnEq	Divers	
BPI Canadian Resource Fund Inc.	CdnEq	Resorc	79.1
BPI Canadian Small Companies	CdnEq	SCDivr	83.9
BPI Corporate Bond	FixInc	CdnBnd	
BPI Corporate Bond Segregated			
BPI Dividend Equity	CdnEq	LCDivr	
BPI Dividend Equity Segregated			
BPI Dividend Income	CdnEq	Divdnd	116.0
BPI Dividend Income Segregated	CdnEq	Divdnd	
BPI Emerging Markets	FgnEq	Emerg	

Fund	Category	Type	MVA
BPI Global Equity Value	FgnEq	Global	100.9
BPI Global Equity Value Segregated	FgnEq	Global	
BPI Global Opportunities	FgnEq	Global	120.8
BPI Global RSP Bond	FixInc	GlbBnd	89.4
BPI Global Small Companies	FgnEq	Global	83.2
BPI High Income	CdnEq	Divdnd	
BPI High Income Segregated	CdnEq	Divdnd	
BPI Income & Growth	Balan	CdnSAA	
BPI Income & Growth Segregated	Balan	CdnSAA	
BPI International Eq Value Segregated	FgnEq	IntlEq	
BPI International Equity Value	FgnEq	IntlEq	
BPI T-Bill	FixInc	CdnMkt	97.0
BPI T-Bill Segregated	FixInc	CdnMkt	
BPI U.S. Money Market	FixInc	USMkt	
C.I. American	USEq	LgCap	89.1
C.I. American RSP	USEq	LgCap	89.7
C.I. American Sector	USEq	LgCap	87.6
C.I. American Segregated	USEq	LgCap	
C.I. Canadian Balanced	Balan	CdnSAA	93.7
C.I. Canadian Bond	FixInc	CdnBnd	102.5
C.I. Canadian Growth	CdnEq	Divers	95.3

Fund	Type	Category	Value
C.I. Canadian Income	Balan	CdnSAA	100.1
C.I. Canadian Resource	CdnEq	Resorc	
C.I. Canadian Sector	CdnEq	Divers	93.7
C.I. Covington	Labour	LSVC	101.8
C.I. Dividend	CdnEq	Divdnd	
C.I. Emerging Markets	FgnEq	Emerg	75.6
C.I. Emerging Markets Sector	FgnEq	Emerg	74.8
C.I. Global	FgnEq	Global	98.7
C.I. Global Bond RSP	FixInc	GlbBnd	91.8
C.I. Global Boomernomics RSP	Balan	GblSAA	
C.I. Global Boomernomics Sector	Balan	GblSAA	
C.I. Global Consumer Products Sector	FgnEq	Global	
C.I. Global Energy Sector	FgnEq	Global	
C.I. Global Equity RSP	FgnEq	Global	89.6
C.I. Global Financial Services Sector	FgnEq	Global	
C.I. Global Health Sciences Sector	Spclty	GlobST	
C.I. Global High Yield	FixInc	GlbBnd	70.5
C.I. Global Resource Sector	CdnEq	Resorc	
C.I. Global Sector	FgnEq	Global	97.3
C.I. Global Segregated	FgnEq	Global	
C.I. Global Technology Sector	Spclty	GlobST	

Fund	Spclty	GlobST
C.I. Global Telecommunications Sector		
C.I. International Balanced	Balan	109.3
C.I. International Balanced RSP	Balan	101.7
C.I. Japanese Sector	FgnEq	
C.I. Latin American	FgnEq	Latin 68.2
C.I. Latin American Sector	FgnEq	Latin 68.1
C.I. Money Market	FixInc	CdnMkt 96.1
C.I. Money Market Segregated	FixInc	CdnMkt
C.I. Pacific	FgnEq	PacRim 94.6
C.I. Pacific Sector	FgnEq	PacRim 93.7
C.I. Short-term Sector	FixInc	CdnMkt 98.2
C.I. US Money Market	FixInc	USMkt 97.8
C.I. World Bond	FixInc	GlbBnd 93.0
Cambridge American Growth	USEq	SmCap 77.7
Cambridge Americas	FgnEq	NrthAm 84.8
Cambridge Balanced	Balan	CdnSAA 62.8
Cambridge China	FgnEq	China 85.5
Cambridge Global	FgnEq	Global 69.8
Cambridge Growth	CdnEq	SCDivr 72.3
Cambridge Pacific	FgnEq	PacRim 92.1
Cambridge Precious Metals	CdnEq	PrMetl

Fund	Category	Type	Value
Cambridge Resource	CdnEq	Resorc	67.2
Cambridge Special Equity	CdnEq	SCGrwt	81.1
Canada Life Asia Pacific Equity	FgnEq	PacRim	105.5
Canada Life Canadian Equity	Equity	Divers	98.3
Canada Life Enhanced Dividend	Equity	CdnDiv	
Canada Life European Equity	FgnEq	Europe	92.3
Canada Life Fixed Income	FixInc	CdnBnd	95.5
Canada Life Gen Asset Alloc (Fidelity)	Balan	CdnAll	
Canada Life Gen Balanced (Bissett)	Balan	CdnBal	
Canada Life Gen Balanced (Trimark)	Balan	CdnBal	
Canada Life Gen Boomernomics (CI)	Balan	SAA	
Canada Life Gen Canadian Bond (AGF)	FixInc	CdnBnd	
Canada Life Gen Canadian Eq (Bissett)	Equity	Divers	
Canada Life Gen Canadian Eq (Scudder)	Equity	Divers	
Canada Life Gen Canadian Eq (Templeton)	Equity	Divers	
Canada Life Gen Canadian Eq (Trimark)	Equity	Divers	
Canada Life Gen Canadian Equity (AGF)	Equity	SCValu	
Canada Life Gen Canadian Equity (AIC)	Equity	Divers	
Canada Life Gen Canadian Equity(Laketon)	Equity	Divers	
Canada Life Gen Cdn S-Term Bond(Scudder)	FixInc	STBnd	
Canada Life Gen Continuum Aggr Gth Mod	Balan	CdnBal	

Canada Life Gen Continuum Conserv Module	Balan	CdnBal
Canada Life Gen Continuum Growth Module	Balan	CdnBal
Canada Life Gen Continuum Max Gth Module	Balan	CdnBal
Canada Life Gen Continuum Moderate Mod	Balan	CdnBal
Canada Life Gen Dividend (AGF)	Equity	CdnDiv
Canada Life Gen Enhancd Dividnd(Laketon)	Equity	CdnDiv
Canada Life Gen European Equity(Laketon)	FgnEq	Europe
Canada Life Gen Fixed Income (Bissett)	FixInc	CdnBnd
Canada Life Gen Fixed Income (Laketon)	FixInc	CdnBnd
Canada Life Gen Global Equity (Laketon)	FgnEq	Global
Canada Life Gen Global Equity (Scudder)	FgnEq	Global
Canada Life Gen Global Equity (Trimark)	FgnEq	Global
Canada Life Gen Global Equity RSP (CI)	FgnEq	Global
Canada Life Gen Greater Europe (Scudder)	FgnEq	Europe
Canada Life Gen Gth America (Fidelity)	FgnEq	USDiv
Canada Life Gen Harbour Canadian (CI)	Equity	Divers
Canada Life Gen Harbour Gth & Income(CI)	Balan	CdnBal
Canada Life Gen Indexed Balanced (TDQC)	Balan	CdnBal
Canada Life Gen Indexed Cdn Bond (TDQC)	FixInc	CdnBnd
Canada Life Gen Indexed Cdn Eq (TDQC)	Equity	Divers
Canada Life Gen Indexed Global Eq (TDQC)	FgnEq	IntlEq

Canada Life Gen Indexed U.S. Eq (TDOC)	FgnEq	USDiv	
Canada Life Gen Intl Bond (Laketon)	FixInc	FgnBnd	
Canada Life Gen Intl Equity (Templeton)	FgnEq	IntlEq	
Canada Life Gen Intl Pfl (Fidelity)	FgnEq	Global	
Canada Life Gen Managed (Laketon)	Balan	CdnBal	
Canada Life Gen Money Market (Laketon)	Cash	CdnMkt	
Canada Life Gen NLoad Money Mkt(Laketon)	Cash	CdnMkt	
Canada Life Gen Small Cap Eq (Bissett)	Equity	SCDivr	
Canada Life Gen True North (Fidelity)	Equity	Divers	
Canada Life Gen U.S. Equity (Scudder)	FgnEq	USDiv	
Canada Life Gen U.S. Value (AIC)	FgnEq	USDiv	
Canada Life Gen World Equity (AIC)	FgnEq	IntlEq	
Canada Life International Bond	FixInc	FgnBnd	83.8
Canada Life Managed	Balan	CdnBal	98.5
Canada Life Money Market	Cash	CdnMkt	90.9
Canada Life S-2	Equity	Divers	100.6
Canada Life U.S. & International Equity	FgnEq	Global	94.9
Canadian Medical Discoveries	Labour	LSVC	74.3
Canadian Protected	CdnEq	Divers	96.7
Canadian Venture Opportunities	Labour	LSVC	88.3
Canso Canadian Equity	CdnEq	Divers	

Fund	Category	Code	Score
Canso Value Bond	FixInc	CdnBnd	
Capital Alliance Ventures	Labour	LSVC	77.2
Capstone Balanced Trust	Balan	CdnSAA	102.0
Capstone Cash Management	FixInc	CdnMkt	97.1
Capstone International Investment	FgnEq	Global	83.9
Chou Associates	USEq	SmCap	115.6
Chou RRSP	CdnEq	Divers	145.6
CIBC 5 Year Protected Balanced Index	Balan	CdnSAA	
CIBC 5-Year Protected Canadian Index	CdnEq	Divers	
CIBC 5-Year Protected Cdn Bond Index	FixInc	CdnBnd	
CIBC 5-Year Protected International Indx	FgnEq	IntlEq	
CIBC 5-Year Protected U.S. Index	USEq	Divers	
CIBC Balanced	Balan	CdnTAA	100.1
CIBC Canadian Bond	FixInc	CdnBnd	98.8
CIBC Canadian Bond Index	FixInc	CdnBnd	
CIBC Canadian Emerging Companies	CdnEq	SCDivr	
CIBC Canadian Imperial Equity	CdnEq	Divers	
CIBC Canadian Index	CdnEq	LCDivr	
CIBC Canadian Real Estate	Spclty	CdnRE	
CIBC Canadian Resources	CdnEq	Resorc	92.2
CIBC Canadian Short-Term Bond Index	FixInc	ST Bnd	93.1

CIBC Canadian Small Companies	CdnEq	SCDivr	
CIBC Canadian T-Bill	FixInc	CdnMkt	92.0
CIBC Capital Appreciation	CdnEq	Divers	97.7
CIBC Core Canadian Equity	CdnEq	Divers	100.4
CIBC Dividend	CdnEq	Divdnd	101.2
CIBC Emerging Economies	FgnEq	Emerg	71.1
CIBC Energy	CdnEq	Resorc	
CIBC European Equity	FgnEq	Europe	88.6
CIBC European Index	FgnEq	Europe	
CIBC Far East Prosperity	FgnEq	PacRim	96.9
CIBC Financial Companies	CdnEq	FinSer	
CIBC Global Bond	FixInc	GlbBnd	93.1
CIBC Global Bond Index	FixInc	GlbBnd	
CIBC Global Equity	FgnEq	Global	100.3
CIBC Global Technology	Spclty	GlobST	91.8
CIBC International Index	FgnEq	IntlEq	
CIBC International Index RRSP	FgnEq	IntlEq	
CIBC International Small Companies	FgnEq	IntlEq	
CIBC Japanese Equity	FgnEq	Japan	112.4
CIBC Latin American	FgnEq	Latin	
CIBC Money Market	FixInc	CdnMkt	92.8

Fund	Class	Category	MVA
CIBC Monthly Income	FixInc	CdnBnd	
CIBC Mortgage	FixInc	Mortge	94.7
CIBC North American Demographics	FgnEq	NrthAm	
CIBC Precious Metal	CdnEq	PrMetl	
CIBC Premium Canadian T-Bill	FixInc	CdnMkt	96.6
CIBC U.S. SMoney Market	FixInc	USMkt	95.0
CIBC U.S. Equity Index	USEq	LgCap	92.3
CIBC U.S. Index RRSP Fund	USEq	Divers	
CIBC U.S. Small Companies	USEq	SmCap	63.3
Clarica Alpine Asian	FgnEq	PacRim	
Clarica Alpine Canadian Resources	CdnEq	Resorc	
Clarica Alpine Growth Equity	CdnEq	Divers	
Clarica Amerifund	USEq	LgCap	89.3
Clarica Bond	FixInc	CdnBnd	93.2
Clarica Diversifund 40	Balan	CdnTAA	101.8
Clarica Equifund	CdnEq	Divers	95.7
Clarica Money Market	FixInc	CdnMkt	92.2
Clarica Premier America	USEq	LgCap	88.2
Clarica Premier Blue Chip	CdnEq	LCDivr	97.5
Clarica Premier Bond	FixInc	CdnBnd	93.6
Clarica Premier Diversified	Balan	CdnTAA	94.7

Clarica Premier Emerging Markets	FgnEq	Emerg	62.8
Clarica Premier Growth	CdnEq	SCGrwt	103.5
Clarica Premier International	FgnEq	IntlEq	99.8
Clarica Premier Mortgage	FixInc	Mortge	92.6
Clarica Summit Canadian Equity	CdnEq	LCDivr	
Clarica Summit Dividend Growth	CdnEq	Divdnd	
Clarica Summit Foreign Equity	FgnEq	Global	
Clarica Summit Growth and Income	Balan	CdnSAA	
Clarington Asia Pacific	FgnEq	PacRim	
Clarington Canadian Balanced	Balan	CdnSAA	
Clarington Canadian Equity	CdnEq	LCDivr	
Clarington Canadian Income	Balan	CdnSAA	
Clarington Canadian Micro-Cap	CdnEq	SCDivr	
Clarington Canadian Small Cap	CdnEq	SCDivr	
Clarington Global Communications	Spclty	GlobST	
Clarington Global Equity	FgnEq	Global	
Clarington Global Opportunities	FgnEq	Global	
Clarington International Equity	FgnEq	IntlEq	
Clarington Money Market	FixInc	CdnMkt	
Clarington U.S. Equity	USEq	Divers	
Clarington U.S. Smaller Company Growth	USEq	Divers	

Fund	Category	Type	MVA
Clean Environment Balanced	Balan	CdnTAA	96.4
Clean Environment Equity	CdnEq	Growth	104.4
Clean Environment International Equity	FgnEq	Global	93.4
Common Sense Asset Builder I	Balan	CdnTAA	113.2
Common Sense Asset Builder II	Balan	CdnTAA	113.4
Common Sense Asset Builder III	Balan	CdnTAA	112.0
Common Sense Asset Builder IV	Balan	CdnTAA	110.0
Common Sense Asset Builder V	Balan	CdnTAA	109.1
Co-Operators Balanced	Balan	CdnAll	92.6
Co-Operators Canadian Equity	Equity	LCDivr	96.4
Co-Operators Fixed Income	FixInc	CdnBnd	97.2
Co-Operators Money Market	Cash	CdnMkt	
Co-Operators U.S. Equity	FgnEq	USLgC	64.6
Co-Operators US Diversified	Balan	SAA	
Crocus Investment Fund (LSIF)	Labour	LSVC	111.8
CT AmeriGrowth-Inv	USEq	LgCap	87.5
CT AsiaGrowth-Inv	FgnEq	PacRim	96.2
CT Balanced Index-Inv	Balan	CdnSAA	
CT Balanced-Inv	Balan	CdnSAA	99.9
CT Bond-Inv	FixInc	CdnBnd	94.8
CT Canadian Bond Index-Inv	FixInc	CdnBnd	

Fund	Type	Category	Value
CT Canadian Equity Index-Inv	CdnEq	LCDivr	
CT Dividend Income-Inv	CdnEq	Divdnd	106.9
CT Emerging Markets-Inv	FgnEq	Emerg	62.5
CT EuroGrowth-Inv	FgnEq	Europe	87.4
CT GlobalGrowth-Inv	FgnEq	Global	
CT High Yield Income-Inv	FixInc	GlbBnd	
CT International Bond-Inv	FixInc	GlbBnd	71.7
CT International Equity Index-Inv	FgnEq	IntlEq	
CT International Equity-Inv	FgnEq	IntlEq	100.6
CT Money Market-Inv	FixInc	CdnMkt	91.5
CT Monthly Income-Inv	FixInc	CdnBnd	
CT Mortgage-Inv	FixInc	B & M	95.3
CT North American-Inv	FgnEq	NrthAm	83.1
CT Premium Money Market-Inv	FixInc	CdnMkt	
CT Retirement Balanced-Inv	Balan	CdnSAA	
CT Short Term Bond-Inv	FixInc	ST Bnd	
CT Special Equity-Inv	CdnEq	SCGrwt	102.3
CT Stock-Inv	CdnEq	LCDivr	97.7
CT U.S. Equity Index-Inv	USEq	Divers	
CT U.S. Equity-Inv	USEq	LgCap	85.2
Cundill Canadian Security Series A	CdnEq	SCValu	134.9

Fund			MVA
Cundill Canadian Security Series B	CdnEq	SCValu	
Cundill Canadian Security Series C	CdnEq	SCValu	
Cundill Recovery Series C	FgnEq	Global	
Cundill Value Series A	FgnEq	Global	79.5
Cundill Value Series B	FgnEq	Global	
Cundill Value Series C	FgnEq	Global	
Desjardins American Market	USEq	LgCap	97.0
Desjardins Balanced	Balan	CdnSAA	94.5
Desjardins Bond	FixInc	CdnBnd	96.3
Desjardins Distinct - Bond	FixInc	CdnBnd	104.4
Desjardins Distinct - Diversified	Balan	CdnSAA	99.0
Desjardins Distinct - Equity	CdnEq	LCDivr	97.0
Desjardins Distinct - Mortgage	FixInc	Mortge	103.6
Desjardins Divers Ambitious	Balan	CdnSAA	
Desjardins Divers Audacious	Balan	CdnSAA	96.8
Desjardins Divers Moderate	Balan	CdnSAA	101.7
Desjardins Divers Secure	Balan	CdnSAA	104.3
Desjardins Dividend	CdnEq	Divdnd	106.2
Desjardins Environment	CdnEq	Divers	104.3
Desjardins Equity	CdnEq	Divers	94.5
Desjardins Europe	FgnEq	Europe	

Desjardins Growth	CdnEq	SCDivr	112.2
Desjardins High Potential Sector	CdnEq	SciTec	
Desjardins International	FgnEq	IntlEq	99.3
Desjardins Money Market	FixInc	CdnMkt	90.3
Desjardins Mortgage	FixInc	Mortge	95.2
Desjardins Quebec	Balan	CdnSAA	
Desjardins Select American	USEq	Divers	
Desjardins Select Balanced	Balan	CdnSAA	
Desjardins Select Canadian	CdnEq	Divers	
Desjardins Select Cartier	Balan	CdnSAA	
Desjardins Select Global	FgnEq	Global	
Desjardins Worldwide Balanced	Balan	GblSAA	100.9
Dominion Equity Resource	CdnEq	Resorc	104.1
Dundee Dollar-Cost Averaging	FixInc	ST Bnd	
Dundee Fund of Funds	Balan	CdnTAA	87.9
Dynamic Americas	USEq	Divers	92.4
Dynamic Canadian Growth	CdnEq	Divers	89.4
Dynamic Canadian Real Estate	Spclty	CdnRE	
Dynamic Canadian Resource	CdnEq	Resorc	
Dynamic Dividend	CdnEq	Divdnd	107.3
Dynamic Dividend Growth	CdnEq	Divdnd	106.5

Fund	Category	Sub	MVA
Dynamic Europe	FgnEq	Europe	85.2
Dynamic Far East	FgnEq	PacRim	113.0
Dynamic Fund of Canada	CdnEq	LCDivr	93.1
Dynamic Global Bond	FixInc	GlbBnd	59.4
Dynamic Global Income & Growth	Balan	GblSAA	
Dynamic Global Partners	Balan	GblTAA	87.5
Dynamic Global Precious Metals	Spclty	GlPrMt	
Dynamic Global Resource	FgnEq	Resourc	58.7
Dynamic Income	FixInc	CdnBnd	77.7
Dynamic International	FgnEq	Global	91.1
Dynamic Israel Growth	FgnEq	IntlEq	
Dynamic Latin American	FgnEq	Latin	
Dynamic Money Market	FixInc	CdnMkt	92.4
Dynamic Partners	Balan	CdnTAA	96.5
Dynamic Power American	USEq	LgCap	
Dynamic Power Balanced	Balan	CdnSAA	
Dynamic Power Bond	FixInc	CdnBnd	
Dynamic Power Canadian	CdnEq	LCDivr	
Dynamic Precious Metals	CdnEq	PrMetl	90.0
Dynamic Protected Americas	USEq	Divers	
Dynamic Protected Dividend Growth	CdnEq	Divdnd	

Fund	Category	Code	Value
Dynamic Protected Global Partners	Balan	GblTAA	
Dynamic Protected International	FgnEq	IntlEq	
Dynamic Protected Partners	Balan	CdnTAA	
Dynamic Quebec	CdnEq	Divers	
Dynamic Real Estate Equity	Spclty	GlobRE	106.4
Dynamic Small Cap	CdnEq	SCDivr	
Elliott & Page Active Bond	FixInc	CdnBnd	
Elliott & Page American Growth	USEq	LgCap	97.1
Elliott & Page Asian Growth	FgnEq	PacRim	103.0
Elliott & Page Balanced	Balan	CdnTAA	89.6
Elliott & Page Emerging Markets	FgnEq	Emerg	69.8
Elliott & Page Equity	CdnEq	LCDivr	89.3
Elliott & Page European Equity	FgnEq	Europe	
Elliott & Page Generation Wave	CdnEq	Divers	
Elliott & Page Global Equity	FgnEq	Global	89.7
Elliott & Page Growth Opportunities	CdnEq	Divers	
Elliott & Page Money	FixInc	CdnMkt	95.3
Elliott & Page Monthly High Income	CdnEq	Divdnd	
Elliott & Page Sector Rotation	CdnEq	LCDivr	
Elliott & Page T-Bill	FixInc	CdnMkt	84.4
Elliott & Page U.S. Mid-Cap	USEq	Divers	

Fund	Category	Subcategory	MVA
Elliott & Page Value Equity	CdnEq	LCValu	
Empire Asset Allocation	Balan	CdnAll	96.6
Empire Balanced	Balan	CdnBal	98.7
Empire Bond	FixInc	CdnBnd	92.5
Empire Elite Dividend Growth	Equity	CdnDiv	
Empire Elite Equity	Equity	LCDivr	101.0
Empire Elite Small Cap Equity	Equity	SCDivr	
Empire Equity Growth #3	Equity	LCDivr	103.9
Empire Foreign Currency Canadian Bond	FixInc	CdnBnd	82.6
Empire International Growth	FgnEq	Global	91.9
Empire Money Market	Cash	CdnMkt	89.0
Empire Premier Equity	Equity	LCDivr	102.7
Empire US Equity Index	FgnEq	USDiv	
ENSIS Growth Fund Inc. (LSVCC)	Labour	LSVC	
Enterprise Fund	Labour	LSVC	69.2
Equitable Life American Growth	FgnEq	USDiv	
Equitable Life Canada Accum. Income	FixInc	CdnBnd	98.3
Equitable Life Canada Asset Allocation	Balan	CdnAll	92.5
Equitable Life Canada Canadian Bond	FixInc	CdnBnd	89.9
Equitable Life Canada Canadian Stock	Equity	Divers	94.6
Equitable Life Canada Common Stock	Equity	Divers	96.9

Fund	Type	Category	Value
Equitable Life Canada International	FgnEq	Global	85.6
Equitable Life Canada Money Market	Cash	CdnMkt	89.7
Equitable Life Canadian Equity Value	Equity	Value	
Equitable Life Global Growth	FgnEq	Global	
Equitable Life Intl Fixed Income	FixInc	FgnBnd	
Ethical Balanced	Balan	CdnSAA	94.4
Ethical Global Bond	FixInc	GlbBnd	82.7
Ethical Growth	CdnEq	LCDivr	100.6
Ethical Income	FixInc	CdnBnd	95.7
Ethical Money Market	FixInc	CdnMkt	91.1
Ethical North American Equity	USEq	LgCap	94.5
Ethical Pacific Rim	FgnEq	PacRim	97.6
Ethical Special Equity	CdnEq	SCDivr	107.4
Fidelity Canadian Asset Allocation	Balan	CdnTAA	109.0
Fidelity Canadian Balanced	Balan	CdnSAA	
Fidelity Canadian Bond	FixInc	CdnBnd	97.4
Fidelity Canadian Growth Company	CdnEq	SCGrwt	123.6
Fidelity Canadian Income	FixInc	ST Bnd	95.2
Fidelity Canadian Short Term Asset	FixInc	CdnMkt	90.1
Fidelity Capital Builder	CdnEq	Growth	86.8
Fidelity Disciplined Equity	CdnEq	Divers	

Fidelity Emerging Markets Bond	FixInc	GlbBnd	76.5
Fidelity Emerging Mkts Portfolio	FgnEq	Emerg	52.5
Fidelity European Growth	FgnEq	Europe	93.0
Fidelity Far East	FgnEq	PacRim	112.5
Fidelity Focus Consumer Industries	USEq	Divers	
Fidelity Focus Financial Services	USEq	Divers	
Fidelity Focus Health Care	SpcIty	GlobST	
Fidelity Focus Natural Resources	CdnEq	Resorc	
Fidelity Focus Technology	SpcIty	GlobST	
Fidelity Global Asset Allocation	Balan	GblSAA	107.5
Fidelity Growth America	USEq	LgCap	91.0
Fidelity International Portfolio	FgnEq	Global	100.0
Fidelity Japanese Growth	FgnEq	Japan	110.2
Fidelity Latin American Growth	FgnEq	Latin	76.6
Fidelity North American Income	FixInc	GlbBnd	98.8
Fidelity Small Cap America	USEq	SmCap	70.9
Fidelity True North	CdnEq	Divers	
Fidelity U.S. Money Market	FixInc	USMkt	93.7
FIRM Canadian Growth	CdnEq	Divers	
First Canadian Asset Allocation	Balan	CdnTAA	98.9
First Canadian Bond	FixInc	CdnBnd	98.4

Fund	Type	Category	Value
First Canadian Dividend	CdnEq	Divdnd	110.9
First Canadian Emerging Markets	FgnEq	Emerg	64.9
First Canadian Equity	CdnEq	LCDivr	104.2
First Canadian Equity Index	CdnEq	LCDivr	98.5
First Canadian European	FgnEq	Europe	86.6
First Canadian Far East	FgnEq	PacRim	100.3
First Canadian Global Science & Tech	Spclty	GlobST	
First Canadian International Bond	FixInc	GlbBnd	74.2
First Canadian International Equity	FgnEq	IntlEq	96.0
First Canadian Japanese	FgnEq	Japan	96.2
First Canadian Latin America	FgnEq	Latin	
First Canadian Money Market	FixInc	CdnMkt	91.9
First Canadian Mortgage	FixInc	Mortge	86.6
First Canadian NAFTA Advantage	FgnEq	NrthAm	81.7
First Canadian Precious Metals	CdnEq	PrMetl	
First Canadian Premium Money Market	FixInc	CdnMkt	
First Canadian Resource	CdnEq	Resorc	93.5
First Canadian Special Equity	CdnEq	SCGrwt	107.2
First Canadian T-Bill	FixInc	CdnMkt	91.0
First Canadian U.S. Dollar Bond	FixInc	GlbBnd	
First Canadian U.S. Dollar Equity Index	USEq	Divers	

Fund	Category	Score
First Canadian U.S. Dollar Money Market	FixInc	USMkt
First Canadian U.S. Equity Index RSP	USEq	Divers
First Canadian U.S. Growth	USEq	LgCap	95.7
First Canadian U.S. Special Equity	USEq	Divers
First Canadian U.S. Value	USEq	Divers
First Heritage	Labour	LSVC	89.4
First Ontario	Labour	LSVC	113.9
First Trust DJIA Target 10 Trust 1996	USEq	Divers	101.0
First Trust DJIA Target 10 Trust 1997	USEq	Divers
First Trust DJIA Target 10 Trust 1998	USEq	Divers
First Trust Global Target 15 Trust 1997	FgnEq	Global
First Trust N.A. Fin Institutions Tr 97	CdnEq	FinSer
First Trust N.A. Fin Institutions Tr 98	CdnEq	FinSer
First Trust North American Tech Tr 97	SpcIty	GlobST
First Trust North American Tech Tr 98	SpcIty	GlobST
First Trust Pharmaceutical Trust 1996	SpcIty	GlobST
First Trust Pharmaceutical Trust 1997	SpcIty	GlobST
First Trust Pharmaceutical Trust 1998	FgnEq	Global
First Trust REIT & Real Estate Gth Tr 98	SpcIty	CdnRE
First Trust Wealth Management Trust 1997	CdnEq	FinSer
First Trust World's Leading Brands Tr 98	FgnEq	IntlEq

Fund	Type	Category	Value
FMOO Balanced	Balan	CdnSAA	
FMOO Bond	FixInc	CdnBnd	87.7
FMOO Canadian Equity	CdnEq	LCDivr	104.3
FMOO Fonds De Placement	Balan	CdnSAA	105.9
FMOO International Equity	FgnEq	Global	101.0
FMOO Money Market	FixInc	CdnMkt	99.4
FMOO Omnibus	Balan	CdnSAA	105.4
Fonds de Croissance Select	USEq	Divers	93.1
Fonds D'Investissement REA	CdnEq	SCDivr	131.8
Franklin U.S. Small Cap Growth	USEq	SmCap	
Friedberg Currency	Spclty	Crrncy	119.3
Friedberg Diversified	Spclty	Crrncy	
Friedberg Foreign Bond	FixInc	GlbBnd	
Friedberg Futures	Spclty	Crrncy	
Friedberg Toronto Trust Equity-Hedge	Spclty	Other	
Friedberg Toronto Trust Intl Securities	Spclty	Other	
GBC Canadian Bond	FixInc	CdnBnd	96.0
GBC Canadian Growth	CdnEq	SCGrwt	120.1
GBC International Growth	FgnEq	IntlEq	95.8
GBC Money Market	FixInc	CdnMkt	91.6
GBC North American Growth	USEq	Divers	75.1

Fund	Type	Category	Score
Global Strategy Bond	FixInc	ST Bnd	91.0
Global Strategy Canada Growth	CdnEq	Value	94.4
Global Strategy Canadian Opportunities	CdnEq	Divers	
Global Strategy Canadian Small Cap	CdnEq	SCDivr	107.0
Global Strategy Divf Europe	FgnEq	Europe	94.4
Global Strategy Divf Japan Plus	FgnEq	Japan	95.7
Global Strategy Divf World Bond	FixInc	GlbBnd	87.4
Global Strategy Divf World Equity	FgnEq	Global	94.5
Global Strategy Europe Plus	FgnEq	Europe	91.8
Global Strategy Gold Plus	CdnEq	PrMetl	88.9
Global Strategy Income Plus	Balan	CdnSAA	107.0
Global Strategy Money Market	FixInc	CdnMkt	92.0
Global Strategy U.S. Equity	USEq	Divers	86.2
Global Strategy World Balanced	Balan	GblSAA	97.9
Global Strategy World Bond	FixInc	GlbBnd	86.3
Global Strategy World Companies	FgnEq	Global	90.9
Global Strategy World Equity	FgnEq	Global	92.7
Global Strategy World Opportunities	FgnEq	IntlEq	
Global Strategy World Trust	FgnEq	Global	
Goldfund Limited	Spclty	GlPrMt	84.3
Goldtrust	CdnEq	PrMetl	87.5

Great-West Life American Growth(A) A	Divers	USEq	
Great-West Life American Growth(A) B	Divers	USEq	
Great-West Life Asian Growth(A) A	PacRim	FgnEq	
Great-West Life Asian Growth(A) B	PacRim	FgnEq	
Great-West Life Balanced(B) A	CdnSAA	Balan	
Great-West Life Balanced(B) B	CdnSAA	Balan	
Great-West Life Balanced(M) A	CdnSAA	Balan	
Great-West Life Balanced(M) B	CdnSAA	Balan	
Great-West Life Balanced(S) A	CdnSAA	Balan	
Great-West Life Balanced(S) B	CdnSAA	Balan	
Great-West Life Bond(B) A	CdnBnd	FixInc	
Great-West Life Bond(B) B	CdnBnd	FixInc	
Great-West Life Bond(S) A	CdnBnd	FixInc	
Great-West Life Bond(S) B	CdnBnd	FixInc	
Great-West Life Canadian Bond(G) A	CdnBnd	FixInc	93.3
Great-West Life Canadian Bond(G) B	CdnBnd	FixInc	94.4
Great-West Life Canadian Equity(G) A	Growth	CdnEq	93.9
Great-West Life Canadian Equity(G) B	Growth	CdnEq	94.2
Great-West Life Canadian Resources(A) A	Resorc	CdnEq	
Great-West Life Canadian Resources(A) B	Resorc	CdnEq	
Great-West Life Cdn Opportunity(M) A	SciTec	CdnEq	

Fund	Category	MVA
Great-West Life Cdn Opportunity(M) B	CdnEq	SciTec
Great-West Life Cdn Real Estate(G) A	Spclty	CdnRE	128.3
Great-West Life Cdn Real Estate(G) B	Spclty	CdnRE	129.5
Great-West Life Diversified Rs(G) A	Balan	CdnSAA	98.3
Great-West Life Diversified Rs(G) B	Balan	CdnSAA	98.8
Great-West Life Dividend(G) A	CdnEq	Divdnd
Great-West Life Dividend(G) B	CdnEq	Divdnd
Great-West Life Dividend/Growth(M) A	CdnEq	LCDivr
Great-West Life Dividend/Growth(M) B	CdnEq	LCDivr
Great-West Life Equity Index(G) A	CdnEq	LCDivr	96.8
Great-West Life Equity Index(G) B	CdnEq	LCDivr	97.1
Great-West Life Equity(M) A	CdnEq	Divers
Great-West Life Equity(M) B	CdnEq	Divers
Great-West Life Equity(S) A	CdnEq	Value
Great-West Life Equity(S) B	CdnEq	Value
Great-West Life Equity/Bond(G) A	Balan	CdnSAA	92.7
Great-West Life Equity/Bond(G) B	Balan	CdnSAA	93.1
Great-West Life European Equity(S) A	FgnEq	Europe
Great-West Life European Equity(S) B	FgnEq	Europe
Great-West life Global Income(A) A	FixInc	GlbBnd
Great-West Life Global Income(A) B	FixInc	GlbBnd

Great-West Life Government Bond(G) A	FixInc	CdnBnd	89.6
Great-West Life Government Bond(G) B	FixInc	CdnBnd	90.9
Great-West Life Growth & Income(A) A	Balan	CdnSAA	
Great-West Life Growth & Income(A) B	Balan	CdnSAA	
Great-West Life Growth & Income(M) A	Balan	CdnSAA	
Great-West Life Growth & Income(M) B	Balan	CdnSAA	
Great-West Life Growth Equity(A) A	CdnEq	Growth	
Great-West Life Growth Equity(A) B	CdnEq	Growth	
Great-West Life Income (M) A	FixInc	CdnBnd	
Great-West Life Income (M) B	FixInc	CdnBnd	
Great-West Life Income(G) A	Balan	CdnSAA	109.2
Great-West Life Income(G) B	Balan	CdnSAA	110.1
Great-West Life International Bond(P) A	FixInc	GlbBnd	70.6
Great-West Life International Bond(P) B	FixInc	GlbBnd	71.3
Great-West Life International Eq(P) A	FgnEq	IntlEq	103.5
Great-West Life International Eq(P) B	FgnEq	IntlEq	103.9
Great-West Life Intl Opportunity(P) A	FgnEq	IntlEq	
Great-West Life Intl Opportunity(P) B	FgnEq	IntlEq	
Great-West Life Larger Company(M) A	CdnEq	LCDivr	
Great-West Life Larger Company(M) B	CdnEq	LCDivr	
Great-West Life Mid Cap Canada(G) A	CdnEq	Growth	

Great-West Life Mid Cap Canada(G) B	CdnEq	Growth		◆																	◆			◆			◆	
Great-West Life Money Market(G) A	FixInc	CdnMkt	87.1											◆	◆													◆
Great-West Life Money Market(G) B	FixInc	CdnMkt	89.6											◆	◆													◆
Great-West Life Mortgage(G) A	FixInc	Mortge	98.5									◆				◆								◆	◆			
Great-West Life Mortgage(G) B	FixInc	Mortge	99.9									◆				◆								◆	◆			
Great-West Life North American Eq(B) A	CdnEq	Divers		◆																		◆		◆			◆	
Great-West Life North American Eq(B) B	CdnEq	Divers		◆																		◆		◆			◆	
Great-West Life Smaller Company(M) A	CdnEq	Divers		◆																◆				◆			◆	
Great-West Life Smaller Company(M) B	CdnEq	Divers		◆																◆				◆			◆	
Great-West Life U.S. Equity(G) A	USEq	LgCap	91.4		◆													◆				◆		◆	◆			
Great-West Life U.S. Equity(G) B	USEq	LgCap	91.8		◆													◆				◆		◆	◆			
Green Line Asian Growth	FgnEq	PacRim	103.0					◆										◆				◆	◆				◆	
Green Line Balanced Growth	Balan	CdnSAA	102.1	◆								◆				◆						◆	◆				◆	
Green Line Balanced Income	Balan	CdnSAA	99.0	◆								◆				◆						◆		◆	◆			
Green Line Blue Chip Equity	CdnEq	LCDivr	95.7	◆																		◆		◆		◆	◆	
Green Line Canadian Bond	FixInc	CdnBnd	101.0									◆				◆							◆			◆	◆	
Green Line Canadian Equity	CdnEq	Divers	102.5	◆																		◆	◆			◆	◆	
Green Line Canadian Govt Bond Index	FixInc	CdnBnd	98.4									◆				◆							◆			◆	◆	
Green Line Canadian Index	CdnEq	Divers	99.1	◆																		◆						◆
Green Line Canadian Money Market	FixInc	CdnMkt	96.6											◆	◆													◆
Green Line Canadian Small-Cap Equity	CdnEq	SCDivr		◆																◆				◆			◆	

Fund	Category	Code	Value
Green Line Canadian T-Bill	FixInc	CdnMkt	94.6
Green Line Dividend	CdnEq	Divdnd	105.5
Green Line Dow Jones Industrial Avg Indx	USEq	LgCap	
Green Line Emerging Markets	FgnEq	Emerg	65.2
Green Line Energy	CdnEq	Resorc	93.5
Green Line Entertainment & Communication	Spclty	GlobST	
Green Line European Growth	FgnEq	Europe	92.6
Green Line European Index	FgnEq	Europe	
Green Line Global Government Bond	FixInc	GlbBnd	80.1
Green Line Global RSP Bond	FixInc	GlbBnd	90.8
Green Line Global Select	FgnEq	Global	91.1
Green Line Health Sciences	Spclty	GlobST	
Green Line International Equity	FgnEq	IntlEq	95.6
Green Line International RSP Index	FgnEq	IntlEq	
Green Line Japanese Growth	FgnEq	Japan	102.7
Green Line Japanese Index	FgnEq	Japan	
Green Line Latin American Growth	FgnEq	Latin	76.7
Green Line Monthly Income	FixInc	CdnBnd	
Green Line Mortgage	FixInc	Mortge	91.4
Green Line Mortgage-Backed	FixInc	B & M	92.1
Green Line Precious Metals	CdnEq	PrMetl	98.8

Fund	Category	Sub-Category	MVA Score
Green Line Premium Money Market	FixInc	CdnMkt	
Green Line Real Return Bond	FixInc	CdnBnd	85.9
Green Line Resource	CdnEq	Resorc	87.1
Green Line Science & Technology	Spclty	GlobST	86.6
Green Line Short Term Income	FixInc	ST Bnd	94.5
Green Line U.S. Blue Chip Equity	USEq	LgCap	
Green Line U.S. Index	USEq	Divers	102.7
Green Line U.S. Mid-Cap Growth	USEq	Divers	80.3
Green Line U.S. Money Market	FixInc	USMkt	95.1
Green Line U.S. RSP Index	USEq	Divers	
Green Line U.S. Small-Cap Equity	USEq	SmCap	
Green Line Value	CdnEq	Value	99.0
Greystone Managed Global	FgnEq	Global	97.3
Greystone Managed Wealth	Balan	CdnSAA	103.7
GS American Equity	USEq	Divers	
GS Canadian Balanced	Balan	CdnSAA	
GS Canadian Equity	CdnEq	LCDivr	
GS International Bond	FixInc	GlbBnd	
GS International Equity	FgnEq	Global	
Guardian American Equity Classic	USEq	LgCap	84.6
Guardian American Equity Mutual	USEq	LgCap	83.3

Fund	Category	Sub-category	Value
Guardian American Large Cap Classic	USEq	LgCap	
Guardian American Large Cap Mutual	USEq	LgCap	
Guardian Canadian Balanced Classic	Balan	CdnSAA	90.2
Guardian Canadian Balanced Mutual	Balan	CdnSAA	88.4
Guardian Canadian Bond Classic	FixInc	CdnBnd	
Guardian Canadian Bond Mutual	FixInc	CdnBnd	
Guardian Canadian High Yield Classic	FixInc	CdnBnd	
Guardian Canadian High Yield Mutual	FixInc	CdnBnd	
Guardian Canadian Income Classic	FixInc	ST Bnd	89.3
Guardian Canadian Income Mutual	FixInc	ST Bnd	85.7
Guardian Canadian Large Cap Classic	CdnEq	LCDivr	
Guardian Canadian Large Cap Mutual	CdnEq	LCDivr	
Guardian Canadian Money Market Classic	FixInc	CdnMkt	93.7
Guardian Canadian Money Market Mutual	FixInc	CdnMkt	87.3
Guardian Emerging Markets Bond Classic	FixInc	GlbBnd	
Guardian Emerging Markets Bond Mutual	FixInc	GlbBnd	
Guardian Emerging Markets Classic	FgnEq	Emerg	61.9
Guardian Emerging Markets Mutual	FgnEq	Emerg	60.8
Guardian Enterprise Classic	CdnEq	SCGrwt	107.2
Guardian Enterprise Mutual	CdnEq	SCGrwt	
Guardian European Equity Classic	FgnEq	Europe	

Fund	Category	Score
Guardian European Equity Mutual	FgnEq	Europe
Guardian Foreign Income Class A	FixInc	GlbBnd	96.7
Guardian Foreign Income Class B	FixInc	GlbBnd	94.3
Guardian Global Equity Classic	FgnEq	Global	88.3
Guardian Global Equity Mutual	FgnEq	Global	87.5
Guardian Global Small Cap Classic	FgnEq	IntlEq
Guardian Global Small Cap Mutual	FgnEq	IntlEq
Guardian Growth & Income Classic	Balan	CdnSAA
Guardian Growth & Income Mutual	Balan	CdnSAA
Guardian Growth Equity Classic	CdnEq	Divers	96.9
Guardian Growth Equity Mutual	CdnEq	Divers	96.2
Guardian International Balanced Classic	Balan	GblSAA	93.7
Guardian International Balanced Mutual	Balan	GblSAA	91.7
Guardian International Income Classic	FixInc	GlbBnd	99.1
Guardian International Income Mutual	FixInc	GlbBnd
Guardian Monthly Dividend Fund Ltd. C	CdnEq	DivdInd	94.3
Guardian Monthly Dividend Fund Ltd. M	CdnEq	DivdInd	92.6
Guardian Monthly High Income Classic	CdnEq	DivdInd
Guardian Monthly High Income Mutual	CdnEq	DivdInd
Guardian U.S. Money Market Classic	FixInc	USMkt	95.9
Guardian U.S. Money Market Mutual	FixInc	USMkt

Hansberger Asian	FgnEq	PacRim	95.7
Hansberger Asian Sector	FgnEq	PacRim	94.7
Hansberger Developing Markets	FgnEq	Emerg	
Hansberger Developing Markets Sector	FgnEq	Emerg	
Hansberger European	FgnEq	Europe	80.5
Hansberger European Sector	FgnEq	Europe	79.0
Hansberger Global Small Cap	FgnEq	Global	
Hansberger Global Small Cap Sector	FgnEq	Global	
Hansberger International	FgnEq	IntlEq	
Hansberger International Sector	FgnEq	IntlEq	
Hansberger Value	FgnEq	Global	
Hansberger Value Sector	FgnEq	Global	
Hansberger Value Segregated	FgnEq	Global	
Harbour Explorer	CdnEq	SCGrwt	
Harbour Explorer Sector	CdnEq	SCGrwt	
Harbour Fund	CdnEq	Value	
Harbour Growth & Income	Balan	CdnSAA	
Harbour Growth & Income Segregated	Balan	CdnSAA	
Harbour Mid-Cap	CdnEq	Divers	
Harbour Mid-Cap Sector Shares	CdnEq	Divers	
Harbour Sector	CdnEq	Value	

Fund	Category	Subcategory	MVA
Harbour Segregated	CdnEq	Value	
Hartford Aggressive Growth	CdnEq	SCGrwt	
Hartford Asset Allocation	Balan	CdnTAA	
Hartford Canadian Advanced Technology	CdnEq	SciTec	
Hartford Canadian Equity	CdnEq	LCDivr	
Hartford Canadian Income	FixInc	CdnBnd	
Hartford Money Market	FixInc	CdnMkt	
Hartford Real Estate Income	Spclty	CdnRE	
Hartford Select World Economies	FgnEq	Global	
Hemisphere Value	Balan	CdnSAA	89.4
Hillsdale LS American Equity	Spclty	Crrncy	
Hirsch Balanced	Balan	CdnSAA	
Hirsch Canadian Growth	CdnEq	Divers	
Hirsch Fixed Income	FixInc	CdnBnd	
Hirsch Natural Resource	CdnEq	Resorc	
HSBC Asia Pacific	FgnEq	PacRim	99.5
HSBC Canadian Balanced	Balan	CdnTAA	99.3
HSBC Canadian Bond	FixInc	CdnBnd	97.5
HSBC Canadian Money Market	FixInc	CdnMkt	95.3
HSBC Dividend Income	CdnEq	Divdnd	109.7
HSBC Emerging Markets	FgnEq	Emerg	59.6

HSBC Equity	CdnEq	LCDivr	101.9
HSBC European	FgnEq	Europe	99.9
HSBC Global Equity	FgnEq	Global	
HSBC Mortgage	FixInc	Mortge	94.7
HSBC Small Cap Growth	CdnEq	SCGrwt	105.9
HSBC U.S. Equity	USEq	Divers	98.9
HSBC US$ Money Market	FixInc	USMkt	
HSBC World Bond	FixInc	GlbBnd	82.1
ICM Balanced	Balan	CdnSAA	97.5
ICM Bond	FixInc	CdnBnd	101.2
ICM Equity	CdnEq	Divers	93.1
ICM International	FgnEq	IntlEq	100.9
ICM Short Term Investment	FixInc	CdnMkt	102.8
ICM U.S. Small Cap Equity	USEq	SmCap	
ICM U.S. Value Growth	USEq	Divers	
Ideal Balanced	Balan	CdnSAA	103.1
Ideal Bond	FixInc	CdnBnd	93.0
Ideal Equity	CdnEq	Divers	105.3
Ideal Money Market	FixInc	CdnMkt	104.2
IG Beutel Goodman Canadian Balanced	Balan	CdnSAA	
IG Beutel Goodman Canadian Equity	CdnEq	LCDivr	

Fund	Category 1	Category 2	Score
IG Beutel Goodman Canadian Small Cap	CdnEq	SCDivr	
IG Merrill Lynch Canadian Equity	CdnEq	Divers	83.8
IG Merrill Lynch Emerging Markets	FgnEq	Emerg	64.5
IG Merrill Lynch U.S. Allocation	Balan	GblSAA	108.8
IG Merrill Lynch World Allocation	Balan	GblSAA	88.2
IG Merrill Lynch World Bond	FixInc	GlbBnd	76.5
IG Sceptre Canadian Balanced	Balan	CdnSAA	
IG Sceptre Canadian Bond	FixInc	CdnBnd	
IG Sceptre Canadian Equity	CdnEq	Divers	
Imperial Growth Canadian Equity	CdnEq	LCDivr	93.7
Imperial Growth Diversified	Balan	CdnSAA	94.7
Imperial Growth Money Market	FixInc	CdnMkt	85.9
Imperial Growth North American Equity	FgnEq	NrthAm	86.3
Industrial Alliance Bissett Bonds BBS	FixInc	CdnBnd	
Industrial Alliance Bissett Cdn Eq ABS	Equity	Divers	
Industrial Alliance Bond BNL	FixInc	CdnBnd	
Industrial Alliance Bond Fund Series 2	FixInc	CdnBnd	
Industrial Alliance Bonds	FixInc	CdnBnd	94.9
Industrial Alliance Can Advantage	Equity	Divers	
Industrial Alliance Diver Opportunity DO	Balan	CdnBal	
Industrial Alliance Diversified	Balan	CdnBal	93.8

Fund	Type	Code																																	
Industrial Alliance Diversified DNL	Balan	CdnBal	•										•							•							•							•		•
Industrial Alliance Diversified Secu DS	Balan	CdnBal	•										•							•							•							•		•
Industrial Alliance Diversified Services	Balan	CdnAll	•										•							•							•							•		•
Industrial Alliance Dividend	Balan	CnHIBa	•										•							•							•							•		•
Industrial Alliance Ecoflex A	Equity	Value 91.5	•						•				•							•							•							•		•
Industrial Alliance Ecoflex B	FixInc	CdnBnd 93.6																		•							•							•		•
Industrial Alliance Ecoflex Bond BNL	FixInc	CdnBnd																																		
Industrial Alliance Ecoflex Bonds BBS	FixInc	CdnBnd																																		
Industrial Alliance Ecoflex Cdn Eq ABS	Equity	Divers	•										•							•						•									•	
Industrial Alliance Ecoflex Cdn Gth NFI	Equity	SCGrwt	•										•							•										•						•
Industrial Alliance Ecoflex D	Balan	CdnBal 92.3	•						•				•							•							•							•		•
Industrial Alliance Ecoflex Diver Opp DO	Balan	CdnBal	•					•					•							•							•							•		•
Industrial Alliance Ecoflex Diver Sec DS	Balan	CdnBal	•									•	•							•							•				•					•
Industrial Alliance Ecoflex Divers DNL	Balan	CdnBal	•																	•							•									
Industrial Alliance Ecoflex E	FgnEq	Emerg			•																				•		•									
Industrial Alliance Ecoflex Euro Gth KFI	FgnEq	Europe				•																			•											
Industrial Alliance Ecoflex G	FixInc	FgnBnd								•																	•							•		
Industrial Alliance Ecoflex H	FixInc	Mortge 94.7							•				•							•										•						•
Industrial Alliance Ecoflex I	FgnEq	USDiv 101.7			•																				•										•	
Industrial Alliance Ecoflex M	Cash	CdnMkt 89.2																														•				•
Industrial Alliance Ecoflex N	Equity	Divers										•																							•	

Fund	Category	Subcategory	Score
Industrial Alliance Ecoflex R	FixInc	CdnBnd	
Industrial Alliance Ecoflex S	FgnEq	USDiv	
Industrial Alliance Ecoflex Stock ANL	Equity	LCValu	
Industrial Alliance Ecoflex T	Equity	LCDivr	
Industrial Alliance Ecoflex Tr N Stk AFI	Equity	Divers	
Industrial Alliance Ecoflex U	FgnEq	USDiv	
Industrial Alliance Ecoflex V	Balan	CnHlBa	
Industrial Alliance Emerging Markets	FgnEq	Emerg	
Industrial Alliance Fide Cdn Gth Co NFI	Equity	SCGrwt	
Industrial Alliance Fide Tr Nth Stck AFI	Equity	Divers	
Industrial Alliance Fidelity Eur Gth KFI	FgnEq	Europe	
Industrial Alliance Global Bond	FixInc	FgnBnd	
Industrial Alliance Income	FixInc	CdnBnd	
Industrial Alliance International	FgnEq	USDiv	102.8
Industrial Alliance Money Market	Cash	CdnMkt	86.7
Industrial Alliance Mortgages	FixInc	Mortge	96.8
Industrial Alliance Stock ANL	Equity	Value	
Industrial Alliance Stock Series 2	Equity	LCDivr	
Industrial Alliance Stocks	Equity	Value	92.5
Industrial Alliance U.S. Advantage	FgnEq	USDiv	
Industrial Alliance U.S. Equity	FgnEq	USDiv	

Fund	Type	Category	Value
Industrial American	USEq	LgCap	82.9
Industrial Balanced	Balan	CdnSAA	95.7
Industrial Bond	FixInc	CdnBnd	97.4
Industrial Cash Management	FixInc	CdnMkt	95.3
Industrial Dividend Growth	CdnEq	Divdnd	102.2
Industrial Equity	CdnEq	SCValu	84.1
Industrial Growth	CdnEq	Divers	83.9
Industrial Horizon	CdnEq	LCDivr	96.5
Industrial Income Class A	Balan	CdnSAA	102.1
Industrial Income Fund (S.40) Units	Balan	CdnSAA	
Industrial Mortgage Securities	FixInc	B & M	77.7
Industrial Pension	Balan	CdnSAA	100.6
Industrial Short-Term	FixInc	CdnMkt	86.9
Infinity Canadian	CdnEq	Growth	
Infinity Income & Growth	CdnEq	Divdnd	
Infinity International	USEq	Divers	
Infinity T-Bill	FixInc	CdnMkt	
Infinity Wealth Management	CdnEq	FinSer	
InvesNat Aggressive Diversified	Balan	CdnSAA	94.4
InvesNat American Index Plus	USEq	Divers	
InvesNat American RSP Index	USEq	Divers	

Fund	Category	Score
InvesNat Bond	FixInc	CdnBnd	95.4
InvesNat Canadian Equity	CdnEq	LCDivr	93.7
InvesNat Canadian Index	CdnEq	Divers	
InvesNat Canadian Index Plus	CdnEq	LCDivr	
InvesNat Conservative Diversified	Balanc	CdnSAA	
InvesNat Corporate Cash Management	FixInc	CdnMkt	99.3
InvesNat Dividend	CdnEq	Dividnd	108.1
InvesNat European Equity	FgnEq	Europe	92.5
InvesNat Far East Equity	FgnEq	PacRim	103.2
InvesNat International RSP Bond	FixInc	GlbBnd	84.4
InvesNat International RSP Index	FgnEq	IntlEq	
InvesNat Intrepid Diversified	Balan	CdnSAA	
InvesNat Japanese Equity	FgnEq	Japan	97.0
InvesNat Moderate Diversified	Balan	CdnSAA	
InvesNat Money Market	FixInc	CdnMkt	93.8
InvesNat Mortgage	FixInc	Mortge	94.2
InvesNat Presumed Sound Investments	FixInc	CdnMkt	
InvesNat Protected Canadian Bond	FixInc	CdnBnd	
InvesNat Protected Canadian Equity	CdnEq	Divers	
InvesNat Protected Growth Balanced	Balan	CdnSAA	
InvesNat Protected International	FgnEq	Global	

Fund	Category	Type	Value
InvesNat Protected Retirement Balanced	Balan	CdnSAA	
InvesNat Retirement Balanced	Balan	CdnSAA	94.3
InvesNat Secure Diversified	Balan	CdnSAA	
InvesNat Short-Term Government Bond	FixInc	ST Bnd	90.9
InvesNat Small Capitalization	CdnEq	SCDivr	114.2
InvesNat T-Bill Plus	FixInc	CdnMkt	96.0
InvesNat Treasury Management	FixInc	CdnMkt	
InvesNat US Money Market	FixInc	USMkt	94.7
Investors Asset Allocation	Balan	CdnTAA	93.4
Investors Canadian Balanced	Balan	CdnSAA	
Investors Canadian Enterprise	CdnEq	LCDivr	
Investors Canadian Equity	CdnEq	Divers	91.9
Investors Canadian Money Market	FixInc	CdnMkt	91.8
Investors Canadian Natural Resource	CdnEq	Resorc	
Investors Canadian Small Cap	CdnEq	SCDivr	
Investors Canadian Small Cap II	CdnEq	SCDivr	
Investors Corporate Bond	FixInc	CdnBnd	95.4
Investors Dividend	CdnEq	Dividnd	108.5
Investors European Growth	FgnEq	Europe	93.4
Investors Global	FgnEq	Global	93.8
Investors Global Bond	FixInc	GlbBnd	79.9

Fund		Spclty	GlobST
Investors Global Science and Technology			
Investors Government Bond	FixInc	CdnBnd	96.0
Investors Growth Plus Portfolio	Balan	GblSAA	103.6
Investors Growth Portfolio	FgnEq	Global	92.7
Investors Income Plus Portfolio	Balan	CdnSAA	109.1
Investors Income Portfolio	FixInc	CdnBnd	96.4
Investors Japanese Growth	FgnEq	Japan	96.8
Investors Latin American Growth	FgnEq	Latin	
Investors Mortgage	FixInc	Mortge	95.6
Investors Mutual	Balan	CdnSAA	94.1
Investors N.A. High Yield Bond	FixInc	GlbBnd	
Investors North American Growth	FgnEq	NrthAm	78.9
Investors Pacific International	FgnEq	PacRim	97.3
Investors Real Property	Spclty	CdnRE	139.0
Investors Retirement Growth Portfolio	CdnEq	Divers	94.3
Investors Retirement High Gth Portfolio	FgnEq	Global	
Investors Retirement Mutual	CdnEq	Divers	91.6
Investors Retirement Plus Portfolio	Balan	CdnSAA	95.1
Investors Special	FgnEq	NrthAm	77.1
Investors Summa	CdnEq	Divers	109.4
Investors U.S. Growth	USEq	LgCap	101.6

Fund	Category 1	Category 2	Value
Investors U.S. Money Market	FixInc	USMkt	
Investors U.S. Opportunities	USEq	Divers	
Investors World Growth Portfolio	FgnEq	Global	79.4
Ivy Canadian	CdnEq	LCValu	111.5
Ivy Enterprise	CdnEq	SCDivr	111.3
Ivy Foreign Equity	FgnEq	Global	105.1
Ivy Growth & Income	Balan	CdnSAA	110.8
Ivy Mortgage	FixInc	Mortge	96.8
Jones Heward American	USEq	LgCap	93.5
Jones Heward Bond	FixInc	CdnBnd	98.2
Jones Heward Canadian Balanced	Balan	CdnSAA	95.1
Jones Heward Fund Limited	CdnEq	Divers	97.6
Jones Heward Money Market	FixInc	CdnMkt	94.4
Leith Wheeler Balanced	Balan	CdnSAA	104.0
Leith Wheeler Canadian Equity	CdnEq	Value	103.6
Leith Wheeler Fixed Income	FixInc	CdnBnd	100.6
Leith Wheeler Money Market	FixInc	CdnMkt	95.6
Leith Wheeler U.S. Equity	USEq	Divers	76.9
London Life American Equity (MAXXUM)	FgnEq	USDiv	
London Life American Growth (AGF)	FgnEq	USDiv	
London Life Asian Growth (AGF)	FgnEq	PacRim	

Fund	Type	Category	Score
London Life Balanced (BG)	Balan	CdnAll	
London Life Balanced (Sceptre)	Balan	CdnBal	
London Life Balanced Growth (LLIM)	Balan	CdnBal	
London Life Bond	FixInc	CdnBnd	92.7
London Life Canadian Balanced (MAXXUM)	Balan	CdnBal	
London Life Canadian Equity	Equity	LCDivr	99.2
London Life Canadian Equity (GWLIM)	Equity	Divers	
London Life Canadian Equity Gth (MAXXUM)	Equity	Divers	
London Life Canadian Opportunity (MF)	Sector	CdnRE	100.3
London Life Diversified	Balan	CdnBal	
London Life Dividend (LLIM)	Equity	CdnDiv	
London Life Dividend (MAXXUM)	Equity	CdnDiv	
London Life Equity (MF)	Equity	Divers	
London Life Equity (Sceptre)	Equity	Divers	
London Life Equity/Bond (GWLIM)	Balan	CdnBal	
London Life European Equity (Sceptre)	FgnEq	Europe	
London Life Global Equity (LLIM)	FgnEq	Global	
London Life Global Equity (MAXXUM)	FgnEq	Global	
London Life Government Bond (GWLIM)	FixInc	CdnBnd	
London Life Growth & Income (AGF)	Balan	CdnAll	
London Life Growth & Income (MF)	Balan	CdnAll	

Fund	Type	Category	Value
London Life Growth Equity (AGF)	Equity	Divers	
London Life Growth Equity (LLIM)	Equity	Divers	
London Life Income (LLIM)	FixInc	CdnBnd	
London Life Income (MAXXUM)	FixInc	CdnBnd	
London Life Income (MF)	FixInc	CdnBnd	
London Life International Equity	FgnEq	IntlEq	91.7
London Life Larger Company (MF)	Equity	LCDivr	
London Life Mid Cap Canada(GWLIM)	Equity	SCDivr	
London Life Money Market	Cash	CdnMkt	91.5
London Life Mortgage	FixInc	Mortge	104.0
London Life Natural Resource (MAXXUM)	Sector	CnPrMt	
London Life Nth American Balanced (LLIM)	Balan	CdnBal	
London Life Nth American Equity (BG)	Equity	Divers	
London Life Precious Metals (MAXXUM)	Sector	CdnST	
London Life Real Estate (GWLIM)	Sector	Consum	
London Life U.S. Equity	FgnEq	USDiv	92.9
Mackenzie Sentinel Canada Equity	CdnEq	Divers	89.5
Mackenzie Sentinel Global	FgnEq	IntlEq	96.0
Manulife AGF American Growth GIF encore	USEq	LgCap	
Manulife AGF Canadian Bond GIF encore	FixInc	CdnBnd	
Manulife AGF Canadian Equity GIF encore	CdnEq	Growth	

Fund	Category	Sub-category	MVA Score
Manulife AGF Dividend GIF encore	CdnEq	Divdnd	
Manulife AGF Global Government Bond GIF encore	FixInc	GlbBnd	
Manulife AGF Growth & Income GIF encore	Balan	CdnTAA	
Manulife AGF High Income GIF encore	CdnEq	Divdnd	
Manulife AIM GT America Growth Class GIF encore	USEq	Divers	
Manulife AIM GT Canada Growth Class GIF encore	CdnEq	Growth	
Manulife Atlas Canadian Balanced GIF encore	Balan	CdnSAA	
Manulife Atlas Canadian Large Cap Growth GIF encore	CdnEq	LCDivr	
Manulife C.I. Harbour GIF encore	CdnEq	Value	
Manulife C.I. Harbour Growth & Income GIF encore	Balan	CdnSAA	
Manulife Cabot Blue Chip	CdnEq	LCDivr	103.8
Manulife Cabot Canadian Equity	CdnEq	LCDivr	100.6
Manulife Cabot Canadian Growth	CdnEq	SCDivr	104.7
Manulife Cabot Diversified Bond	FixInc	CdnBnd	86.4
Manulife Cabot Emerging Growth	CdnEq	SCGrwt	103.6
Manulife Cabot Global Equity	FgnEq	Global	97.0
Manulife Cabot Money Market	FixInc	CdnMkt	89.2
Manulife Canadian Equity Index GIF encore	CdnEq	Divers	
Manulife Dynamic Dividend Growth GIF encore	CdnEq	Divdnd	
Manulife Dynamic Global Bond GIF encore	FixInc	GlbBnd	
Manulife Dynamic Partners GIF encore	Balan	CdnTAA	

Manulife Elliott & Page American Growth GIF encore	USEq / LgCap
Manulife Elliott & Page Balanced GIF encore	Balan / CdnTAA
Manulife Elliott & Page Money Market A GIF encore	FixInc / CdnMkt
Manulife Elliott & Page Money Market B GIF encore	FixInc / CdnMkt
Manulife Elliott & Page Sector Rotation GIF encore	CdnEq / LCDivr
Manulife Elliott & Page Value Equity GIF encore	CdnEq / LCValu
Manulife Fidelity Canadian Asset Alloc GIF encore	Balan / CdnTAA
Manulife Fidelity Canadian Bond GIF encore	FixInc / CdnBnd
Manulife Fidelity Cap Builder GIF encore	CdnEq / Growth
Manulife Fidelity Growth America GIF encore	USEq / LgCap
Manulife Fidelity International Portfolio GIF encore	FgnEq / Global
Manulife Hyperion Value Line U.S. Equity GIF encore	USEq / LgCap
Manulife Merrill Lynch Global Growth GIF encore	FgnEq / Global
Manulife Merrill Lynch U.S. Basic Value GIF encore	USEq / Divers
Manulife O'Donnell Canadian GIF encore	CdnEq / LCDivr
Manulife O'Donnell Select GIF encore	CdnEq / Divers
Manulife Sceptre Balanced Growth GIF encore	Balan / CdnSAA
Manulife Sceptre Canadian Equity GIF encore	CdnEq / Divers
Manulife Talvest Canadian Asset Alloc GIF encore	Balan / CdnTAA
Manulife Talvest Income GIF encore	FixInc / ST Bnd
Manulife Trimark Select Balanced GIF encore	Balan / CdnSAA

Fund			MVA
Manulife Trimark Select Canadian Growth GIF encore	CdnEq	Value	
Manulife Trimark Select Growth GIF encore	FgnEq	Global	
Manulife U.S. Equity Index GIF encore	USEq	Divers	
Manulife VistaFund 1 Am Stock	USEq	Divers	
Manulife VistaFund 1 Bond	FixInc	CdnBnd	
Manulife VistaFund 1 Capital Gains	CdnEq	Divers	
Manulife VistaFund 1 Diversified	Balan	CdnSAA	
Manulife VistaFund 1 Equity	CdnEq	LCDivr	
Manulife VistaFund 1 Global Bond	FixInc	GlbBnd	
Manulife VistaFund 1 Global Equity	FgnEq	IntlEq	
Manulife VistaFund 1 Short-Term Sec.	FixInc	CdnMkt	
Manulife VistaFund 2 Am Stock	USEq	Divers	
Manulife VistaFund 2 Bond	FixInc	CdnBnd	
Manulife VistaFund 2 Capital Gains	CdnEq	Divers	
Manulife VistaFund 2 Diversified	Balan	CdnSAA	
Manulife VistaFund 2 Equity	CdnEq	LCDivr	
Manulife VistaFund 2 Global Bond	FixInc	GlbBnd	
Manulife VistaFund 2 Global Equity	FgnEq	IntlEq	
Manulife VistaFund 2 Short-Term Sec.	FixInc	CdnMkt	
Marathon Equity	CdnEq	SCGrwt	92.6
Marathon Performance Canadian Balanced	Balan	CdnSAA	

Fund	Type	Category	Value
Marathon Performance Canadian Cash	FixInc	CdnMkt	
Marathon Performance Large Cap Canadian	CdnEq	LCDivr	
Marathon Performance Large Cap U.S.	USEq	LgCap	
Marathon Performance Nth Amer Lg-Short	FgnEq	NrthAm	
Marathon Resource	CdnEq	Resorc	
Mawer Canadian Balanced RSP	Balan	CdnSAA	103.3
Mawer Canadian Bond	FixInc	CdnBnd	99.6
Mawer Canadian Diversified Investment	Balan	CdnTAA	101.6
Mawer Canadian Equity	CdnEq	LCDivr	99.4
Mawer Canadian High Yield Bond	FixInc	CdnBnd	
Mawer Canadian Income	FixInc	CdnBnd	97.2
Mawer Canadian Money Market	FixInc	CdnMkt	95.7
Mawer New Canada	CdnEq	SCValu	108.2
Mawer U.S. Equity	USEq	LgCap	87.4
Mawer World Investment	FgnEq	IntlEq	103.5
MAXXUM American Equity	USEq	LgCap	92.4
MAXXUM Canadian Balanced	Balan	CdnSAA	96.3
MAXXUM Canadian Equity Growth	CdnEq	Divers	93.3
MAXXUM Dividend	CdnEq	DivdInd	103.9
MAXXUM Global Equity	FgnEq	Global	94.5
MAXXUM Income	FixInc	CdnBnd	96.5

Fund			MVA
MAXXUM Money Market	FixInc	CdnMkt	97.4
MAXXUM Natural Resource	CdnEq	Resorc	84.4
MAXXUM Precious Metals	CdnEq	PrMetl	93.3
MB Balanced Growth Pension	Balan	CdnSAA	
MB Canadian Equity Growth	CdnEq	LCDivr	
MB Fixed Income - Pooled	FixInc	CdnBnd	
MB Global Equity	FgnEq	Global	
McLean Budden American Growth	USEq	LgCap	92.0
McLean Budden Balanced Growth	Balan	CdnSAA	103.6
McLean Budden Canadian Equity Growth	CdnEq	LCDivr	100.6
McLean Budden Fixed Income	FixInc	CdnBnd	99.6
Mclean Budden International Growth	FgnEq	IntlEq	
McLean Budden Money Market	FixInc	CdnMkt	98.9
Merrill Lynch Global Growth	FgnEq	Global	
Merrill Lynch U.S. Basic Value	USEq	Divers	
Middlefield Canadian Realty	Spclty	CdnRE	
Middlefield Enhanced Yield	CdnEq	Divdnd	
Middlefield Growth	CdnEq	Resorc	100.8
Middlefield Money Market	FixInc	CdnMkt	
Millennia III American Equity Series 1	FgnEq	USDiv	82.9
Millennia III American Equity Series 2	FgnEq	USDiv	82.5

Fund	Category	Style	Rating
Millennia III American Equity Series 3	FgnEq	USDiv	
Millennia III American Equity Series 4	FgnEq	USDiv	
Millennia III Canadian Balanced Series 1	Balan	CdnBal	93.6
Millennia III Canadian Balanced Series 2	Balan	CdnBal	93.1
Millennia III Canadian Balanced Series 3	Balan	CdnBal	
Millennia III Canadian Balanced Series 4	Balan	CdnBal	
Millennia III Canadian Dividend Series 1	Equity	CdnDiv	
Millennia III Canadian Dividend Series 2	Equity	CdnDiv	
Millennia III Canadian Dividend Series 3	Equity	CdnDiv	
Millennia III Canadian Dividend Series 4	Equity	CdnDiv	
Millennia III Canadian Equity Series 1	Equity	Divers	93.5
Millennia III Canadian Equity Series 2	Equity	Divers	93.3
Millennia III Canadian Equity Series 3	Equity	Divers	
Millennia III Canadian Equity Series 4	Equity	Divers	
Millennia III European Equity Series 3	FgnEq	Europe	
Millennia III European Equity Series 4	FgnEq	Europe	
Millennia III Global Balanced Series 3	Balan	SAA	
Millennia III Global Balanced Series 4	Balan	SAA	
Millennia III Income Series 1	FixInc	CdnBnd	92.4
Millennia III Income Series 2	FixInc	CdnBnd	91.1
Millennia III Income Series 3	FixInc	CdnBnd	

Fund	Class 1	Class 2	Score
Millennia III Income Series 4	FixInc	CdnBnd	
Millennia III International Equity 1	FgnEq	Global	97.1
Millennia III International Equity 2	FgnEq	Global	96.7
Millennia III International Equity 3	FgnEq	Global	
Millennia III International Equity 4	FgnEq	Global	
Millennia III Money Market Series 1	Cash	CdnMkt	87.4
Millennia III Money Market Series 2	Cash	CdnMkt	85.0
Millennia III Money Market Series 3	Cash	CdnMkt	
Millennia III Money Market Series 4	Cash	CdnMkt	
Millennia III Nth American Small Comp 1	FgnEq	NrthAm	
Millennia III Nth American Small Comp 2	FgnEq	NrthAm	
Millennia III Nth American Small Comp 3	FgnEq	NrthAm	
Millennia III Nth American Small Comp 4	FgnEq	NrthAm	
MLI AGF American Growth GIF	USEq	Divers	
MLI AGF Canadian Bond GIF	FixInc	CdnBnd	
MLI AGF Canadian Stock GIF	CdnEq	LCDivr	
MLI AGF Dividend GIF	CdnEq	Divdnd	
MLI AGF Global Government Bond GIF	FixInc	GlbBnd	
MLI AGF Growth & Income GIF	Balan	CdnSAA	
MLI AGF High Income GIF	CdnEq	Divdnd	
MLI AIM GT America Growth Class GIF	USEq	Divers	

MLI AIM GT Canada Growth Class GIF	CdnEq	Divers
MLI C.I. Harbour GIF	CdnEq	LCDivr
MLI C.I. Harbour Growth & Income GIF	Balan	CdnSAA
MLI Canadian Equity Index GIF	CdnEq	LCDivr
MLI Dynamic Dividend Growth GIF	CdnEq	Dividnd
MLI Dynamic Global Bond GIF	FixInc	GlbBnd
MLI Dynamic Partners GIF	Balan	CdnTAA
MLI Elliott & Page American Growth GIF	USEq	Divers
MLI Elliott & Page Balanced GIF	Balan	CdnSAA
MLI Elliott & Page Equity GIF	CdnEq	LCDivr
MLI Elliott & Page Money Market A GIF	FixInc	CdnMkt
MLI Elliott & Page Money Market B GIF	FixInc	CdnMkt
MLI Elliott & Page Value Equity GIF	CdnEq	LCValu
MLI Fidelity Canadian Asset Alloc GIF	Balan	CdnTAA
MLI Fidelity Canadian Bond GIF	FixInc	CdnBnd
MLI Fidelity Cap Builder GIF	CdnEq	Divers
MLI Fidelity Growth America GIF	USEq	Divers
MLI Fidelity International Portfolio GIF	FgnEq	Global
MLI Fidelity True North GIF	CdnEq	Divers
MLI O'Donnell Canadian GIF	CdnEq	LCDivr
MLI O'Donnell Select GIF	CdnEq	Divers

Fund			MVA
MLI Talvest Canadian Asset Alloc GIF	Balan	CdnTAA	
MLI Talvest Income GIF	FixInc	CdnBnd	
MLI Talvest Value Line U.S. Equity GIF	USEq	Divers	
MLI Trimark Select Balanced GIF	Balan	CdnSAA	
MLI Trimark Select Canadian Growth GIF	CdnEq	Divers	
MLI Trimark Select Growth GIF	FgnEq	Global	
MLI U.S. Equity Index GIF	USEq	Divers	
NAL-Balanced Growth	Balan	CdnSAA	102.5
NAL-Canadian Bond	FixInc	CdnBnd	91.1
NAL-Canadian Diversified	Balan	CdnSAA	87.8
NAL-Canadian Equity	CdnEq	LCDivr	87.3
NAL-Canadian Money Market	FixInc	CdnMkt	90.3
NAL-Equity Growth	CdnEq	LCDivr	101.4
NAL-Global Equity	FgnEq	Global	88.8
NAL-U.S. Equity	USEq	Divers	94.3
National Balanced	Balan	CdnSAA	98.4
National Dividend Income	CdnEq	Divdnd	
National Equities	CdnEq	LCDivr	99.9
National Fixed Income	FixInc	CdnBnd	93.8
National Global Equities	FgnEq	Global	84.3
National International Equity	FgnEq	IntlEq	

National Money Market	FixInc	CdnMkt	85.9
National US Equity Index	USEq	Divers	
Navigator American Growth	USEq	Divers	82.2
Navigator American Value	USEq	LgCap	94.1
Navigator Asia Pacific	FgnEq	PacRim	107.7
Navigator Canadian Focused Growth Pfl	CdnEq	SCGrwt	91.7
Navigator Canadian Growth	CdnEq	Growth	
Navigator Canadian Growth & Income	Balan	CdnSAA	
Navigator Canadian Income	FixInc	CdnBnd	93.8
Navigator Canadian Technology	CdnEq	SciTec	
Navigator Money Market	FixInc	CdnMkt	
NN American Asset Allocation	Balan	GblSAA	
NN American Equity Index	USEq	Divers	
NN Asset Allocation	Balan	CdnTAA	103.9
NN Bond	FixInc	CdnBnd	95.2
NN Canadian 35 Index	CdnEq	LCDivr	99.9
NN Canadian Communications	CdnEq	SciTec	
NN Canadian Financial Services	CdnEq	FinSer	
NN Canadian Growth	CdnEq	LCDivr	100.2
NN Canadian Resources	CdnEq	Resorc	
NN Canadian Small Cap	CdnEq	SCDivr	

Fund	Category	Type	MVA Score
NN Can-Am	USEq	Divers	88.3
NN Can-Asian	FgnEq	PacRim	107.6
NN Can-Daq 100	USEq	Divers	
NN Can-Emerge	FgnEq	Emerg	
NN Can-Euro	FgnEq	Europe	90.8
NN Can-Global Bond	FixInc	GlbBnd	
NN Dividend	CdnEq	Divdnd	103.5
NN Elite	Balan	GblSAA	78.2
NN European Equity Index	FgnEq	Europe	
NN Information Technology	SpcIty	GlobST	
NN International Bond Index	FixInc	GlbBnd	
NN International Brands	FgnEq	IntlEq	
NN Money Market	FixInc	CdnMkt	98.6
NN T-Bill	FixInc	CdnMkt	89.9
Northwest Balanced	Balan	CdnTAA	94.9
Northwest Dividend	CdnEq	Divdnd	97.4
Northwest Growth	CdnEq	Divers	98.8
Northwest Income	FixInc	CdnBnd	89.0
Northwest International	FgnEq	Global	91.9
Northwest Money Market	FixInc	CdnMkt	91.7
O'Donnell American Sector Growth	USEq	LgCap	

Fund	Type	Category	Value
O'Donnell Balanced	Balan	CdnSAA	
O'Donnell Canadian	CdnEq	LCDivr	
O'Donnell Canadian Emerging Growth	CdnEq	SCGrwt	
O'Donnell Growth	CdnEq	SCGrwt	
O'Donnell High Income	FixInc	CdnBnd	
O'Donnell Money Market	FixInc	CdnMkt	
O'Donnell Select	CdnEq	Divers	
O'Donnell Short Term	FixInc	CdnMkt	
O'Donnell U.S. High Income	FixInc	GlbBnd	
O'Donnell U.S. Mid-Cap	USEq	Divers	
O'Donnell World Equity	FgnEq	Global	
O'Donnell World Precious Metals	Spclty	GlPrMt	
Optima Strategy- Canadian Equity	CdnEq	Value	105.3
Optima Strategy- Canadian Fixed Income	FixInc	CdnBnd	101.0
Optima Strategy- Global Fixed Income	FixInc	GlbBnd	83.4
Optima Strategy- International Equity	FgnEq	IntlEq	93.3
Optima Strategy- Real Estate Investment	Spclty	GlobRE	
Optima Strategy- Short Term	FixInc	ST Bnd	99.7
Optima Strategy- U.S. Equity	USEq	LgCap	105.9
Optimum Actions	CdnEq	Divers	104.2
Optimum Croissance Et Revenus	Balan	CdnSAA	

Fund			MVA
Optimum Epargne	FixInc	CdnMkt	93.9
Optimum Equilibre	Balan	CdnSAA	106.3
Optimum International	FgnEq	Global	95.5
Optimum Obligations	FixInc	CdnBnd	99.0
Perigee Accufund	Balan	CdnSAA	
Perigee Active Bond	FixInc	CdnBnd	
Perigee Canadian Agressive Growth Equity	CdnEq	SCDivr	
Perigee Canadian Sector Equity	CdnEq	Divers	
Perigee Canadian Value Equity	CdnEq	Value	101.9
Perigee Diversifund	Balan	CdnSAA	
Perigee Index Plus Bond	FixInc	CdnBnd	98.3
Perigee International Equity	FgnEq	IntlEq	96.0
Perigee North American Equity	CdnEq	LCDivr	102.3
Perigee Symmetry Balanced	Balan	CdnSAA	101.4
Perigee T-Plus	FixInc	CdnMkt	100.7
Perigee U.S. Equity	USEq	Divers	84.3
PH & N S U.S. Money Market	FixInc	USMkt	100.4
PH & N Balance Pension Trust	Balan	CdnSAA	103.9
PH & N Balanced	Balan	CdnSAA	102.4
PH & N Bond	FixInc	CdnBnd	100.9
PH & N Canadian Equity	CdnEq	Divers	100.5

Fund	Type	Category	Value
PH & N Canadian Equity Plus	CdnEq	Divers	100.9
PH & N Canadian Equity Plus Pension Tr	CdnEq	Divers	104.2
PH & N Canadian Money Market	FixInc	CdnMkt	97.8
PH & N Dividend Income	CdnEq	DivInd	115.9
PH & N Euro-Pacific Equity	FgnEq	IntlEq	95.8
PH & N North American Equity	FgnEq	NrthAm	79.3
PH & N Pooled U.S. Pension	USEq	LgCap	
PH & N Short-Term Bond & Mortgage	FixInc	ST Bnd	99.7
PH & N U.S. Equity	USEq	LgCap	90.6
PH & N Vintage	CdnEq	Growth	102.5
Primerica Canadian Aggressive Growth Pfl	Equity	Growth	
Primerica Canadian Balanced Portfolio	Balan	CdnBal	
Primerica Canadian Conservative Pfl	Balan	CdnBal	
Primerica Canadian Growth Portfolio	Equity	Growth	
Primerica Canadian High Growth Portfolio	Equity	Growth	
Primerica Canadian Income Portfolio	FixInc	CdnBnd	
Primerica International Growth Portfolio	FgnEq	Global	
Primerica International High Growth Pfl	FgnEq	Global	
Primerica Intl Aggressive Growth Pfl	FgnEq	Global	
Primus Canadian Equity	CdnEq	Divers	
Primus Canadian Fixed Income	FixInc	CdnBnd	

Fund			Score
Primus EAFE Equity	FgnEq	IntlEq	
Primus Emerging Markets Equity	FgnEq	Emerg	
Primus Enhanced Global Bond	FixInc	GlbBnd	
Primus International Synthetic	FgnEq	IntlEq	
Primus Prime Credit Money Market	FixInc	CdnMkt	
Primus S&P 500 Synthetic	USEq	Divers	
Primus U.S. Equity	USEq	Divers	
Protected American	Balan	GblSAA	81.8
Pursuit Canadian Bond	FixInc	CdnBnd	78.5
Pursuit Canadian Equity	CdnEq	Growth	101.4
Pursuit Global Bond	FixInc	GlbBnd	72.4
Pursuit Global Equity	FgnEq	IntlEq	95.1
Pursuit Growth	FgnEq	Global	
Pursuit Money Market	FixInc	CdnMkt	99.2
Resolute Growth	CdnEq	SCGrwt	99.7
Retrocom Growth	Labour	LSVC	112.2
Royal & SunAlliance Balanced	Balan	CdnBal	101.9
Royal & SunAlliance Canadian Growth	Equity	SCDivr	99.7
Royal & SunAlliance Dividend	Equity	CdnDiv	
Royal & SunAlliance Equity	Equity	LCDivr	104.5
Royal & SunAlliance Global Emerging Mkt	FgnEq	Emerg	

Royal & SunAlliance Income	FixInc	CdnBnd	95.3
Royal & SunAlliance International Equity	FgnEq	IntlEq	99.1
Royal & SunAlliance Money Market	Cash	CdnMkt	98.2
Royal & SunAlliance U.S. Equity	FgnEq	USDiv	100.3
Royal Asian Growth	FgnEq	PacRim	98.6
Royal Balanced	Balan	CdnSAA	96.9
Royal Balanced Growth	Balan	CdnTAA	
Royal Bond	FixInc	CdnBnd	93.0
Royal Canadian Equity	CdnEq	LCDivr	98.4
Royal Canadian Growth	CdnEq	SCGrwt	102.1
Royal Canadian Index	CdnEq	Divers	
Royal Canadian Money Market	FixInc	CdnMkt	93.3
Royal Canadian Small Cap	CdnEq	SCGrwt	96.4
Royal Canadian Strategic Index	CdnEq	LCDivr	
Royal Canadian T-Bill	FixInc	CdnMkt	93.1
Royal Canadian Value	CdnEq	Value	
Royal Dividend	CdnEq	Dividnd	112.0
Royal Energy	CdnEq	Resorc	105.1
Royal European Growth	FgnEq	Europe	92.8
Royal Global Bond	FixInc	GlbBnd	80.8
Royal Global Education	FgnEq	Global	

Fund			MVA
Royal International Equity	FgnEq	IntlEq	100.0
Royal International RSP Index	FgnEq	IntlEq	
Royal Japanese Stock	FgnEq	Japan	104.1
Royal Latin American	FgnEq	Latin	76.0
Royal Life Science & Technology	Spclty	GlobST	85.7
Royal Monthly Income	CdnEq	Divdnd	
Royal Mortgage	FixInc	Mortge	92.7
Royal Precious Metals	CdnEq	PrMetl	92.5
Royal Premium Canadian Index	CdnEq	Divers	
Royal Premium Money Market	FixInc	CdnMkt	
Royal Premium U.S. Index	USEq	Divers	
Royal Trust Advantage Balanced	Balan	CdnSAA	
Royal Trust Advantage Growth	Balan	CdnSAA	
Royal Trust Advantage Income	Balan	CdnSAA	
Royal U.S. Equity	USEq	LgCap	89.7
Royal U.S. Growth Strategic Index	USEq	Divers	
Royal U.S. Index	USEq	Divers	
Royal U.S. RSP Index	USEq	Divers	
Royal U.S. Value Strategic Index	USEq	Divers	
Royal U.S.$ Money Market	FixInc	USMkt	95.1
Saxon Balanced	Balan	CdnSAA	95.9

Fund	Category	Type	Value
Saxon High Income	CdnEq	DivdInd	
Saxon Small Cap	CdnEq	SCDivr	122.8
Saxon Stock	CdnEq	Divers	100.0
Saxon World Growth	FgnEq	Global	80.1
Sceptre Balanced Growth	Balan	CdnSAA	96.8
Sceptre Bond	FixInc	CdnBnd	98.9
Sceptre Canadian Equity	CdnEq	Divers	
Sceptre Equity Growth	CdnEq	Divers	89.2
Sceptre International	FgnEq	Global	79.0
Sceptre Money Market	FixInc	CdnMkt	96.6
Sceptre U.S. Equity	USEq	Divers	
Scotia American Growth	USEq	Divers	85.3
Scotia American Stock Index	USEq	Divers	
Scotia Canadian Balanced	Balan	CdnSAA	104.9
Scotia Canadian Blue Chip	CdnEq	LCDivr	92.7
Scotia Canadian Dividend	CdnEq	DivdInd	112.6
Scotia Canadian Growth	CdnEq	Divers	93.9
Scotia Canadian Income	FixInc	CdnBnd	99.4
Scotia Canadian Mid-Large Cap	CdnEq	LCDivr	98.8
Scotia Canadian Short Term Income	FixInc	ST Bnd	89.8
Scotia Canadian Small Cap	CdnEq	SCGrwt	105.7

Fund	Type	Category	MVA Score
Scotia Canadian Stock Index	CdnEq	LCDivr	
Scotia CanAm Stock Index	USEq	LgCap	90.1
Scotia CanAm U.S.S Income	FixInc	GlbBnd	86.4
Scotia CanAm USS Money Market	FixInc	USMkt	
Scotia CanGlobal Income	FixInc	CdnBnd	84.1
Scotia Emerging Markets	FgnEq	Emerg	61.1
Scotia European Growth	FgnEq	Europe	
Scotia Global Income	FixInc	GlbBnd	79.9
Scotia International Growth	FgnEq	Global	90.5
Scotia Latin American	FgnEq	Latin	76.8
Scotia Money Market	FixInc	CdnMkt	92.7
Scotia Mortgage Income	FixInc	Mortge	95.6
Scotia Pacific Rim	FgnEq	PacRim	99.1
Scotia Precious Metals	CdnEq	PrMetl	94.5
Scotia Premium T-Bill	FixInc	CdnMkt	96.4
Scotia T-Bill	FixInc	CdnMkt	91.3
Scotia Total Return	Balan	CdnTAA	97.9
Scudder Canadian Bond	FixInc	CdnBnd	
Scudder Canadian Equity	CdnEq	Value	112.5
Scudder Canadian Money Market	FixInc	CdnMkt	
Scudder Canadian Short Term Bond	FixInc	ST Bnd	101.8

Scudder Canadian Small Company	CdnEq	SCDivr	
Scudder Emerging Markets	FgnEq	Emerg	72.8
Scudder Global	FgnEq	Global	101.4
Scudder Greater Europe	FgnEq	Europe	96.4
Scudder Pacific	FgnEq	PacRim	108.1
Scudder US Growth & Income	USEq	Divers	
Signature Canadian	CdnEq	Divers	
Signature Canadian Balanced	Balan	CdnSAA	
Spectrum United American Equity	USEq	LgCap	86.5
Spectrum United American Growth	USEq	Divers	81.1
Spectrum United Asian Dynasty	FgnEq	PacRim	92.5
Spectrum United Asset Allocation	Balan	CdnTAA	99.9
Spectrum United Canadian Balanced Pfl	Balan	CdnSAA	95.2
Spectrum United Canadian Equity	CdnEq	LCDivr	99.6
Spectrum United Canadian Growth	CdnEq	SCDivr	97.1
Spectrum United Canadian Growth Pfl	Balan	CdnSAA	
Spectrum United Canadian Income Pfl	FixInc	CdnBnd	
Spectrum United Canadian Investment	CdnEq	LCValu	109.2
Spectrum United Canadian Money Market	FixInc	CdnMkt	93.5
Spectrum United Canadian Resource	CdnEq	Resorc	
Spectrum United Canadian Small-Mid Cap	CdnEq	SCDivr	

Fund			MVA
Spectrum United Canadian Stock	CdnEq	LCDivr	99.3
Spectrum United Cdn Conservative Pfl	Balan	CdnSAA	
Spectrum United Cdn Maximum Growth Pfl	CdnEq	Divers	
Spectrum United Diversified	Balan	CdnSAA	99.8
Spectrum United Dividend	CdnEq	Divdnd	116.7
Spectrum United Emerging Markets	FgnEq	Emerg	69.6
Spectrum United European Growth	FgnEq	Europe	93.7
Spectrum United Glob Telecommunications	Spclty	GlobST	95.8
Spectrum United Global Bond	FixInc	GlbBnd	79.2
Spectrum United Global Diversified	Balan	GblSAA	100.6
Spectrum United Global Equity	FgnEq	Global	91.1
Spectrum United Global Growth	FgnEq	Global	78.3
Spectrum United Global Growth Portfolio	FgnEq	Global	
Spectrum United Long-Term Bond	FixInc	CdnBnd	95.8
Spectrum United Mid-Term Bond	FixInc	CdnBnd	93.6
Spectrum United Optimax U.S.A.	USEq	Divers	90.8
Spectrum United RSP International Bond	FixInc	GlbBnd	72.5
Spectrum United Savings	FixInc	CdnMkt	92.6
Spectrum United Short-Term Bond	FixInc	ST Bnd	94.2
Spectrum United U.S. Dollars Money Mkt	FixInc	USMkt	91.8
Standard Life Balanced	Balan	CdnSAA	102.5

Fund	Type	Category	Rating
Standard Life Bond	FixInc	CdnBnd	95.4
Standard Life Canadian Dividend	CdnEq	Divdnd	110.0
Standard Life Equity	CdnEq	Divers	107.5
Standard Life Growth Equity	CdnEq	Divers	94.8
Standard Life International Bond	FixInc	GlbBnd	81.8
Standard Life International Equity	FgnEq	IntlEq	102.5
Standard Life Money Market	FixInc	CdnMkt	98.4
Standard Life Natural Resources	CdnEq	Resorc	93.9
Standard Life U.S. Equity	USEq	LgCap	88.4
Stone & Co Flagship Global Growth	FgnEq	IntlEq	
Stone & Co Flagship Growth & Income	Balan	CdnSAA	
Stone & Co Flagship Money Market	FixInc	CdnMkt	
Stone & Co Flagship Stock Canada	CdnEq	LCDivr	97.0
Strategic Value	FgnEq	Global	
Strategic Value American Equity	USEq	LgCap	84.8
Strategic Value Asia Pacific	FgnEq	PacRim	95.4
Strategic Value Canadian Balanced	Balan	CdnSAA	95.3
Strategic Value Canadian Equity	CdnEq	LCDivr	97.6
Strategic Value Canadian Equity Value	CdnEq	Divers	
Strategic Value Canadian Small Companies	CdnEq	SCGrwt	111.2
Strategic Value Commonwealth	FgnEq	Global	85.3

Fund	Category	Subcategory	Score
Strategic Value Dividend	CdnEq	Divdnd	105.7
Strategic Value Emerging Markets	FgnEq	Emerg	63.0
Strategic Value Europe	FgnEq	Europe	93.5
Strategic Value Global Balanced	Balan	GblSAA	96.9
Strategic Value Global Balanced RSP	Balan	CdnSAA	
Strategic Value Government Bond	FixInc	ST Bnd	92.5
Strategic Value Income	FixInc	CdnBnd	96.2
Strategic Value International	FgnEq	Global	83.8
Strategic Value Money Market	FixInc	CdnMkt	90.8
Synergy Canadian Growth Class	CdnEq	Growth	
Synergy Canadian Momentum Class	CdnEq	Divers	
Synergy Canadian Short Term Income Class	FixInc	CdnBnd	
Synergy Canadian Small Cap Class	CdnEq	SCDivr	
Synergy Canadian Style Management	CdnEq	Divers	
Synergy Canadian Value Class	CdnEq	Value	
Synergy Global Style Management Class	FgnEq	Global	
Synergy Tactical Asset Allocation	Balan	CdnTAA	
Talvest Asian	FgnEq	PacRim	97.7
Talvest Bond	FixInc	CdnBnd	94.9
Talvest Canadian Asset Allocation	Balan	CdnTAA	100.2
Talvest Canadian Equity Growth	CdnEq	Growth	

Fund	Category	Name	Value
Talvest Canadian Equity Value	CdnEq	Divers	96.5
Talvest Canadian Resource	CdnEq	Resorc	
Talvest Cash Management	FixInc	CdnMkt	
Talvest China Plus	FgnEq	China	
Talvest Dividend	CdnEq	Dividnd	104.0
Talvest European	FgnEq	Europe	97.7
Talvest Foreign Pay Canadian Bond	FixInc	GlbBnd	96.4
Talvest Global Asset Allocation	Balan	GblTAA	92.3
Talvest Global Equity	FgnEq	Global	
Talvest Global Health Care	Spclty	GlobST	
Talvest Global R.R.S.P	FgnEq	Global	99.5
Talvest Global Science & Technology	Spclty	GlobST	
Talvest Global Small Cap	FgnEq	Global	
Talvest High Yield Bond	FixInc	CdnBnd	
Talvest Income	FixInc	ST Bnd	92.1
Talvest Millennium High Income	CdnEq	Divdnd	
Talvest Millennium Next Generation	CdnEq	SCDivr	113.6
Talvest Money	FixInc	CdnMkt	96.3
Talvest Small Cap Canadian Equity	CdnEq	SCGrwt	117.5
Talvest Value Line U.S. Equity	USEq	LgCap	83.9
Templeton Balanced	Balan	CdnSAA	101.1

Fund	Category	Type	Score
Templeton Canadian Asset Allocation	Balan	CdnTAA	99.4
Templeton Canadian Balanced GIF	Balan	CdnSAA	
Templeton Canadian Bond	FixInc	CdnBnd	88.1
Templeton Canadian Stock	CdnEq	Divers	103.2
Templeton Canadian Stock GIF	CdnEq	Divers	
Templeton Emerging Markets	FgnEq	Emerg	74.8
Templeton Global Balanced	Balan	GblSAA	99.3
Templeton Global Bond	FixInc	GlbBnd	71.8
Templeton Global Smaller Companies	FgnEq	Global	80.7
Templeton Growth	FgnEq	Global	90.8
Templeton Growth GIF	FgnEq	Global	
Templeton International Balanced	Balan	GblSAA	90.6
Templeton International Stock	FgnEq	IntlEq	105.6
Templeton International Stock GIF	FgnEq	IntlEq	
Templeton Mutual Beacon	USEq	Divers	
Templeton Mutual Beacon GIF	USEq	Divers	
Templeton Treasury Bill	FixInc	CdnMkt	92.6
Templeton Treasury Bill GIF	FixInc	CdnMkt	
Transamerica Balanced Investment Growth	Balan	CdnSAA	99.1
Transamerica Growsafe Canadian 60 Index	CdnEq	Divers	
Transamerica Growsafe Canadian Balanced	Balan	CdnSAA	100.3

Transamerica Growsafe Canadian Bond	FixInc	CdnBnd	93.2
Transamerica Growsafe Canadian Equity	CdnEq	LCDivr	102.0
Transamerica Growsafe Canadian Money Mkt	FixInc	CdnMkt	93.8
Transamerica Growsafe Cdn Divid & Income	CdnEq	Dividnd	
Transamerica Growsafe European 100	FgnEq	Europe	
Transamerica Growsafe Intl Balanced	Balan	GblSAA	98.3
Transamerica Growsafe Japanese 225	FgnEq	Japan	
Transamerica Growsafe U.S. 21st Century	USEq	Divers	
Transamerica Growsafe U.S. 500 Index	USEq	Divers	99.7
Transamerica Growsafe U.S. Balanced	Balan	GblSAA	
Transamerica Growsafe U.S. Bond	FixInc	GlbBnd	
Transamerica Growsafe U.S. Equity	USEq	Divers	
Trans-Canada Bond	FixInc	CdnBnd	80.6
Trans-Canada Dividend	CdnEq	Dividnd	81.2
Trans-Canada Money Market	FixInc	CdnMkt	97.8
Trans-Canada Pension	Balan	CdnTAA	91.0
Trans-Canada Value	CdnEq	Value	91.0
Triax Growth	Labour	LSVC	
Trillium Growth Capital Inc.	Labour	LSVC	56.3
Trimark Advantage Bond	FixInc	CdnBnd	99.2
Trimark Advantage Bond Segregated	FixInc	CdnBnd	

Fund	Code	Score
Trimark Americas	FgnEq	Amrcas	75.2
Trimark Americas Segregated	FgnEq	Amrcas	
Trimark Canadian	CdnEq	LCDivr	98.8
Trimark Canadian Bond	FixInc	CdnBnd	98.5
Trimark Canadian Bond Segregated	FixInc	CdnBnd	
Trimark Canadian Resources	CdnEq	Resorc	
Trimark Canadian Resources Segregated	CdnEq	Resorc	
Trimark Canadian Small Companies	CdnEq	SCDivr	
Trimark Canadian Small Coms Segregated	CdnEq	SCDivr	
Trimark Discovery	Spclty	GlobST	
Trimark Discovery Segregated	Spclty	GlobST	
Trimark Europlus	FgnEq	Europe	
Trimark Europlus Segregated	FgnEq	Europe	
Trimark Fund	FgnEq	Global	89.7
Trimark Government Income	FixInc	ST Bnd	94.7
Trimark Government Income Segregated	FixInc	ST Bnd	
Trimark Income Growth	Balan	CdnSAA	92.0
Trimark Indo-Pacific	FgnEq	PacRim	103.4
Trimark Indo-Pacific Segregated	FgnEq	PacRim	
Trimark Interest	FixInc	CdnMkt	95.8
Trimark Interest Segregated	FixInc	CdnMkt	

Fund	Type	Style	Value
Trimark RSP Equity	CdnEq	LCDivr	92.5
Trimark Select Balanced	Balan	CdnSAA	95.9
Trimark Select Balanced Segregated	Balan	CdnSAA	
Trimark Select Canadian Growth	CdnEq	Value	97.2
Trimark Select Canadian Grth Segregated	CdnEq	Value	
Trimark Select Growth	FgnEq	Global	86.8
Trimark Select Growth Segregated	FgnEq	Global	
Universal Americas	FgnEq	Amrcas	82.9
Universal Canadian Balanced	Balan	CdnSAA	
Universal Canadian Growth	CdnEq	Divers	109.7
Universal Canadian Resource	CdnEq	Resorc	98.9
Universal European Opportunities	FgnEq	Europe	97.7
Universal Far East	FgnEq	PacRim	97.9
Universal Future	CdnEq	Divers	99.9
Universal International Stock	FgnEq	IntlEq	97.1
Universal Japan	FgnEq	Japan	107.7
Universal Precious Metals	CdnEq	PrMetl	93.4
Universal Select Managers	FgnEq	Global	
Universal U.S. Emerging Growth	USEq	SmCap	61.2
Universal U.S. Money Market	FixInc	USMkt	87.2
Universal World Asset Allocation	Balan	GblTAA	91.1

Fund	Type	MVA
Universal World Balance RRSP	Balan	GblSAA	95.9
Universal World Emerging Growth	FgnEq	Emerg	68.3
Universal World Growth RRSP	FgnEq	Global	85.4
Universal World High Yield	FixInc	GlbBnd	
Universal World Income RRSP	FixInc	GlbBnd	91.5
Universal World Real Estate	Spclty	GlobRE	
Universal World Science & Technology	Spclty	GlobST	
Universal World Tactical Bond	FixInc	GlbBnd	79.9
Universal World Value	FgnEq	Global	
University Avenue Balanced	Balan	CdnSAA	86.2
University Avenue Canadian	CdnEq	Divers	71.7
University Avenue Canadian Small Cap	CdnEq	SCDivr	
University Avenue Money	FixInc	CdnMkt	
University Avenue U.S. Growth	USEq	Divers	81.1
University Avenue U.S. Small Cap	USEq	Divers	
University Avenue World	FgnEq	Global	
Valorem Canadian Bond-Value	FixInc	CdnBnd	
Valorem Canadian Equity-Value	CdnEq	Divers	
Valorem Demographic Trends	CdnEq	Divers	
Valorem Diversified	Balan	CdnSAA	
Valorem Global Equity-Value	FgnEq	Global	

Valorem Government Short Term	FixInc	CdnMkt	
Valorem U.S. Equity-Value	USEq	Divers	
VenGrowth Fund	Labour	LSVC	112.0
Workers Investment	Labour	LSVC	
Working Opportunity (EVCC)	Labour	LSVC	101.3
Working Ventures Canadian	Labour	LSVC	89.3
YMG American Growth	USEq	Divers	
YMG Balanced	Balan	CdnSAA	87.0
YMG Bond	FixInc	CdnBnd	
YMG Canadian Value	CdnEq	Value	
YMG Emerging Companies	CdnEq	SCDivr	
YMG Enterprise	CdnEq	Divers	
YMG Growth	CdnEq	Divers	101.7
YMG Hedge	Spclty	Other	
YMG Income	FixInc	CdnBnd	61.9
YMG International	FgnEq	IntlEq	95.1
YMG Money Market	FixInc	CdnMkt	96.8
YMG Strategic Fixed Income	FixInc	CdnBnd	
Zweig Global Balanced	Balan	GblSAA	116.0
Zweig US Equity	USEq	Divers	75.7
Zweig Strategic Growth	CdnEq	Divers	

GENERAL INDEX

FUND INDEX